BETWEEN
FREEDOM AND
BONDAGE

BETWEEN FREEDOM AND BONDAGE

Race, Party, and Voting Rights in the Antebellum North

CHRISTOPHER MALONE

Routledge
Taylor & Francis Group
New York   London

Chapter 1 reprinted with permission from *New Political Science*, vol. 27, no. 2 (June 2005), pp. 177–196.

Chapter 3 reprinted with permission, *Journal of Pennsylvania History*, volume 72, no. 4 (Winter): 468–506.

Routledge
Taylor & Francis Group
270 Madison Avenue
New York, NY 10016

Routledge
Taylor & Francis Group
2 Park Square
Milton Park, Abingdon
Oxon OX14 4RN

© 2008 by Taylor & Francis Group, LLC
Routledge is an imprint of Taylor & Francis Group, an Informa business

Printed in the United States of America on acid-free paper
10 9 8 7 6 5 4 3 2 1

International Standard Book Number-13: 978-0-415-95697-0 (Softcover) 978-0-415-95696-3 (Hardcover)

Library of Congress Cataloging-in-Publication Data

Malone, Christopher.
   Between freedom and bondage : race, party, and voting rights in the antebellum North / Christopher Malone.
       p. cm.
       ISBN 978-0-415-95696-3 (hardback : alk. paper) -- ISBN 978-0-415-95697-0 (pbk. : alk. paper)
       1. African Americans--Suffrage--History--19th century. 2. African Americans--History--To 1863. 3. African Americans--Politics and government--19th century. 4. United States--Politics and government--1783-1865. I. Title.

JK1924.M35 2007
324.6'208996073074--dc22   2007007661

Visit the Taylor & Francis Web site at
http://www.taylorandfrancis.com

and the Routledge Web site at
http://www.routledge.com

For Mom,
Who has taught me the meaning
Of strength
Of compassion
Of mercy
Of joy and sorrow
Of courage and intelligence
Of unconditional love.

Contents

Acknowledgments   ix

1 The Beginning of the Story: Black Enfranchisement
  in the Antebellum Era   1

2 "The Minds of Blacks Are not Competent to Vote":
  Racial Voting Restrictions in New York   23

3 "An Asylum for the Oppressed Injured Sons of Europe":
  The Disenfranchisement of Blacks in Pennsylvania   57

4 "Servility Is not Confined to Color":
  The Disenfranchisement and Reenfranchisement
  of Blacks in Rhode Island   101

5 "The Vaunted Superiority of the White Race Imposes
  Corresponding Duties": Massachusetts—The "Exception"
  to the Rule   143

6 Epilogue Reconstructing the Two Reconstructions:
  Antebellum Race Formation and the Nationalization of
  Party Politics   195

Endnotes   207

Selected Bibliography   231

Index   241

Acknowledgments

Like many first books, this one began as a loose set of ideas during a frantic search for an "original" dissertation topic in the late 1990s while I was a graduate student at my wonderful alma mater, The City University of New York's Graduate Center. My dissertation was defended in late 2001 in a small room in midtown Manhattan as the ruins of the World Trade Center still smoldered to the south. That same year, I had also taken my first full-time teaching position at Pace University in New York, whose main campus is located just three blocks from Ground Zero.

Revisions to the manuscript were done primarily in those somber but compassionate New York days in the wake of 9/11. However, a good deal of the work was also completed during summer and winter breaks back home in my beloved New Orleans while visiting family and friends. The finishing touches were put on the work in the days and months after Hurricane Katrina chased my family, friends, and the rest of the noble people of New Orleans into exile. Eighteen months later as I write this, more than half the city has still not returned.

One will not find a discussion of either 9/11 or Hurricane Katrina in the pages that follow. And yet, the shadows of these two events cast themselves everywhere. For the sentences in this book were strung together through the tears and suffering of both 9/11 and Katrina. More aptly, it was written in the space in my mind between New York and New Orleans.

It may be said that, in the dawn of the twenty-first century, all of us in the United States live between these two events—between 9/11 and Katrina—and these two cities—between New York and New Orleans. My adult life has been spent between them. Despite the tragedies—and, in many ways, because of these tragedies—I am blessed to call these two great American cities "home."

I want to thank first and foremost my family. Although far away and perhaps unsure of what exactly it is I do from day to day, they are always with me. The pride they may feel in having the first member of their clan publish a book pales in comparison to the love and strength I have received from them over these years.

I want to thank the Dyson College of Arts and Sciences at Pace University for providing funding and release time for research and writing. I also want to acknowledge some of my wonderful colleagues at Pace University who have made me a better teacher and scholar through the endless conversations about politics and life. Most especially, Greg Julian, the chair of my department who is responsible for bringing me to Pace, and Meghana Nayak, my officemate and travel-course buddy—thank you both for your friendship and your love.

Because this project began as a dissertation, I would like to acknowledge the numerous colleagues going back to my grad school and teaching days at CUNY who have commented and provided excellent feedback on parts of the manuscript at dissertation workshops, conferences, colloquia, and seminars. First among firsts on this list is Frances Fox Piven. Without her guidance and mentoring, I would not be where I am or who I am today—it is as simple as that. I came to the CUNY Graduate Center to study under her. It is rare that you meet someone who is actually nicer, funnier, more caring, more charming, and more intelligent in real life than they are in the books they write. So it is with Fran Piven. I learned from her that teaching, mentoring students, producing solid scholarship, and engaging in the struggles of politics are not mutually exclusive things. Alas, after years of her mentorship, I am most proud to call her friend.

I also thank all of my friends and colleagues who sat with me at the Roundtable at Fran Piven's Upper Westside apartment month after month for her now famous Dissertation Workshop Dinners/Meetings. It was peculiarly refreshing to know you could eat a great home-cooked meal while having your intellectual work shredded apart by a smart and lovely bunch of people—and nonetheless leave with a smile on your face.

I also would not have made it through the demands of graduate school without the direction and friendship of Andy Polsky, who over the course of my days as an adjunct at Hunter College taught me how to be a better teacher and a better scholar. To his current and former students, Andy is best known for his meticulous scholarship and his legendary red pen. He went through dozens of them on draft after draft of my own work—which no doubt made it better, sharper, more nuanced.

There were many colleagues in the field who commented on parts of this work over the years at conferences and other opportunities where I had the chance to present my work. Ira Katznelson, Ruth O'Brien, Joan Tronto, all the members of the New York Colloquium on American Political Development, Tali Mendelberg, Phillip Klinkner, Richard Valelly, to name a few.

I want to thank the various librarians and staff at the institutions where I conducted a bulk of my research: the New York Public Library, the New York Historical Society, the New York State Archives, the Massachusetts Historical Society, the Massachusetts State Archive, the Pennsylvania Historical Society and State Archive, and the Rhode Island Historical Society and the State Archive of Rhode Island.

I want to thank *New Political Science* and *Pennsylvania History* for allowing me to reprint here updated versions of manuscripts that appeared in those journals.

I thank Routledge Press and especially my editor Kimberly Guinta who has stuck with the manuscript over several years of review and revision.

Last but not least, I want to thank all of the students I have had the good fortune to teach and learn from over the years—at Pace where I have been since 2001, and Hunter College, York College, and Baruch College from 1995 to 2000. After more than a decade of teaching, the classroom remains a pure source of my intellectual nutrition. One still marvels at the idea that he can get paid for doing something he loves so much. I would almost do it for no material compensation whatsoever—almost.

Christopher Malone

Pace University
New York City, February 2007

CHAPTER 1

The Beginning of the Story

Black Enfranchisement in the Antebellum Era

These two races are fastened to each other without intermingling; and they are unable to separate entirely or to combine. The most formidable of all ills that threaten the future of the Union arises from the presence of a black population upon its territory; and in contemplating the causes of present embarrassments, or of future dangers in the United States, the observer is invariably led to this as a primary fact.

Alexis de Tocqueville, *Democracy in America*[1]

On July 27, 2006, President George W. Bush signed the Voting Rights Act Reauthorization and Amendments Act of 2006. The law extended most of the provisions first put in place by the landmark Voting Rights Act of 1965, and then amended and reauthorized in 1982. In outlining the significance of the legislation, Bush drew on the exceptional dangers that race prejudice had posed to American democracy. "The right of ordinary men and women to determine their own political future lies at the heart of the American experiment, and it is a right that has been won by the sacrifice of patriots," he stated. "The amendments to our Constitution that outlawed slavery and guaranteed the right to vote came at the price of a terrible civil war." The false start of Reconstruction was followed by nearly another hundred years of state-sponsored second-class citizenship; by the 1960s, all three branches of the federal government had at last found the political will to provide the basic parameters of political equality for black Americans. "For some parts of our country," Bush continued, "the Voting Rights Act [of 1965] marked the first appearance of African Americans on the voting rolls since Reconstruction. And in the primaries and elections that followed the signing of this act, many African Americans pulled the voting lever for the first time in their lives." Championing the strides made at the same time underscoring the lingering problems the act was meant to address, he concluded, "in four decades since the Voting Rights Act was first passed, we've made progress toward equality, yet the work for a more perfect union is never ending. We'll continue to build on the legal equality won by the civil rights movement to help ensure that every person enjoys the opportunity that this great land of liberty offers."[2]

Civil rights leaders roundly applauded the reauthorization of the Voting Rights Act as a victory in the unending quest for political equality for blacks in the United States. Rightfully so. Yet, placed in a certain context, the passage of the law in the summer of 2006 was cause for some degree of ambivalence. On the one hand, that a Republican Congress with a power base in the old Confederacy passed—and a Republican president from Texas signed—the legislation indicated to some extent the advances in racial attitudes made by the New South since the days of Jim Crow. To be sure, when it came to race matters this crowd bared little resemblance to the Party of Lincoln or the Radical Republicans of the Thirty-Ninth Congress: George Bush had received a scant 11 percent of the black vote in 2004, and by then the only black Republican in Congress in the modern era had retired. Yet the legislation passed with overwhelming majorities in both Houses. On the other hand, the very idea that the provisions of the Voting Rights Act would remain in place well into the fourth decade of the twenty-first century also underscored the general sense that racial discrimination was still a real cause for concern in these United States. Given the reported problems in voting for blacks in Florida in the presidential election of 2000 and Ohio in 2004, one could not deny that, in the most fundamental act undertaken by citizens in our democracy, race still mattered. So, too, did laws designed to prevent racial discrimination at the ballot box.

Yes, despite what progress the nation had made, race still mattered. That was the message conveyed by the passage of the Voting Rights Act Reauthorization and Amendments Act of 2006. But when it came to voting and the other fundamental tenets of our democracy, race had *always* mattered. This is not a particularly new or shocking statement, even if the ways in which race still matters has the uncanny ability to shock us out of our slumber. Witness, for example, New Orleans in the days after Katrina.

President Bush was right to contextualize the reauthorization of the act by alluding to the history of the Reconstruction period. This is, after all, where the narrative of black enfranchisement supposedly "all began." In its most simplistic form, that story goes something like this: After the Civil War, the Fifteenth Amendment to the Constitution was ratified in 1870 and granted black males the right to vote in both the North and the South. With the end of Reconstruction and the beginning of what Southern whites called "Redemption," state after state in the South erected formidable barriers to the franchise—grandfather clauses, literacy tests, poll taxes, understanding clauses, prohibitive residency requirements, and, when these failed, outright physical violence. The discriminatory laws and acts of intimidation effectively disenfranchised blacks across the South for the next eighty years. It was not until the ratification of the Twenty-Fourth Amendment and the passage of the Voting Rights Act of 1965 that African Americans won back the right to vote in the South once and for all. Despite very difficult obstacles and lingering racist attitudes, the enforcement of legislation such as the Voting Rights Act and its reauthorization in the summer of 2006 would ensure that the long steady march of democracy for black Americans would continue on its way.

Although grossly simplified, this nonetheless passes for an accurate abstract of the history of voting rights for blacks over the last century and a half. But to begin the story of black enfranchisement with the Fifteenth Amendment would be leaving out an important part—the beginning of it, if you will. It also would rob us of a rich context by which we might be able to understand the struggles since Reconstruction that Bush alluded to on that summer day in 2006. For, although much is known about the period following Reconstruction, relatively little is known about voting rights for blacks *before* the ratification of the Fifteenth Amendment—particularly in the North after gradual emancipation took hold in the opening decades of the nineteenth century. In the broadest sense, that is the subject of this book.

Much has been written on the expansion of the suffrage in the early national period and, to a lesser extent, on the condition of free blacks in both North and South during this time. Yet a comprehensive attempt to address black enfranchisement in the antebellum North within the larger context of race and American political development has not been undertaken. A quick glance reveals that transformations in racial voting restrictions before the Civil War do not fit neatly into most accounts of change and continuity in American politics. It should be noted that disenfranchisement of black Americans was occurring across both time and space in an ostensibly random manner for most of the first century of the country's history. It spanned the years of the Federalist regime, the Jeffersonian Republicans, Jacksonian Democracy, the rise and demise of the

Table 1.1 States Restricting the Franchise to White Males[3]

Virginia (1762)	Rhode Island (1822)[4]
Georgia (1777)	North Carolina (1835)
South Carolina (1790)	Tennessee (1834)
Delaware (1792)	Arkansas (1836)
Kentucky (1799)	Michigan (1837)
Maryland (1801)	Pennsylvania (1838)
Ohio (1803)	Florida and Texas (1845)
New Jersey (1807)	Iowa (1846)
Louisiana (1812)	Wisconsin (1848)
Indiana (1816)	California (1850)
Mississippi (1817)	Minnesota (1858)
Illinois and Connecticut (1818)	Oregon (1859)
Alabama (1819)	Kansas (1861)
Missouri and New York (1821)[5]	West Virginia (1863)

Whig Party, the formation of the Republican Party, and the onset of the Civil War. Black disenfranchisement even occurred during Reconstruction until the eve of the ratification of the Fifteenth Amendment in 1870 (see Table 1.1). Disenfranchisement was not necessarily confined to any one section of the country, nor was it exactly uniform in the way it was applied in each section of the country. States themselves underwent drastic changes over time. Finally, when we consider those cases in which no racial disenfranchisement was enacted at all, we are left with a sort of Rorschach test of facts and events without a coherent viewpoint by which they might be understood.

Until the appearance of work such as Piven and Cloward's *Why Americans Don't Vote*, and more recently Rogers Smith's *Civic Ideals: Conflicting Visions of U.S. Citizenship*, Alexander Keyssar's *The Right to Vote: The Contested History of Democracy in the United States*, and Ron Hayduk's *Democracy for All: Restoring Immigrant Voting Rights in the United States*, a consensus had more or less formed around the history of the right to vote in the United States.[6] Again, to put it rather simplistically: at the time of the country's founding, only white men with property could vote. The vote was then expanded in turn to propertyless white men, to African-American males (although soon denied in practice), to women, to African Americans again, and then finally to those between the ages of eighteen and twenty-one. The history of the United States is thus portrayed as the history of a unidirectional extension of democracy. As Keyssar points out, as early as 1928 the Harvard historian and political scientist William Munro wrote in *The Government of American Cities* that "the history of the American suffrage has been one of steady and irresistible expansion." Most scholars in the twentieth century have agreed: E. E. Schattschneider called the expansion of the suffrage "astonishingly easy." Thus, credence has always been given to the perception that democracy in America, with the expansion of the suffrage as its irresistible force, was nothing short of inevitable.[7]

Piven and Cloward, Smith, Keyssar, and Hayduk all demonstrate in their excellent analyses that nothing is ever inevitable when it comes to the basic rights in American democracy. Recently, Richard Valelly has demonstrated a similar point in the history of black enfranchisement in his important work.[8] I shall follow their lead here and propose that the story of black enfranchisement in the antebellum period does not fit into a simple, unidirectional synthesis either. There was no long steady march toward democracy for northern blacks. The right to vote was not characterized by irresistible expansion. Neither was its attainment, when it did occur, astonishingly easy. With no federal statutes on the books to which blacks could appeal to for protection, it was unclear whether blacks were meant to be included in the social contract instantiated in the first state constitutions drafted after the Revolutionary War. Some states placed no restrictions on black males,[9] some placed a property restriction higher for black males than for white males,[10] and most explicitly restricted the vote to white males either through state constitutional revision or statute.[11] And in at least one state, blacks had the right to vote, lost it, and reacquired it in the wake of a virtual intrastate civil war.[12] In short, all across the North throughout the antebellum period blacks lived somewhere, to quote the noted historian Charles Wesley, "between freedom and bondage."[13]

The upshot is that a gap exists in our understanding of the history of the right to vote for black Americans in the United States, and consequently in the tale of American democracy itself. Once again, I take seriously the caution offered by Alexander Keyssar: "The history of the right to vote in the United States has received far less scrutiny than the subject would seem to warrant."[14] *Between Freedom and Bondage* picks up Keyssar's challenge by scrutinizing the right to vote for African Americans in great detail in four states in the antebellum North: New York, Pennsylvania, Massachusetts, and Rhode Island.

I have chosen these four states primarily because of the divergent ways in which blacks were treated in their quest to share in the democratic ideal of the United States. New York placed a $250 property qualification on black males at the same time as it dropped most property qualifications for white males in 1821. Pennsylvania disenfranchised black males completely in 1838 after allowing them to vote for nearly a half-century. Massachusetts granted black males the right to vote in the early 1780s and never legally denied them that right. And Rhode Island, the most bizarre case, disenfranchised black males by state statute in 1822 and reenfranchised them in the wake of the Dorr War in 1843. Thus, these four states present us with a puzzle: given these differences, can we explain the outcomes in some coherent fashion that sheds light not only on the problem of voting rights for blacks in the antebellum North but also on the larger question of racial conflict in American politics?

My response is found in what follows. The circumstances leading up to these outcomes; how political leaders reached their conclusions; the partisan, ideological, and institutional forces at work within each state but also across state lines—these are all subjects of this book. I shall make the broad point that, despite the political contingencies that led to these different outcomes, what happened in New York, Pennsylvania, Massachusetts, and Rhode Island was indeed structured and the product of similar social, economic, and cultural undercurrents. My goal is to sort out these currents and show how their contingent interaction led to such divergent results. Events across state lines can, I argue, be explained with reference to three key variables that changed over time and combine in different ways to structure what I shall call "race formation":

- the changing economic structure of racial conflict;
- the changing partisan structure of race affiliation; and
- the changing discursive structure of racial coalitions.

Conflict, Continuity, and Change: Race Formation and the Contours of American Politics in the Antebellum North

Traveling across the United States in the 1830s, Alexis de Tocqueville went in search of what writers before and since have struggled to find: the distinctive or "exceptional" quality of American democracy. What set Americans apart, Tocqueville contended, was the basic equality of social condition that Americans enjoyed. As Raymond Aron points out in his *Essay on Freedom,* Tocqueville in most cases used the word "democracy" to designate a condition of society rather than a specific form of government.[15] And yet, the America he observed was in the throes of a fundamental transformation in the very concept of representative, democratic government. By the early 1830s, state after state had dropped property qualifications for voting. Thus, the impulse for a more "democratic" condition of American society had already translated into a more "democratic" system of constitutional government. But however democracy is defined, we need to understand how Tocqueville took exception to his own formula, a fact that is often overlooked particularly by scholars who may be grouped within what Katznelson calls the "national character tradition."[16]

As early as the 1830s, the unique feature of the black experience in the United States—politically, socially, economically, culturally—had come into such sharp focus that Tocqueville believed the white and black races incapable of complete integration or, for that matter, complete separation. In fact, by the time that Tocqueville had concluded his extended trip across America, both the promise of complete integration of blacks into a dominant white society and the desire for complete separation of the races had been attempted—with little success. It is telling that Tocqueville would call this predicament a "primary fact" of American life, as the quote at the beginning of this chapter indicates. If there was an "exceptional" quality to American democracy—if indeed an outer limit to American liberalism was to be identified—its location lay in the intractability of the color line.

Tocqueville went on later to make special mention of conditions for blacks living in the North. "The prejudice of race appears to be stronger in the states that have abolished slavery than in those where it still exists; and nowhere is it so intolerant as in those states where servitude has never been known."[17] Without any federal guarantee of life or liberty, Northern blacks were left to the mercy of state politics. The conditions for blacks in Northern states varied tremendously—from near-full citizenship rights in Massachusetts, to quasi-citizenship and quasi-freedom in New York and Pennsylvania, to attempted expulsion in Ohio. If conditions for blacks were not the same across Northern states throughout the antebellum period, neither were they the same *within* Northern states over the course of the antebellum period. Each state underwent its own changes and development in the period from the Founding to the Civil War. This is not to suggest that the changes and development were random, haphazard, or unintelligible. On the contrary, I will argue that in fact the development of each state was highly structured. Explaining that path of development within each state is a crucial benefit in applying the analytical concept of race formation.

I borrow the term "race formation" largely from Michael Omi and Howard Winant's *Racial Formation in the United States from the 1960s to the 1990s*.[18] Omi and Winant define "racial formation" as "the sociohistorical process by which categories are created, transformed and destroyed."[19] Racial formation "connect[s] what race means in a particular discursive practice and the ways in which both social structures and everyday experience are racially organized, based upon that meaning."[20] For Omi and Winant, the category of race then encompasses both social structures and the cultural representations of individuals existing in a racialized society within a given historical epoch. Linking the structural constraints of the "macro-level" social processes of race to the everyday, lived experience of racialized beings is the key. These are linked through what the authors term "racial projects," which serve a mediating role between the two.

Race formation is similar in that it serves to connect the quotidian experience of race to the larger racialized institutional structures and the limits they impose upon individual and group actors. Yet, I depart from Omi and Winant on a key issue. My use of race formation goes beyond the "socio-historical process" to include an overtly "political" process of how decisions on race get institutionalized by political actors. That political process lies at the core of why I believe the outcomes on voting rights for blacks in these four states have an underlying logic and occurred in the manner that they did. I take my bearings from three broad areas of scholarship that, considered separately, do not fully satisfy my search for an explanation. Broadly speaking, they can be defined as: (1) the socioeconomic approach, (2) the historical-institutional argument, and (3) the discursive/ideological perspective.

Bringing to bear different bodies of scholarship on big questions of race and American political development has been proven to have significant explanatory power. Richard Valelly's recent excellent work on black enfranchisement during what he calls the "two reconstructions" is a case in point.[21] I seek here a similar solution: a methodological mix applied to the puzzle of black enfranchisement in parts of the antebellum North in particular, which I hope proves useful when directed at other questions of race and American political development beyond the issue of black suffrage in these four states. I will now look at each of these scholarly fields, where I draw on them and believe they fall short individually, and how I employ them collectively in my pursuit of the development of race formation.

The Economic Structure of Racial Conflict

The first federal Census taken in 1790 indicates that about sixty-six thousand of all blacks (slave and free) lived in Northern states—or roughly 8 percent of the entire black population of the country. At the time, a total of 59,553 free blacks lived in the United States, with nearly 60 percent of them (approximately thirty-four thousand) living in the South.[22] By 1800, the free black population in the United States nearly doubled to 110,000. Over the course of the opening decades of the nineteenth century, the percentage of free blacks living in the Northern states compared to the overall free black population increased substantially. Manumitted slaves were moving to the North, fugitive slaves were fleeing to the North, and the abolition of slavery was taking hold throughout the North. In the case of New York, for example, manumission played the largest role. An act was passed in New York in 1799 providing for the manumission of black males at the age of

TABLE 1.2 Percentages of Blacks in the Population by Region, 1790–1850[23]

Region	1790 (%)	1800 (%)	1810 (%)	1820 (%)	1830 (%)	1840 (%)	1850 (%)
(United States)	19.3	18.9	19.0	18.4	18.1	16.8	15.7
New England	1.7	1.5	1.4	1.3	1.1	1.0	0.8
Middle Atlantic	5.3	4.6	4.1	3.3	2.9	2.6	2.1
East North Central	—	1.2	1.3	1.0	1.1	1.0	1.0
West North Central	—	—	17.4	15.9	18.3	15.6	13.2

TABLE 1.3 Percentage of Population of Blacks by States, 1790–1850[24]

State	1790 (%)	1800 (%)	1810 (%)	1820 (%)	1830 (%)	1840 (%)	1850 (%)
Massachusetts	1.4	1.5	1.4	1.3	1.2	1.1	0.9
Rhode Island	6.3	5.3	4.8	4.3	3.7	3.0	2.5
New York	7.6	5.3	4.2	2.9	2.3	2.1	1.6
Connecticut	2.3	2.5	2.6	2.9	2.7	2.6	2.1
New Jersey	7.7	8.0	7.6	7.2	6.4	5.8	4.9
Pennsylvania	2.4	2.7	2.9	2.9	2.8	2.8	2.8

twenty-eight and black females at the age of twenty-five. At that time, black males could vote if they owned a freehold of twenty pounds value or if they rented a tenement of the annual fee of forty shillings.[25] In a twenty-year period, the number of slaves in New York decreased from 20,613 in 1800 to 10,046 in 1820.[26] By 1840, there were but four slaves in the entire state.

However, although the number of blacks in the North increased in this time period, it is important to note that *the density of blacks in the overall population did not.* In most cases, black density either remained stable or decreased throughout the antebellum period. Tables 1.2 and 1.3 detail the percentage of blacks in the population by region of the country and by selected Northern states.

Although different regions and states of the North contained a variance of black densities at the time of the first Census, all of the regions and nearly all of the states highlighted here witnessed declines in black density in the population during the antebellum period. Only Pennsylvania's black density increased—although very slightly. Most of this decline can be attributed to the immigration of ethnic whites in the first half of the nineteenth century into some of the major Northern urban centers such as New York City, Philadelphia, Boston, and Providence.

These numbers are significant because they tell us that the steady increase of the black population did not significantly change the racial makeup of those states or the region of the country as a whole. Thus, in terms of what Rodney Hero calls "social diversity,"[27] the North changed ethnically but not racially. Nonetheless, the racial and ethnic makeup, along with rapid economic changes in each state, bear heavily on the outcome of black disenfranchisement, as I will show.

In the wake of the Revolutionary War, most Northern states passed gradual abolition laws, referred to as *post nati* statutes. Of the four states I cover, only Massachusetts did not pass such a law: slavery was outlawed there through constitutional interpretation in 1783. Massachusetts also was the only Northern state covered here that listed no slaves in the first national census of 1790. For New York, Pennsylvania, and Rhode Island, the process of emancipation was gradual as the eighteenth century closed and the nineteenth century commenced. The deliberate nature of emancipation in the post-Revolutionary period took place against a backdrop of tremendous social and economic change in the North. In each of the four states I examine, the onset of the nineteenth century signaled the transition from an agrarian (New York, Pennsylvania, and Massachusetts) or maritime (Massachusetts again and Rhode Island) economy to one increasingly based on manufacturing. At the same time, immigration was altering the ethnic makeup of many northern states. By the opening decade of the nineteenth century, New York and Pennsylvania had witnessed a significant influx of immigrants, particularly those of Irish descent. By contrast, significant levels of immigration were delayed in Rhode Island and Massachusetts for several decades. The timing of immigration played a large role in the levels of racial animosity in each of these states.

Just emerging from slavery, blacks were faced with the difficult task of carving out independent lives for themselves and providing the means of economic sustenance. Of course, slavery operated much differently in the North than in the South. Rather than toiling on large sprawling plantations, slaves were mostly concentrated in Northern urban centers and worked as "domestics" in their owners' homes. As free blacks moved out of white households and into their own (segregated) communities, they sought work anywhere they could find it. Naturally, they competed on the lowest rung of the economic ladder with poor whites—many of whom were recent immigrants in places such as Philadelphia and New York City. Economic competition thus caused racial tensions in those areas where urbanization, immigration, and industrialization were the most pronounced. On the one hand, the larger the growing free black population, the more visible blacks were and, hence, the more resentment they faced. On the other hand, the earlier that immigration, urbanization, and industrialization took place, the more likelihood that racial animosities would flare up. As we shall see, New York and Pennsylvania experienced more racial conflict earlier than

Rhode Island and Massachusetts as a result of earlier immigration of white ethnics. In general, the social and economic milieu of the early nineteenth century across the North tested what Joanne Pope Melish has described as "the stability of social identity and the meaning of citizenship for whites as well as for people of color."[28]

By the early decades of the nineteenth century, these socioeconomic forces combined to structure racial conflict in Northern states. I accept the premises of a large body of literature that focuses on the socioeconomic origins of race discrimination and the ideology of "whiteness." Whiteness among poorer whites, goes this line of thinking, is born of socioeconomic conflicts and is used as a form of social control by white elites on the (black) minority. Racial conflict, in other words, is instigated in the first instance by the demands of the labor market. A considerable number of scholars analyzing American history from the seventeenth century to the present have argued more or less along these lines. Edmund Morgan's *American Slavery/American Freedom: The Ordeal of Colonial Virginia;* Lerone Bennett's *The Shaping of Black America;* Alexander Saxton's *The Rise and Fall of the White Republic;* David Roediger's *Wages of Whiteness: Race and the Making of the American Working Class;* Noel Ignatiev's *How the Irish Became White;* and Theodore Allen's *The Invention of the White Race* are cases in point.[29]

Across the four states under consideration over the opening decades of the nineteenth century, we shall see that a set of economic factors provided the context for the structure of racial conflict between blacks and poor whites as gradual manumission took hold against the backdrop of urbanization and immigration. However, these socioeconomic arguments alone cannot explain the outcomes. Racial antagonisms did play out; yet, although rooted in economic competition, they needed to find a political voice, and then get channeled through a set of political institutions. In other words, they needed to become part of a larger narrative constructed around race and located in a specific form of institutional patterning. Although the white working classes were indeed "agents" and played a role in the construction of their own racial identity, leaving the analysis there would ignore *how* political elites sought advantage by piecing together a racial narrative out of the conflict and the institutional means they sought to solve the problems that the conflict presented. Piven and Cloward understand this point intuitively when they analyze the logic of social movements: "Just as political leaders play an influential role in stimulating mass arousal, so do they play an important role in shaping the demands of the aroused."[30] If economic competition "aroused" the white working classes into racial conflict in the early nineteenth century, political leaders played an influential role in both stimulating that arousal and shaping the direction that it took.

The Racial Structure of Partisan Competition

How that dynamic took place leads me to the second and third perspectives—the historical-institutionalist argument about partisan competition, on the one hand, and the discursive/ideological argument about racial coalition formation, on the other. Let me take up partisan competition first.

It is a fundamental fact that the principal structuring institution of political conflict in the United States is the electoral-representative system. Political parties are the linkages in any electoral-representative system between the citizenry and those elected. As Klinkner and Smith state, "as political scientists we must insist that any analysis ... must come to grips with the incentives that shape the behavior of political parties."[31] Most political party scholars have placed parties at the center of democratic political life, and many have argued that they are essential for the creation and extension of democratic values.[32] Socioeconomic concerns need to be augmented with an analysis of how racial conflict structured partisan competition and how political discourse structured racial coalition formation.

With regard to the historical-institutionalist argument, I take my bearings here from several recent works. Valelly's analysis of the "two reconstructions" has already been mentioned. His comparison of the post-Reconstruction era to the civil rights era leads him to a compelling theory about the development of coalition formation. Party actors were in conflict with one another during both periods in the struggle for black enfranchisement; in order to maintain and/or capture power, party leaders needed to expand their coalition by incorporating new members. In explaining why the first reconstruction failed and the second succeeded, Valelly incorporates Skowronek's work on the courts and parties, Riker's theory of the "minimum winning coalition," and Waldner's view that elites expand coalitions only when their status is jeopardized.[33] Paul Frymer's *Uneasy Alliances* argues other important points for my purposes here. Frymer contends that parties in the United States have compelling incentives *not* to incorporate and mobilize blacks into the political system because doing so would disrupt existing coalition formation within the political party. "The success of broad-based parties," Frymer writes, "rests on the marginalization of black interests."[34] As a consequence, blacks, more than any other group, suffer from what he calls "electoral capture," which he defines as those circumstances when the group has no choice but to remain in the party.[35] Once part of the coalition that forms a political party, blacks have nowhere to go politically. Political leaders are aware of the dilemma that blacks face. At the same time, they engage in their own political calculus; electoral incentives to win and maintain political offices lead them to downplay the interests of blacks because articulating these interests would lead to alienating the "median" white voter. Party leaders thus maximize votes while minimizing the articulation of black interests.

Much of what Valelly and Frymer argue has relevance in the cases of New York, Pennsylvania, Massachusetts, and Rhode Island. I will maintain that the expansion of a broad-based winning coalition by political actors was a motivating factor in all of these states. For example, blacks in New York were a "captured" group of the Federalists in the first party era and then of the Whigs in the second. As early as 1800, the black vote in New York was decisive in certain municipal elections. Jeffersonian Republicans quickly moved to eliminate the electoral advantage of the Federalists by first intimidating blacks and then moving to disenfranchise them through a change in the state constitution. As I point out in Chapter 2, electoral incentive plays a large role in the motivations of the political actors. After the constitution of 1821 placed a property qualification on blacks of $250, those blacks still qualified to vote continued to vote the Whig ticket—even though the New York Whig Party refused to articulate forcefully the rights of blacks during the second party period.

In Pennsylvania, the Democratic Party was able to disrupt the coalition of blacks and Whigs when Democratic leaders were successful in disenfranchising blacks in the state constitution adopted in 1838. Their efforts came on the heels of a controversial county election in which the black vote proved to be decisive. The Whig Party had captured the black vote, and the Democratic Party disrupted it through constitutional disenfranchisement. Democrats were successful in maintaining electoral advantage in Pennsylvania for the remainder of the antebellum period.

A similar experience obtains in Rhode Island in the wake of the Dorr War. Granted the franchise after the Law and Order Party put down Thomas Dorr's rebellion, blacks were part of the winning coalition put in place by the Whigs. They voted the Whig ticket loyally until the party's demise in the mid-1850s. As we will see in Chapter 4, the Whig Party did little to articulate black interests during this period. For example, blacks in Rhode Island were pressed hard by Whig leaders to vote for presidential candidate Zachary Taylor in 1848 over the Free Soil candidate Martin Van Buren—even though Taylor was a slaveholder. Whig leaders consistently reminded blacks that they had been granted the franchise by the Whig Party. The distribution of the franchise was to be repaid with black loyalty come election time. Yet, white Rhode Island Whigs refused to press for the advancement of black rights. For example, Whigs refused to do anything about school desegregation or the right of blacks to sit on a jury, even though they held political power with the help of blacks after the Dorr War.

Electoral capture of the black vote did not play a major role in Massachusetts. Throughout the antebellum period, black density remained miniscule in the state. Thus, blacks provided neither a decisive electoral advantage nor posed a real electoral threat to either of the parties during the first and second party eras. Although electoral competition was stiff at times, the racial structure of partisan competition was much weaker in Massachusetts than in New York, Pennsylvania, or Rhode Island. Overall in Massachusetts, however, one party dominated most of the time, and lost only to fusion campaigns. By then, black voting rights were firmly established.

The work of Valelly and Frymer furthers my search for an explanation of these particular outcomes, and the racial dynamics involved in partisan coalition formation in general. But if this historical-institutionalist approach assists in understanding the calculations, incentives, and institutional limitations party leaders faced while seeking to maximize votes and minimize black interests, it does not do much work in helping me understand normative questions that remain. Why, for instance, does black marginalization, which Frymer convincingly describes, work in the first place? What is it about race in the United States that ostensibly allows the marginalization of black interests to operate as a norm? At the least, the discursive elements that Omi and Winant emphasize—and that I seek to do as well in the development of race formation—are taken for granted by many historical-institutionalist perspectives. Political interests of groups are part of the equation of party competition; what is needed is an explanation of why or how they arrive at their interests in the first place, which is to say, their normative roots.

The Discursive Structure of Racial Coalition Formation

Hence, I offer a third piece to this puzzle, with an emphasis on the *discursive structure of racial coalition formation* and a concomitant accent on the normative elements of political discourse surrounding race. Like political institutions, political discourse does not appear out of thin air. Political actors inherit a "discourse-in-being" much as they inherit an "institution-in-being" in the pursuit and maintenance of political office. Similarly, political actors must work within a set of political discourses that both limits the political coalition's interests and allows it to maintain its cohesion. Political discourse, in other words, is the glue that helps shape the winning coalition and hold it together; it also forms the normative assumptions on which the coalition acts. Political discourse, I contend, operates on two levels—it is at once constitutive and instrumental. On the one hand, narratives embodied in political discourse already have shaped significant normative aspects of the political and social world in which the political actor seeks advantage. Consequently, these narratives have gone a long way in shaping both the *identity* and the *interests* of the political actor. On the other, the political discourse is employed as a powerful tool in coalition formation and the quest for political advantage.

Philosophers of language such as J. L. Austin,[36] postmodern thinkers such as Michel Foucault,[37] and Critical Race theorists such as Richard Delgado all make a similar point in their respective work. For all of them, human agents learn to "get things done with words"—that is, construct a social world and then operate within it.[38] Derrick Bell and Patricia Williams have infused their scholarly, academic works with "storytelling" as a way of building consensus among members of an "outgroup" and ultimately changing the status quo. Narratives thus help *create* group identity and interests. Much like Delgado, Austin, and Foucault, I argue political discourse should be considered an important variable in explaining political outcomes because the narratives contained in discourse have already shaped the identity and interests of those seeking political outcomes.

With this in mind, I propose here that a set of *racial* narratives should be considered as a key variable in explaining black (dis)enfranchisement in New York, Pennsylvania, Massachusetts, and Rhode Island. As mass-based political parties sprang to life in the second party period, political life became increasingly structured through partisanship and the electoral-representative system. Politicians such as Martin Van Buren saw the benefit of parties in the twin goals of organizing voters to gain office and organizing the government once elected. Political actors then set about creating a durable voting coalition to sustain an electoral majority. In order to win office, political leaders needed to create voting majorities; in order create voting majorities, political leaders had to construct narratives that swayed voters to their side.[39] In short, political leaders had to relate to potential coalition members how they believed the world not only worked but also *should* work—and what place members of the coalition inhabited in that world. That is precisely what party leaders did when the issue of black suffrage arose in either constitutional conventions where it was debated or in the public discourse.

Specifically, I contend that two competing racial belief systems developed and formed the basis of mainstream political discourse on race, not only in these four states but also across the antebellum North.[40] I call them racial paternalism, on the one hand, and racial ascriptivism, on the other. These narratives played a large role in the *formation of racial coalitions*.

Versions of racial paternalism have been elaborated on by various scholars, and I rely particularly on the work of Eugene Genovese, Winthrop Jordan, and James Oakes.[41] Racial paternalism holds that mental, moral, and psychological characteristics were the result of the environment. But the mental, moral, and psychological characteristics found in blacks were to be overcome only under the watchful gaze of paternalistic whites. Winthrop's analysis of Enlightenment thinking and its connection to environmentalist arguments about moral development is telling; similarly, Genovese and Oakes make the compelling point that paternalism, far from being merely a benevolent set of attitudes, suggests a social order that is stable and hierarchical. Racial paternalism dominated the thinking of many northern Revolutionary leaders and persisted in various degrees of strength throughout the antebellum North. Paternalistic whites sought a more inclusive—perhaps even biracial—society founded on some type of equality between the races rather than rooted exclusively in a racial contract premised on notions of whiteness. As we know, abolition in the North did not lead to full citizenship rights for blacks though some Revolutionary leaders argued for it. But this is not to suggest that political actors espousing racial paternalism at the time of the Founding believed fully in either the natural or social equality of blacks and whites. Racial paternalism cannot be considered a mere subset of the "liberal political tradition" espoused by Hartz, Myrdal, or Tocqueville. Neither can it be folded neatly into Smith's "multiple traditions" typology.[42] Many racial paternalists understood blacks to be inferior in some way, but they believed that it was the duty of whites to uplift the black race out of the degraded condition within which blacks found themselves. Giving them the right to vote was one way of achieving those ends.

If racial paternalism dominated Revolutionary thinking on race, by no means was it unchallenged by other views. Duncan Macleod makes the case that developments during the Revolutionary era prompted the reemergence of arguments about racial hierarchy as the South felt the need to justify the continuation and perpetuation of slavery.[43] In the North, these arguments were used to justify the denial of the rights of citizenship to blacks mainly by Jeffersonian Republicans and then Jacksonian Democrats as they sought to incorporate poor whites into their coalition. Jordan argues that the environmentalist philosophy was beginning to erode by the first decade of the nineteenth century. George Fredrickson picks up on this point and contends that, by the 1820s, another set of racial attitudes had taken hold, premised on ascribed differences and "scientific" explanations of race.[44] Inequality and low moral and mental capacity were not a result of environmental factors, went this line of thinking, but, rather, because of the moral and intellectual inferiority of blacks to whites. I contend that this set of racial attitudes, which I call *racial ascriptivism,* also was circulating at the time of the Revolution—although by no means did it have its origins in the Revolution. Indeed, racial ascriptivism provided the ideological justifications for the institutionalization of hereditary, lifetime African slavery in the mid- to late seventeenth century. But, by the turn of the nineteenth century, it had once again become an ascendant narrative about race and citizenship and, as we shall see, would reemerge in the debates around black suffrage in the four Northern states I am analyzing here.

In general, racial ascriptivism holds that blacks were essentially different from, and thereby inherently inferior to, whites. Blacks should not be part of the "white republic"—not only because they were never meant to be part of its citizenry, but also because they were naturally ill-equipped for citizenry. For this reason, blacks should not be granted the franchise. In this view, there is no doubt that the faculties of blacks and whites are fundamentally different, and that no amount of education will lift the black man up from "worthlessness," as one delegate in the Pennsylvania Constitutional Convention of 1837–1838 put it.[45] By the time of the Civil War, racial ascriptivism had become the dominant racial paradigm in the country, as exemplified in the "white republic ideology" of Chief Justice Roger Taney's *Dred Scott* opinion in 1857, where he argued that blacks were *always* considered inherently inferior and could *never* be considered citizens under the proper meaning of the Constitution.

I will seek to make the case that these two racial belief systems—racial paternalism and racial ascriptivism—were employed by those on opposite sides of the debate over black enfranchisement in New York, Pennsylvania, Rhode Island, and Massachusetts. Moreover, they need to be considered as important variables in our search for an explanation of what happened in each state. The ideas embedded in each were certainly used instrumentally for partisan advantage when time came for debate over the franchise; yet, this is not to say those who argued on either side didn't actually believe in what they were saying. On the contrary, I take these political actors at their word. But the more important point I wish to make is that these competing racial belief systems were a vital ideological component in the formation of the (racial) coalitions among the competing parties. They had *a priori* shaped the ideas and interests of members in the coalition. As such, they were the ideological glue that held coalitions together along the lines of race.

Let me briefly conclude here by recapitulating a few points. First, despite different outcomes on black voting rights, the four states under consideration share similar economic, political, and ideological currents with an underlying logic. Second, these outcomes can be explained by applying the changing dynamic of race formation, which combines three interrelated levels of analyses: the changing economic structure of racial conflict; the changing partisan structure of race affiliation; and the changing discursive structure of racial coalitions.

In order for black disenfranchisement to be enacted, I posit that three conditions had to be present: (1) when racial conflict took place as an outgrowth of rapid economic and demographic change; (2) when political actors seeking electoral advantage were in a position to successfully prey on this racial conflict by arousing poorer white working classes; and (3) when an ascriptive racial belief system became the dominant racial paradigm for understanding citizenship rights for blacks.

To Follow

I pursue the question of black enfranchisement in these four states by focusing on these three factors—how racial conflict is structured through economic competition; how partisan competition is structured by racial cleavages; and how racial coalition formation is structured through racial narratives and a racialized discourse. Before laying out what follows in each of the chapters, I wish to offer three notes of caution: one about what the reader will find and two about what the reader will not find in the pages that follow.

In telling the stories of voting rights in New York, Pennsylvania, Rhode Island, and Massachusetts, I have chosen a layered, analytical approach over a linear, chronological restatement of events. In each chapter, I begin by addressing the changing economic structure of racial conflict in each state, which is then followed first by the changing partisan structure of race affiliation in each state, and finally by the changing discursive structure of racial coalitions in each state. The effect, then, is really three "histories" in the development of each state over time—with the expressed aim of weaving together the economic, institutional, and ideological dimensions to the problem at hand. Had it been possible to relay the narrative and offer my explanation in another, more straightforward fashion, I certainly would have. Both political scientists and historians would tend to agree that history is rarely "one darn thing after the other ..." Alas, my narrative follows this belief.

Second, although I clearly address the issue of race in America throughout the book, I refrain from addressing the term in any grand theoretical or paradigmatic terms. There is no extended discussion of the debate, for instance, between those who argue that race is a biological/genetic reality and those who contend that race is purely a social construction. Neither is there a detailed analysis of the origins of racial conflict as a "psychocultural" phenomenon or as a "socioeconomic" formation. That is the subject of other works, and many scholars have taken up that task more competently than I perhaps ever could.[46] Given the framework I have laid out earlier, it should be clear that my concept of "race" has to embody in an integral way the socioeconomic, the historical-institutional, and the discursive-ideological. I have tried to remain true to this framework throughout—which explains the way each chapter unfolds. Furthermore, because much of what I deal with here involves the enactment of laws and changes in state constitutions, it should be clear that the legal arrangements I discuss are by-products of "race" but then serve to reinforce the very demands of race (economically, politically, ideologically) once they are put in place. "Race" is the concept with which I deal—but my analysis assumes that the concept entails what I might call economic race, political race, and ideological race.

Finally, the reader may—and perhaps *should*—be disconcerted to find so few black voices in what follows. Those who commented on earlier versions of the manuscript have uniformly made this critique, and to it I plead guilty as charged. This is not to suggest that either so few black advocates of voting rights existed in the antebellum North, or that the voices that were heard were not significant enough to warrant inclusion here. The scholarship on African Americans in the antebellum period—both North and South—is robust and burgeoning. The appearance of so much quality work has reinforced an idea whose time has come: that black history in America *is* American history, no more, no less. The works of James and Lois Horton, Leslie Harris, William Andrews, David Blight, Nell Irvin Painter, Jean Fagan Yellin, Graham Russell Hodges, Carla Peterson, James Brewer Stewart, Patrick Rael, Maryemma Graham, Frances Smith Foster—just to name a few—are all testament to the importance of black voices during the period I am considering. Put simply, my focus is a different one. I've attempted here to analyze how political actors and party leaders responded to the changing landscape by merely doing what they always do—by explaining reality as they see it back to the citizenry in the hope of shaping enough viewpoints to remain in power. Certainly there were other views on race—both in the black and white communities—than the ones that are offered in the pages that follow. But as they were channeled through the political-institutional structure, my focus is trained on what was said, and who was saying it, when decisions were made on black enfranchisement across these four states.

Chapter 2 addresses the case of New York. A property qualification of $250 was placed on blacks during the Constitutional Convention of 1821—at the very moment that property qualifications were dropped for whites. The property qualification was a product of the attempts by Martin Van Buren's Bucktail Republicans to gain partisan advantage over what was left of the Federalist Party and consolidate political power in the state. Blacks had voted loyally with the Federalists since the turn of the century. Van Buren and his allies perceived the threat and moved to disenfranchise blacks completely. However, the Federalist delegates in the convention of 1821 would not allow complete disenfranchisement. Thus, a compromise was struck—but on racially ascriptive grounds. By the 1820s, racial ascriptivism had replaced paternalism as the dominant race culture in the state.

Chapter 3 looks at Pennsylvania. Of all the states analyzed here, the transformation of Pennsylvania is perhaps the most dramatic. Founded on the ideology of Quakerism, Pennsylvania was one of the most racially liberal colonies during the middle decades of the eighteenth century. The early abolitionist movement was stronger there than anywhere else in the North. During the Revolutionary era, it was one of the first states to abolish slavery and grant blacks the right to vote. However, over the course of the next half-century, it became one of the most racially restrictive states in the North. I argue that heavy immigration by the Irish and the migration of blacks into the state by the opening decades of the nineteenth century played a large role in the transition from a paternalistic race culture to an ascriptive one. Yet, as bad as social conditions became for blacks, they were still allowed to vote in the 1830s. All of this changed when a few black votes helped a Whig candidate defeat a Democrat for county office. During the Constitutional Convention of 1837, blacks were written out of the electorate as Democrats sought to gain electoral advantage. By the late 1830s, Pennsylvania had completed its peculiar journey from racial paternalism to a "white man's republic."

Chapter 4 addresses the case of Rhode Island and the reenfranchisement of blacks in the wake of the Dorr War. Rhode Island was the only state in which blacks gained the right to vote after being denied that right. Disenfranchisement occurred by state statute in 1822. By then, racial ascriptivism had become dominant as the state's small black population endured economic hardship and social ostracization. However, within two decades, the black community had earned a modicum of respectability and had amassed a considerable amount of wealth. Thus, when Thomas Dorr and his suffrage followers moved to first institute a new constitution and then take over the government by arms, blacks had become part of the political equation. Initially, they were aligned with Dorr and the suffrage association. But against Dorr's own inclinations and urgings, the suffrage movement succumbed to ascriptivism. In response, the black community in Rhode Island—with the help of abolitionists—aligned themselves with the Law and Order Party. Blacks displayed both their loyalty and their "worthiness" of citizenship by protecting the streets of Providence during the Dorr Conflict. As a reward, the Law and Order Party granted blacks the right to vote—a right that blacks enjoyed in Rhode Island for the remainder of the antebellum period.

Chapter 5 looks at the case of Massachusetts. Blacks were granted the right to vote in Massachusetts by constitutional interpretation in the early 1780s and were never denied that right. During the first party era, political leaders of both parties were decidedly paternalistic in their racial views. Furthermore, Massachusetts did not experience either the heavy influx of immigrants or free blacks in the opening decades of the nineteenth century. Thus, racial conflict did not materialize as a result of socioeconomic factors to the extent that it did in New York and Pennsylvania. As Massachusetts entered the second party era, it remained racially paternalistic. I argue that the advent of abolitionism in the state in the 1830s furthered the effects of the paternalistic race culture for the remainder of the antebellum period. It is telling that in Massachusetts the rights of blacks were expanded greatly from the 1830s to the Civil War.

I conclude by "reconstructing" the Two Reconstructions, and ask the question of whether the concept of race formation can serve to help us understand better racial conflict and political party development in the period from the Civil War to the present.

CHAPTER 2

"The Minds of Blacks Are not Competent to Vote"

Racial Voting Restrictions in New York

Constitutional and Ideological Change in Old New York

On March 14, 1779, Alexander Hamilton wrote to John Jay, president of the Continental Congress, concerning the conscription of Negro soldiers into the Revolutionary Army. The letter was delivered by Colonel Henry Laurens, who was en route to his native South Carolina to enlist the support of the state's governor and legislature for arming blacks to fight the British. Hamilton reasoned that Revolutionary leaders should make a broad appeal to the slave population of South Carolina before the British beat them to it. In exchange for taking up arms against the Crown, blacks would be "given their freedom with their muskets."[1] He argued that "this will secure their fidelity, animate their courage, and I believe will have a good influence upon those who remain, by opening a door to their emancipation." While asserting the dire need for new troops against the British onslaught, Hamilton also felt compelled to assure Jay that blacks were up to the task. "I have not the least doubt, that the negroes will make very excellent soldiers, with proper management." He went further and defended the mental capabilities of blacks. "I frequently hear it objected to the scheme of embodying negroes that they are too stupid to make soldiers. This is so far from appearing to me a valid objection that I think their want of cultivation (for their *natural* faculties are *probably* as good as ours) joined to that habit of subordination which they acquire from a life of servitude, will make them sooner became soldiers than our White inhabitants."[2] For Hamilton, granting slaves their freedom along with their muskets was both a moral and strategic decision, a blend of ideology and political expediency, "for the dictates of humanity and true policy equally interest me in favour of this unfortunate class of men."[3]

Originally, Hamilton had written that the natural faculties of blacks were "perhaps" as good as whites, but in the end he crossed it out in favor of the stronger word "probably." The truth of the matter is that Hamilton was not sure if blacks and whites were endowed with the same mental abilities. But, like the other Federalist leaders of New York in the Revolutionary years, Hamilton was certain that the "habit of subordination" under the institution of slavery had led to their current degraded condition. Along with John Jay, Rufus King, Governour Morris, and others, Hamilton approached the problem of race through a natural rights philosophical lens, insistently arguing that all men were by nature free and equal. If there were inequalities between the races, it was "probably" a result of environmental factors that led to a want of cultivation on the part of blacks.

This cadre of Federalist leaders at the forefront of the Revolutionary cause in New York shaped the dominant racial discourse of the state, and thereby the politics associated with race, in the last quarter of the eighteenth century. All were staunch abolitionists, and nowhere are the paternalistic views of this generation of New York leaders expressed more clearly than in the words and deeds of Jay himself. Before becoming coauthor of *The Federalist*, Supreme Court Chief Justice, or Governor of New York, Jay was the first president of the New York Manumission Society, founded in 1785. Hamilton was his vice president. Jay was the author of the Society's constitution and wrote in the preamble that "It is our duty ... to endeavor, by lawful ways and means, to enable [blacks] to share equally with us in ... civil and religious liberty ... to which our brethren are, *by nature,* as much entitled as to ourselves." Throughout the Revolutionary and Confederation years, Jay fought for gradual abolition of slavery in New York. He argued vigorously for an abolition clause in the first state constitution drafted in 1777. On March 21, 1784, Jay manumitted one of his two slaves, Benoit, whom he had purchased just five years earlier in Martinique. In doing so, he wrote that "whereas the Children of Men are *by Nature* equally free, and cannot without Injustice be either reduced to, or held in Slavery, And whereas it is therefore right ... [Benoit] should be manumitted."[4] In 1795, Jay was elected governor of New York. During his first four years in office, many bills were sent up to the state legislature providing for the gradual abolition of slavery. All of them were rejected by the state Senate. Finally, in 1799, both houses passed a gradual abolition bill that Jay signed on March

29. It provided that all males born after July 4 of that year would be freed on July 4, 1827, and all females would be freed on July 4, 1822.

Thomas Jefferson's election to the presidency in 1800 ushered in the first party system in American political history, and along with it a period of stiffened party competition in New York. Despite Jefferson's inaugural assertion that "we are all Republicans, we are all Federalists" in the spring of 1801, rancorous partisanship took hold in New York as the Federalists were overthrown after nearly a quarter century of legislative rule.[5] On the national level, Federalists had suffered politically from the passage of—and President Adams' support for—the Alien and Seditions Acts. In New York, the policies of the old Revolutionary aristocracy came under increasing attack by Jeffersonian Republicans—including their dominant racial ideology. Despite the complete demise of the Federalists on the national level by 1816, party competition continued in New York over the opening decades of the nineteenth century as competing factions coalesced, disintegrated, and reorganized into new political parties more or less along the old Federalist–Jeffersonian Republican lines. In short, there was little in the way of an "Era of Good Feelings" in New York. Although most of these factions referred to themselves as "Republicans" in some fashion and thereby claimed the mantle of Jefferson, the conflicts of this early period persisted. Not until the Van Buren–led victory of the Bucktail Republicans after the ratification of the constitution drafted in the convention of 1821 did the last remnants of the old Federalist Party disappear.

My contention in this chapter is that the first constitutional change in New York in nearly fifty years also consolidated a transformation in the dominant racial belief system in state politics that had begun to materialize in the opening decades of the nineteenth century. If the dominant racial paradigm of the Revolutionary period was one that I have characterized in the introduction as racial paternalism, founded on a natural rights philosophy, the dominant ideology in New York by the 1820s was ascriptive in nature, founded on racial hierarchy whereby blacks were considered naturally subordinate to whites. We shall examine this latter dominant racial belief system in detail; but perhaps it suffices for now to offer an example by quoting Samuel Young, ally of Van Buren, at the Constitutional Convention of 1821. When debating the suffrage question for blacks, Young responded bluntly by saying, "The minds of blacks are not competent to vote. They are too degraded to estimate the value, or exercise with fidelity and discretion this important right." Whereas Hamilton and his cohorts were willing to take a chance that blacks possessed the mental capabilities for many of the responsibilities of citizenship, Young and his colleagues were deeply skeptical. This transformation in the discourse surrounding race was fundamental, and as I hope to show was a significant ingredient in the overall ideological differences between the political parties in New York with the advent of Jacksonian democracy and the second party system.

In 1821, Van Buren's burgeoning political machine was successful in partially disenfranchising black males by placing a $250 property qualification on them while dropping most voting qualifications for white males. Despite incessant petitioning, referenda on the question of black suffrage, and state constitutional conventions over the next half-century, black New Yorkers would not receive the full rights of voting until their black brethren in the South would receive them, that is, with the ratification of the Fifteenth Amendment in 1870. Like Hamilton a half-century before, the leaders of the Bucktail Republicans were most certainly driven partly by ideology and partly by political expediency. For, even by the time Jefferson had entered the White House, the patron-client bond between Federalists and blacks had already been sealed and molded into an incipient political coalition. According to the historian Dixon Ryan Fox, those manumitted black males who had served in Federalist households loyally voted the Federalist ticket once they met the suffrage qualifications before 1821.[6] The paternalistic relationship formed between Federalists and blacks in the waning days of slavery would assume a more overtly political character throughout the entire antebellum period. To put it simply, the Federalists and then Whigs consistently favored some type of equal suffrage for blacks—even if they endorsed it halfheartedly—and the Bucktail Republicans and later the Democrats favored the complete disenfranchisement of blacks. Such a political arrangement prompted Fox to write in his groundbreaking study of New York party politics that black New Yorkers in the middle decades of the nineteenth century "were Whigs because their fathers had been Federalists."[7] As early as the opening of the nineteenth century, Democratic Republicans saw the potential impact of the Federalist-black coalition in the political equation for office seekers, and vowed to destroy it. My argument here is that, in order to destroy it as a matter of political expediency, they had to construct an entirely new racial belief system by drawing on a different narrative on race, founded on a certain set of essentialist assumptions about racial difference and citizenship.

The racial alignment of the parties born of the paternalistic relationship between the New York Revolutionary aristocracy and their black servants assumed an overtly class character even as early as the formative days of Tammany Hall in New York City in the late eighteenth century.[8] It was certainly in place with the ascendancy of Van Buren's political machine. Fox intimated that lower-class whites opposing the rights of blacks formed the basis of Bucktail Republican support in the opening decades of the nineteenth century just as the push for an expanded suffrage across the country was taking hold. "The mechanics had opposed emancipation, for they did not like to see the negro change his butler's coat for cap and jeans or his salver for a saw."[9] As I alluded to earlier, similar views on the construction of "whiteness" as an ideology in the first half of the nineteenth century have been suggested by labor historians of the period, including David Roediger.[10] In looking at the politics of New York in this period, I have come to a similar conclusion: race became a fundamental factor in the ideological formation of the political parties during this first party system. In the period between the Revolutionary War and the Constitutional Convention of 1821, the politics of race and the politics of class were deeply intertwined but were played out against the backdrop of partisan conflict and party formation, with each side putting forth competing visions of race and citizenship. Both sides of this conflict were motivated partly by ideology and partly by the desire to win office by maximizing votes come election time.

As we shall see, the political actors and other opinion leaders of this period certainly acted out of naked self-interest and made arguments about race that served to advance their political agendas. But these arguments were nonetheless ideological in nature, and contained within them normative positions on the question of race and citizenship—they were, in short, constructing a narrative about civil society, the meaning of democracy, and the place of African Americans within that vision of civil society and democracy. In advancing their own political agendas, political leaders were both responding to and shaping the racialized world in a period of rapid economic, social, and political change.

Section I begins by looking at some of the economic and social background conditions in New York in the period leading up to the Constitutional Convention of 1821. Blacks in New York faced many of the same difficulties faced by other black northerners during the wrenching political and social changes associated with gradual abolition. In looking at the question of race from this perspective, we shall see that an emerging free black population, on the one hand, and a growing white working-class population, on the other, presented particular problems to New York political leaders who in turn sought to shape the changing social landscape to their political advantage. In Section II, I turn to look at political conflict and partisanship in the period between the Revolution and 1821. The creation of the first party system in the United States also brought stiffened political competition to New York. My contention is that two competing discourses surrounding race—one that was dominant and entrenched, the other emergent—were firmly established in this period as the question of black suffrage was debated. Political leaders on both sides blended their racial ideologies with political expediency to maintain hold on political power. Finally, in Section III, I look at the debates of the Constitutional

Convention of 1821 surrounding the rights of blacks for the franchise as a way of delineating between the two competing racial belief systems of this period. In doing so, I point out the final transformation from racial paternalism that had been predominant in the late eighteenth century in New York, to a racial ascriptivism that came to dominate by the 1820s.

African Americans in New York: Economic and Social Conditions from the Colonial Period to 1821

The Dutch founded the colony of New Netherland in 1624 and placed its administration under the auspices of the Dutch West India Company. Persons of African descent were among the earliest settlers, arriving through the slave trade as early as 1626. Other settlers of the colony included English, French, Swedish, and Germans, and it is estimated that nearly twenty languages were spoken in the early seventeenth century. Under Dutch rule, persons of African descent were owned not by individuals but by the West India Company. The Dutch gave Africans certain freedoms unknown under the peculiar institution of slavery that emerged in the English colonies. For example, African men and women could intermarry, hire themselves out for a wage, bring suit in courts, raise crops and families, and purchase their freedom.[11] People of African descent enjoyed rights usually reserved for white indentured servants under Dutch rule. But all of this changed when the English assumed control of the colony in 1664. According to Leon Higginbotham, African men and women went from "half-freedom to slavery" as New Netherland changed hands from the Dutch to the English and became New York.[12] On taking over the colony, the English quickly moved to abolish what rights persons of African descent had enjoyed under Dutch rule. In 1684, the word "slave" was first attached to the list of those indentured or encumbered. By this time, slavery had taken on a distinctly racial character, with negroes, Indians, and mulattoes relegated to slave status, and whites relegated to indentured status.

In response to a black slave uprising in 1712, the English put in place a new set of laws known as the "Duke's Law," which strictly circumscribed the life of black slaves much like the life of the slave was restricted in the Chesapeake and the lower South. It stipulated, for instance, that slaves could not congregate in groups of more than three unless working for their master or face forty lashes at the discretion of the justice of the peace. Moreover, slaves were to be put to death for murdering or raping whites, or for "willfully burn[ing] any dwelling-house, barn …" In the wake of another ostensible uprising in 1741 in New York City, known as the "Great Negro Plot of 1741," thirteen blacks were burned at the stake, whereas sixteen blacks and four whites were hanged by colonial officials after a rash of fires

Table 2.1 Black Density, 1703–1790[13]

Year	Percentage Black
1703	11.5
1723	14.8
1731	14.3
1737	14.7
1746	14.8
1749	14.4
1756	14.0
1771	11.8
1786	8.5
1790	7.6

erupted all over the city over the course of a week. The residents of lower Manhattan suspected both blacks and Indians in the cause of the fires and whipped up the hysteria that produced the lynch mobs. By the time of the American Revolution, the agricultural regions of New York State had one of the more restrictive slave codes in the North, whereas race relations in New York City were severely strained and problematic. Blacks—both slave and free—living in urban centers of New York did not enjoy the same levels of autonomy that the black communities in other northern urban centers such as Boston, Philadelphia, and Rhode Island enjoyed.[14]

If slavery became more restrictive in New York under English rule, it also proliferated in New York more than in any other northern colony. By the time the Constitution was ratified, New York had the largest black population of any colony north of Maryland. Between 1698 and 1790, the number of blacks in New York increased tenfold, from 2,170 to 21,329.[15] Throughout the colonial period, black density in the overall population of New York remained fairly steady. It peaked in the middle decades of eighteenth century as the demand for labor all across the colonies increased, but began to diminish in the Revolutionary and Confederation years as immigration to New York increased in the wake of the war. In addition, it is estimated that as many as three thousand slaves joined the British forces and were evacuated in 1783 with the signing of the Treaty of Paris.[16]

There is scant data on the number of free blacks living in New York before the first national census was taken in 1790. But the evidence seems to suggest that during the Revolutionary and Confederation years there was a sharp increase in the number of free blacks in the state. Census data for 1790 shows 4,654 free blacks and 21,329 slaves in the state.[17] We can surmise that some were freemen from before the war, some were freed because of their service during the war, and some had been manumitted in other parts of the country and state and had migrated to New York after the war. Surprisingly few of these free blacks were former slaves in New York City manumitted by slavemasters who caught the abolitionist spirit in the wake of the Revolutionary War.[18] In 1799, New York passed a gradual abolition law that freed all males born after the Fourth of July of that year when they turned twenty-seven; women would be freed on reaching the age of twenty-two. As of July 4, 1827, all forms of slavery came to an end in the state. Even before the law took effect, however, the percentage of free blacks in the state rose precipitously and continued to rise over the next three decades. In 1800, the number of free blacks doubled over the previous ten years: there were 8,573 free blacks and 15,602 slaves in New York at that time. By 1810, the free black population had surpassed the slave population, 25,333 to 15,017. On the eve of the Constitutional Convention of 1821, there were 22,332 free blacks and 7,573 slaves in the state.[19] Thus, in the opening decades of the nineteenth century, we see the same phenomenon in New York that occurred in other northern states that passed gradual abolition laws in the late eighteenth century—namely, that blacks were emerging from slavery en masse over a relatively short period of time. But just as in other northern states, the density of blacks in the overall population *declined* significantly in New York throughout the antebellum period, as Table 2.2 shows.

Steady immigration to New York and the opening of lands in the western part of the state in the opening decades of the nineteenth century played significant roles in the declining density of blacks in the overall population. At the time of the ratification of the Constitution, New York's population was 340,000. By 1820, the population of the state rose to 1.3 million—a fourfold increase.[20] Yet black population growth was minimal

Table 2.2 Black Density as a Percentage in New York Population, 1790–1860[21]

Year	Percentage Black
1790	7.6
1800	5.3
1810	4.2
1820	2.9
1830	2.3
1840	2.1
1850	1.6
1860	1.3

in proportion to the overall growth rate. Given this, New York presents us with the same puzzle that we find across much of the North, that is, why was the black community in New York met with rising forms of political, social, and economic discrimination even though their numbers were declining relative to the overall population of the state?

Here we must return to the nature of gradual abolition all across the North, and the potential political, social, and economic conflicts it embodied. Although relatively few in number, an increasing free black population became more visible in every way, particularly in the bustle of an urban center such as New York City. In the latter days of slavery, most blacks in New York City worked as domestics in the houses of the old (Federalist) aristocracy. As laborers, they were not in competition for jobs with whites at the lower end of the economic ladder. As "citizens," they were utterly invisible, both in the political and social sense: most lived in white-headed households rather than their own communities, on the one hand, and all but a few were disqualified from the vote, on the other. With gradual abolition came wrenching political, social, and economic changes that brought with them a backlash against a black community just uplifted from slavery. Economically, blacks were perceived by working-class whites as a potential threat to jobs. Socially, there were considered pariahs or outcasts, consigned to the slums of the city. Politically, they were seen by ascendant Republicans politicians seeking office as a dangerous voting block. These forces came together powerfully at the turn of the nineteenth century in New York as the old Federalists in power were challenged for the first time. Gronowicz asserts that Irish Republican fervor contributed heavily to the development of the Democratic Republican ideology well before the War of 1812, and that New York Republicans drew on the competition between Irish and African-American labor for political support.[22] In short, Tammany Hall taught the Irish that they could climb the ladder of success by shunning any contact with blacks; Tammany leaders road the wave of this hostility to political power. As early as 1804, Republican newspapers such as the *American Citizen* published parodies of black speech patterns in which "Zambo" degraded himself by comparing his skin to the rough rind of a coconut.[23] In 1799, the *New York Journal and Patriotic Register* pointed out not only the Federalist detestation of the Irish, but also its enthusiasm for "the black ones of Santa Domingo [*sic*]."[24] Republican newspapers also never hesitated to remind its readers that "nineteenth-twentieths" of all black voters voted the Federalist ticket, a point to which we shall return shortly.[25]

The rather bleak picture we get of black life in New York in the opening decades of the nineteenth century is buttressed by other economic and social data gathered on the period. The federal government only began keeping occupational census information in 1850. But Shane White has meticulously pieced together through various sources profiles of black economic and social life in New York City from 1790 to 1810, which helps to shed light on the some of the economic and social conditions that blacks endured.[26] White asserts that roughly a third of all free blacks lived in white households from 1790 to 1810. Although percentages remained constant, the real number of blacks living in white households increased by more than six times.[27] Most of these blacks lived and worked in the homes of merchants, artisans, professionals, and retail salesmen as domestic laborers—in other words, the homes of prominent New York City Federalists. But in the same period, the number of free black–headed households went from 157 to 1,228, or about an eightfold increase. By 1810, thriving black communities had sprouted up in New York City, particularly in the Fifth, Sixth, and Seventh Wards.[28] In the public sphere, blacks were being seen physically—and not only as domestic servants doing the shopping for employees or masters, or as chauffeurs driving horse drawn buggies. It was inevitable that the visibility of an increasingly independent black community would lead to entrenched residential segregation by the middle decades of the nineteenth century. White estimates that in 1810 nearly half of all blacks for whom he found occupation statistics were laborers and mariners. A surprising number were skilled artisans—about a third— though the number of black artisans in New York City declined by a fourth from 1800 to 1810.[29] The decline over this ten-year period may point to the increasing attacks and discrimination blacks faced by white artisans. Food service such as waiting tables was also one of the main occupations left to blacks. During this time, black workers dominated the oyster industry: of twenty-seven listed in the 1810 directory, sixteen of them were black, or about 60 percent.[30]

Despite the level of skill blacks possessed, they were increasingly relegated to the most menial jobs and persistently forced to the bottom rung on the economic and social ladder. White immigration to the state made matters worse, but economic downturns were another factor. Jefferson's Embargo of 1804, the depression that followed the War of 1812, and the Panic of 1819 all hit the black community harder than the white community. In the 1810s and 1820s, white immigrants flooded into the domestic service industry, a field that was predominantly African-American since colonial days. According to Herman Bloch, the number of Irish filing for employment with the New York Society for the Encouragement of Faithful Domestics in the late 1820s was more than three times that of blacks; even the number of other "whites" filing for employment surpassed blacks.[31]

Harry Reed has argued that free black communities all across the antebellum North looked to five specific areas in order to form a community identity and "consciousness" to ease the harshness of their increasingly isolated status: the church, self-help organizations, black newspapers, the black convention movement, and the ideology of emigration.[32] In New York in the opening decades of the nineteenth century, education and religion were the most important socioeconomic institutions for blacks. The New York Manumission Society, led by John Jay and Alexander Hamilton, was instrumental in setting up the first school for blacks in New York, the New York African Free School. It was founded in 1806 and had fifty pupils that year. Nine years later, a new school for black girls was funded by William Street. In 1820, a second Free African School was erected on Mulberry Street. According to Gronowicz, in 1823 the free African schools educated 866 black children. The Federalist newspaper *Commercial Advertiser* boasted of the schools' successes and stated that the difference between a black child attending the schools and one not educated is the difference between becoming a productive citizen and being "plunged in scenes of sloth, idleness, dissipation and crime, until they pass from step to step, into the state prison, and at last up to the gallows."[33] The reporter continued that only three of the thousands of black children attending the African Free School had ever been convicted of a crime.

Yet, the success of the African Free School in securing blacks economic opportunities is mixed. According to Bloch, of the thousands of blacks educated in these schools over a ten-year period, three of them had become ministers, two had entered the teaching profession, and the "rest had found little solace in having an education."[34] Most whites in the abolitionist community advocated education as the surest way to lift blacks out from under their degraded and miserable condition. Their paternalistic sentiments are hardly unnoticeable when we consider that in the 1821 Convention delegates were reminded that the careful instruction of blacks was important in their moral development. But in fact many abolitionists were reluctant to practice what they preached and hire well-trained, educated blacks in their own business establishments for fear of reprisals from an increasingly hostile white population. Leon Litwack summarized it best when he asked about the abolitionists' paternalistic push for the rights of blacks: "Of what use, was the right to vote, attend school and to enter the homes of the abolitionists if it was still impossible to gain access to any but the most menial employment."[35]

Other institutions helped to sustain the New York black community throughout the antebellum period. Black New Yorkers took an early active role in the establishment of black churches. In 1796 blacks started a movement for their own church; five years later, the African Methodist Episcopal Zion Church was founded, with Peter Williams at its head. In 1809, the Abyssinian Baptist Church was erected. Over the next two decades, a web of black churches would come to provide blacks not only with places of worship but also homeless shelters, refuges for fugitive slaves, aid to the sick, training grounds for leadership, and meeting places for antislavery struggles.[36] Moreover, the establishment of black churches was encouraged by white religious leaders as means for the mental and moral uplift of the black race. The first black newspaper appeared in New York City in 1827, and the influential *Colored American* was first printed in 1835.

Yet, despite the successes of the New York Free African School, the creation of a complex web of black churches, and the like, blacks in New York found themselves faced with the same political, economic, and social barriers that black communities in other northern states were faced with as gradual abolition laws took hold and a free black population emerged from slavery. They had, for the most part, spent the latter part of the eighteenth century under the paternalistic gaze of the old Federalist aristocracy, working and living in its houses as domestics. The Federalists promoted the moral and mental uplift of blacks by encouraging the creation of strong black religious and educational institutions—these were the keys to the integration of blacks into what everyone on both sides of the debate concerning race and citizenship agreed was a white man's society. We might characterize the racial dynamic propagated by these leaders as an early version of the doctrine of "separate but equal": blacks could be granted a certain amount of economic and political equality, but social equality was out of the question. To the teeming working classes and the new generation of Republicans leaders seeking their support, however, blacks were seen as both a threat and an outcaste community in every respect—politically, socially, and economically. Thus, they preached a form of "separate and unequal" when it came to race and citizenship. And, in order to further diminish the potential impact of blacks, and remake New York society in the image of the white man, this new generation of leaders had to seek a political solution to the social and economic problems that race presented.

Politics, Partisanship, and Competing Racial Narratives up to 1821

Historians still echo Carl Becker's well-known dictum that the political struggles in New York in the years leading up to the Revolutionary war were centered around the question of "home rule," on the one hand, and "who should rule at home," on the other.[37] Becker's doctoral dissertation on the history of New York focused more on the social and economic background forces in New York than on the machinery of politics—parties, committees, conventions, and so on. He concluded that the American Revolution was not only a result of a contest for independence, but more importantly a contest for the democratization of American society—that is, a contest between the haves and the have-nots or, in Becker's words, conservatives and radicals. In writing about the significance of the Stamp Act and the riots it unleashed, Becker asserted that they "revealed the latent opposition of motives and interests between the privileged and unprivileged,—an opposition which the war itself only half suppressed, and which was destined to reappear in the rivalry of Federalist and Republican."[38]

In the years that followed the publication of *The History of Political Parties in the Province of New York,* Becker never returned to analyze the machinery of New York politics—that is, the political conflict between the Federalists and Republicans in the early national period born of the social and economic forces he had described in vivid detail. But historians subsequently picked up on Becker's class-based analysis of the Revolutionary Era, taking for granted Becker's social and economic analysis in order to fill in some of the details of New York politics. Progressive historian Dixon Ryan Fox is perhaps the most notable of these. His *The Decline of Aristocracy in the Politics of New York* is written in the progressive tradition and argues that the conservatism of the old Federalist aristocracy of the Revolutionary Era succumbed to the democratizing forces swirling in New York in the first three decades of the nineteenth century. But where Becker focused on background forces, Fox was certainly more interested in the machinery of politics. Fox sought to fold an analysis of race into his historical narrative of New York.[39] He put racial conflict and political parties into historical perspective when he wrote:

> The attachment of the colored citizen to the Republican Party is usually explained by reference to the memory of Lincoln, Stevens, Grant, and Sumner; but in New York, at least, the freedman learned to vote against St. Tammany before most of the apostles of his "rights" were born, and the jealous hatred of poor mechanics helps far more than reconstruction policies to account for the attitude of New York Democrats towards Negro suffrage.[40]

He concluded that "if there had never been a Negro south of the Potomac, still the Negro in New York would never had voted the Democratic ticket." For Fox, the reason was clear: the social and economic struggles that gave rise to the first party system in New York also shaped the dynamics and parameters of racial conflict in state politics. This occurred independently of the spread of slavery in the South. Well before the rise of the Republican Party and the subsequent racial alignment of the parties in the third party system, Fox correctly asserted that the politics of race had already been stitched in to the political fabric of New York.

In the last section, I focused on the social and economic changes in New York in the period leading up to the Constitutional Convention of 1821. In this section, I want to pick up on Fox's insights into the politics of race in "old New York" but concentrate the discussion on partisan conflict and the discourse surrounding race in the same period. My focus will be not only on the machinery of New York politics but also on the political actors pulling the levers.

I mentioned at the outset that the generation of New York Revolutionary leaders was, for the most part, staunchly abolitionist. John Jay and his colleagues all understood that the Revolutionary rhetoric of freedom rang hollow if the natural rights it espoused did not extend to ending hereditary slavery. Concerning the continuation of slavery in New York, Jay wrote in 1780 from Europe to his friend Egbert Benson that "till America comes into this measure [for abolition], her prayers to Heaven for liberty will be impious. ... I believe God governs this world, and I believe it to be a maxim in his as in our court, that those who ask for equity ought to do it."[41] In 1777, the first New York Constitutional Convention was held and a constitution was drafted. According to Prescott and Zimmerman, the sixty-six men who gathered in New York were influential Whigs.[42] Much like the framers of other state constitutions in the Revolutionary era, the drafters of the New York constitution made no mention of race, creed, or previous condition of servitude as an impediment to the suffrage. The suffrage qualification was afforded to "every male inhabitant of full age" who met the property and residence requirements. For the Assembly, these were (1) the ownership of 20 pounds freehold or (2) the leasing of a tenement at 40 shillings. Voting requirements for the Senate were more stringent: property requirements were set at 100 pounds for the latter.[43] The New York Constitution was peculiar in that it established two bodies that usurped certain powers we now assume to be granted to the executive branch exclusively or to the people: the Council of Appointments and the Council of Revision. The Council of Appointments consisted of the governor and one senator chosen annually from each of the four senatorial districts. It was given the authority to appoint judges, mayors, coroners, district attorney, and so on—in short, all the statewide and local government offices that are currently popularly elected. The Council of Revision was granted the power of the veto over legislation. It was composed of the governor, the chancellor, and the judges of the Supreme Court; the Council could return bills to the legislature for revision—essentially giving it veto power over the legislature—but the legislature could override the Council's rejection with a two-thirds majority in both houses. As we shall see, the Council of Revision quickly became an institutional barricade to many of the efforts by Democratic Republicans to disenfranchise blacks in the period leading up to the Constitutional Convention of 1821. In fact, Bucktail Republicans portrayed the two councils as undemocratic in their persistent calls for a new constitution in the years preceding 1821.

Abolitionists were in the clear majority at the Constitutional Convention of 1777. Although the constitution did not explicitly abolish slavery, the convention did adopt a resolution proposed by Governour Morris urging the legislature to take measures committed to the principle that "every human being who breathes the air of the state shall enjoy the privileges of a freeman."[44] The resolution passed by a vote of 31–5. Four years later, the Assembly passed a law manumitting slaves who had served in the state militia. As we have seen, Alexander Hamilton had urged the legislature of South Carolina in 1779 to take a similar course of action and give slaves "their freedom with their muskets."[45] As we will see, a similar situation occurred in the wake of the Dorr War in Rhode Island, where blacks were granted suffrage rights after displaying their loyalty to the Law and Order Party and assisting in quelling the rebellion. Moreover, the history of the United States is replete with similar types of rewards for blacks who have displayed their patriotism. In fact, Klinkner and Smith have argued loyal military service in times of war has been one of the necessary factors in the advancement of civil rights for blacks throughout U.S. history.[46]

Calls were roundly made throughout New York to end slavery in the early 1780s as pressure was placed on political leaders to follow the lead of its neighboring states. In 1784, the *New York Journal* published a letter from an abolitionist in Pennsylvania to a friend in New York. Pennsylvania was one of the first states to abolish slavery. The Pennsylvanian attacked any type of personal slavery, saying that "the argument in favour of personal slavery are so few, and those few so weak, those in behalf of liberty, and the equal right all men have to freedom, so numerous and cogent, that it is really embarrassing to advocate for the latter, to arrange them and apply them."[47] In 1785, the New York legislature sought to make good on the 1777 convention's resolution on abolition and moved to pass a manumission law. A majority of both houses were clearly prepared to end slavery in New York, but two questions remained: (1) How fast should manumission be enacted? and (2) to what extent should blacks be given political rights? Aaron Burr led a group of militant abolitionists and proposed the immediate abolition of all slavery in the state. The Assembly rejected Burr's proposal 33–13 but approved a more moderate plan of abolition by a majority of 36–11.[48] In actuality, all but one member of the Assembly voted for some form of abolition, as ten of the members that voted against the moderate bill voted with Burr on the more radical measure.[49]

Yet, the bill that emerged from the Assembly stopped short of granting blacks full political equality. Blacks were denied the right to vote or hold political office, forbidden to intermarry with whites or give testimony against whites in a court of law, and barred from serving on juries. The Senate rejected the bill and went on record against the Assembly's measure, arguing that racial restrictions were not only unfair but also dangerous, and could result in civic disorder if a portion of the electorate was denied the rights of citizenship.[50] The "stake in society" argument on voting fell on deaf ears in the Assembly; whereas the latter revised the bill to allow for intermarriage, the holding of public office, and the admissibility of evidence in courts, the Assembly would not budge on the Senate's action. Fearing that an emancipation bill would not be passed, the Senate nonetheless signed off on the measure that denied the right to vote to blacks and sent it to the Council of Revision for consideration.[51]

With the old Federalist Robert Livingston presiding over the Council of Revision as Chancellor, the bill was rejected and sent back to the legislature. In issuing the veto, Livingston made a total of five objections that centered around three main ideas. First, Livingston asserted a natural rights philosophy and argued that voting was an inalienable right of citizenship which could not be abridged on the basis of race. Livingston wrote that blacks are "entitled to all the privileges of citizens" and cannot "be deprived of these essential rights without shocking the principle of equal liberty which every page in that Constitution labors to enforce."[52] Because some blacks had already exercised the right to vote in New York, depriving them now "of this essential privilege, and under the idea of political expediency, without their having been charged with any offence, disfranchises them in direct violation of established rules of justice."[53] Second, Livingston employed a common Revolutionary theme by arguing that disenfranchising blacks deprives them of the very representation that formed the basis of the American insurgency against the British crown. The law passed by the Legislature, in Livingston's words, "either enacts what is wrong, or supposes that those may rightfully be charged with the burdens of government, who have no representative sharing in imposing them." Finally, Livingston warned of the dangers that disenfranchisement would cause in the future: "Because this class of disfranchised and discontented citizens, who at some future period may be both numerous and wealthy, may under the direction of ambitious and factious leaders become dangerous to the State, and effect the ruin of a constitution whose benefits they are not permitted to enjoy."[54] Livingston and the Council then returned the bill to the Legislature. In doing so, he offered to New York's political leaders a vision of society that sought to integrate blacks by giving them a political stake in that society. The alternative was not only political instability and possible insurrection but also a violation of the natural rights of citizens of African descent.

In his veto address, Livingston did no more than what Hamilton sought to do just a few years earlier amid the Revolutionary War: that is, approach the question of race from a standpoint of both policy and humanity. On resubmission of the bill, however, the Senate was now unwavering in its support for the original bill. Apparently, its members wanted an emancipation bill more than the suffrage measure. The Senate passed the bill in unamended form and sent it on to the Assembly.[55] By now, however, the Assembly had changed its mind. Heeding Livingston's veto message, a majority of the Assembly now strongly favored both emancipation and voting rights, and voted down the unrevised bill forwarded by the Senate by a vote of 23–17.[56] The bill died on the floor of the Legislature, thus ending the legislative attempt at emancipation.

With the failure of the New York Legislature to act on full emancipation, calls to abolish the peculiar institution once and for all in the Empire State reached a feverish pitch. That same year, in 1785, the New York Manumission Society was founded, with Jay and Hamilton at its head. During the same period, calls were made from the editorial pages of several New York newspapers. The *New York Gazetteer* attacked slavery as "the deprivation of all the rights which nature has given to man."[57] Other newspapers bellowed that slave owners deserved to be plundered, tormented, and massacred at the hands of their slaves.[58] In the face of heated antislavery rhetoric, the state Legislature moved to curtail the practice of slavery as much as possible by liberalizing slave controls, encouraging private manumissions of slaves who were healthy enough to support themselves, and outlawing the slave trade in the state. But slavery would not be abolished completely until 1799, when Federalist Governor John Jay signed an abolition bill gradually manumitting slaves passed into law by a Federalist Legislature. According to Fox, the vote for manumission was on a straight party line in the legislature, with sixty-eight Federalists supporting the bill and twenty-three Republicans opposing it.[59]

The election of 1800 swept the Republicans into office in New York, in federal office as well as in the executive branch of the state. In the Legislature, the Assembly went Republican, but the Senate was deadlocked at six senators from each party.[60] DeWitt Clinton beat Federalist candidate General Van Rensselaer in the governor's race by a solid majority of four thousand votes. Some historians have made reference to the fact that the Republicans began to move to disenfranchise blacks in the wake of election of 1800 because a single black ward in New York City caused the makeup of the government to become Federalist. Citing Fox, Herman Bloch makes this point in his work *The Circle of Discrimination.*[61] However, nowhere in Fox's work is this assertion made, and no evidence could be found that a single Negro ward in New York caused a change in the makeup of the government at the state or the national level.[62] As was mentioned, the Senate was deadlocked at six senators each after the election of 1800; from this, we can gather that whatever black vote there was in New York City may have helped the Federalists hold seats in the Senate's southern district.[63] But the Republicans clearly won a majority of the seats in the Assembly and took the governor's office.

Nonetheless, the Republican victories that year signaled the onset of party competition in New York in the opening decade of the nineteenth century. It was fueled in large part by issues of both class and race. Leaders of the ascendant Republican Party began to use the political relationship between blacks and the Federalists to stir passions among white immigrants for political support. On the other side, Federalist leaders exploited the constituency of the newly formed Republican coalition, whereas black leaders in New York City decried the bond between the party of slaveholders in the South and the party of Jefferson in the North. In 1807 Federalists protested against the influence of "foreign-born" voters in elections.[64] In April of the next year, blacks held what amounted to the first black political convention in New York City, known as the first "General Meeting of the Electors of Colour." They solidly supported the Federalist ticket for elective office across the state in the elections to be held later that month. In 1809, black leader Joseph Sydney urged black New Yorkers to support the Federalists. In a sermon on abolition, he bellowed against the party of Jefferson, arguing that it was blacks':

> indispensable duty of bestowing our votes on those, and only those, whose talents and whose political, moral and religious principles will most effectively promote the best interest of America. ... How important, then, that we, my countrymen, should unite our efforts with those of our Federal friends in endeavoring to bring about this desirable change, so all-important to commerce, to our own best interests, and the prosperity and glory of our country. ... [The Democratic Republicans] are the very people who hold our African brethren in bondage [in the South]. These people, therefore, are enemies of our rights.[65]

Republican politicians responded in kind to the growing partisan rancor by playing the race card. In the wake of the Republican embargo against the British, the Federalists rebounded from their legislative loss of 1800 to take control of the Assembly in 1809. That same year, Republicans began an all out assault on the Federalist Party, questioning its patriotism in opposing the embargo and asserting that its membership was comprised of Tory (i.e., British) sympathizers. Moreover, Republican newspapers accused the Federalists of being the protectors of blacks at the expense of the Irish immigrants.[66] In 1809, Republicans created a campaign song that not only played on racial animosities but also sought to stir up questions about Federalist motivations in opposing the Republican-led embargo:

Federalists with blacks unite,
And tell us wondrous stories;
And after they have spit their spite,
We prove them to be Tories.[67]

By 1809, the racial divide between the Federalists and the Republicans had escalated into physical intimidation at voting places in New York City. In the statewide election of that year, Republican inspectors at polling places began to question the free status of any black man wishing to cast his vote. Many were turned away because black men had no physical proof of their freedom; Republican inspectors thus assumed any black man arriving at the polls was a slave of the prominent Federalists in the city. Federalist newspapers exposed the practice immediately and called upon citizens to fight against the practice as a violation of the natural rights of blacks to vote. The *New York Commercial Advertiser* ran a column on April 26, 1809, stating the following:

> *Shameful violation of the right of suffrage*—The Republican inspectors of the Fourth Ward yesterday rejected the vote of a free man of colour, on the grounds that one of the inspectors *deemed it convenient to suspect* that he was born in slavery. The person who offered himself to vote declared that he was born in freedom, and was willing to take the oath prescribed by law. Notwithstanding this declaration, his vote was rejected. The principle assumed by the Inspectors was that every man of colour was presumed to be born in slavery: and in order to entitle himself to vote, he must produce legal evidence of his manumission. This principle, so hostile to the true spirit of republicanism, is the result of a systematic plan to disfranchise a large portion of Electors, who possess every requisite qualification, together with sagacity to discern the magnanimity to resist the late encroachments of our rulers on the constitutional liberties of the people. Men of Color! Friends of Humanity! You are imperiously called on to resist, by every honourable effort, this insidious attempt to destroy the most invaluable principle of Freemen—*the elective franchise.*[68]

Three days later, the Federalist-leaning *New York Spectator* ran the same column. In response to the continued practice by Republican inspectors, the Federalists organized among blacks a chapter of the Washington Benevolent Society, a partisan fraternity that helped blacks deal with the restrictive practices. Meanwhile, Republican newspapers defended the practice.[69]

The Republicans once again swept into office in the 1810 elections. Daniel Tompkins won the governor's office, and Republicans captured both Senate and Assembly—the latter by a two-to-one margin. In his firsthand account of the political struggles of the day, Jabez Hammond asserted that the Federalists lost the election of 1810 for three reasons: first, Congress altered the terms of the very unpopular embargo against the British. Second, hostilities against Great Britain were reaching a heightened pitch, and the Republican attempt to paint the Federalists as "Tories" began to gain traction. Finally, Hammond intimated that Madison's popularity midway through his first term gave the Federalists little chance of gaining ground either at the state or national level.[70] Republicans consolidated their gains in the election of 1811 and once again moved to destroy the impact of black voters in New York City. That year, the Legislature passed a harsh bill entitled "a Bill to Prevent Frauds at Elections, and For Other Purposes." Essentially, the bill sought to legalize what Republican inspectors in the city had done by force in previous elections. The main provision of the bill read as follows:

> Whenever any person of color, or black person shall present himself to vote at any election of this state, he shall produce to the inspectors, or persons conducting such an election, a certificate of freedom under the hand and seal of one of the clerks of the counties of this state, or under the hand of a clerk of any town within this state.[71]

In order to receive the certificate, a black man had to obtain the services of a lawyer and appear before a Supreme Court judge, where proof of freedom could be obtained in writing. The total cost to the black voter included the cost of the lawyer, 25 cents to the court, and a shilling to the county clerk for filing the certificate. In addition, the black man had to take an oath saying that he was the person listed on the certificate.

The Council of Revision once again stepped in on the side of blacks and vetoed the legislation. In the objections, the Council offered several reasons for its veto, ranging from the feasibility of carrying out the law, to questions dealing with the scientific basis for the law, and finally to a deep skepticism of its moral underpinnings. The Council first argued that the description of "persons of color" offered in the bill was too vague for inspectors to follow accurately. The "races" had been mixed over the centuries. Should inspectors go on differences presented to the eye, or the "quality of the blood"?[72] In other words, an inspector would have difficulty determining practically who was black and who was not in many cases. But, more important, the Council was hinting that a science of race was nearly impossible. We must keep in mind that the first modern attempts to construct a scientific racism were just underway in the early nineteenth century. Moreover, the emergence of a science of race that placed blacks in a subordinate position to whites formed the basis of much of the rhetoric that justified the disenfranchisement of blacks during this period, as I argued in the opening chapter. As early as 1811, the New York Council of Revision was making a legitimate counterargument to this scientific view of racial difference: how could we really be sure what constituted "race" if the blood of the races was mixed? But, perhaps most important, the Council of Revision once again relied on a natural rights argument for most of its objections. Stating that the bill selects certain persons that "under the constitution and laws of the state, entitled to the elective franchise, many of whom were born free," it violated the rights of blacks:

> whose ancestors have uninterruptedly enjoyed the elective franchise under the colonial as well as this state government, and to whom that right has been transmitted with their freeholds, the humiliating degradation of being challenged in consequence of a supposed taint, and being excluded from voting in common with their fellow citizens, on their own oaths, and thus exposing electors to wanton insult and contumely, merely on account of their complexion, whether produced by the accidental circumstances of birth, climate or disease, while in the act of exercising the noblest right of a freeman.[73]

The bill was not passed over the Council's veto. The War of 1812—labeled by the Federalists as "Mr. Madison's War"—brought new scrutiny on the policies of Republicans. Federalists termed the slate of Republican officials running across the state that year the "War Ticket," whereas the Federalists labeled themselves as the "Peace Ticket." Amid the war, Republicans in other parts of the state continued to support the policy of the disenfranchisement of blacks through statute. However, at the same time, Republicans in New York City still made overtures to blacks and courted their votes assiduously. In a letter entitled "Attention!! People of Colour" published in Alexander Hamilton's *New York Evening Post* on April 27, 1813, a "free man of colour" discussed these overtures made by the "Democratic" Party and urged his brethren not to heed party leaders' calls for support. He stated that the courting of blacks by Democrats were meant to "deceive and coax [blacks] to support their detestable system of administration."[74] He continued by stating that Governor Tompkins was no friend of the black man because he had supported "the law respecting certificates of freedom" that had been proposed two years earlier. He closed by urging his fellow blacks to consider what the Democratic Party stood for when it ostensibly supported a law restricting slavery:

> [The law] states that liberty is the right of all men, and the gift of God, not confined to climate or complexion [sic] etc. If liberty is a universal right, why did not the Democrats pass an act for the general emancipation of all the slaves? It was not for want of power, for they

had a large majority in the national and state legislatures, for many years: if the gift of God to man, how dare they sacrilegiously deprive others of it, except they doubt the existence of the deity, or like their great idol, believe in twenty Gods, or no God at all, for as matters stand, there is no oppression in the law, but lies, notorious lies in their address. *IF THERE IS A SLAVE IN THE UNITED STATES, IT IS THE FAULT OF THE DEMOCRATS!*[75]

Blacks once again voted the Federalist ticket in the spring elections of 1813.[76] It became clear to Republicans that they had no chance of swaying black voters in New York, and they consequently adopted a new hardline strategy. In 1814 the Republican-led Legislature put forth a bill similar to the one proposed in 1811. This later version also forced blacks to present a certificate of freedom on voting. However, the bill only applied to New York City. Once again, the Council of Revision vetoed it. But this time the Republicans overrode the veto. A year later, new amendments and new restrictions were added to a bill passed on April 11, 1815.[77] Once again, the bill was passed over the objection of the Council of Revision. Although the new bill exempted blacks that had obtained certificates before the 1815 passage, it did force blacks to register to vote five days before the election and deliver their affidavits to the mayor for inspection.[78]

The impact of the Republican-led assault on the suffrage rights for blacks in New York City was severe. The 1810 census showed 9,823 blacks in the city; 1,686 were slaves.[79] By 1820, there were 10,886 blacks in New York City, 518 of whom were slaves.[80] A delegate at the Constitutional Convention of 1821 estimated that nearly 300 blacks in New York voted in the statewide election of 1813; in the spring elections of 1821, the figure had dropped to 163.[81] Thus, whereas the number of free blacks increased in New York City by about 20 percent, the number of black voters decreased by nearly 50 percent. To a large extent, the Republicans had achieved the goal they set out to accomplish as early as 1800 when the first assault on the Federalist-black coalition took hold: the "Negro" wards of New York City had been all but nullified in electoral politics.

Although the end to the war left the Federalist Party in pieces across the country, two main factions emerged in New York politics by 1816: the Clintonians and Van Buren's Bucktail Republicans. In 1818, the Bucktails presented a bill in the legislature calling for a constitutional convention, which Governor Clinton and his allies blocked outright. But the following year, the same bill was presented, and this time Clinton agreed to the convention if it only revisited appointive power; the Bucktails refused the measure because of its restrictive character. In 1820, Van Buren's Bucktails gained control of the legislature and immediately passed a bill calling for an unrestricted constitutional convention. The Council of Revision altered the bill, arguing that the people should decide for themselves on the need for a convention. For the referendum, the electorate was expanded to include freeholders, taxpayers, militiamen, and men who worked on public roads. In short, the referendum was to be the most democratic in New York State history. The referendum passed by a margin of three to one.

Race and Suffrage in the Constitutional Convention of 1821

On the eve of the Constitutional Convention, Republican leaders had been successful in building their coalition along the lines of race by continually painting the remnants of the Federalist Party as the party that protected blacks. It resonated with what by 1820 was fast becoming the base of the Bucktail Republican Party: poorer ethnic whites. The economic antagonisms of the first decades of the nineteenth century bred racial hostilities; the Republicans had been successful in turning this into political advantage. As Van Buren and his allies prepared for the convention, the next step would be to completely write blacks out of the electorate and redefine the very meaning of citizenship in the Empire State. Many Republicans would draw on the harshest of racially ascriptivist views in pursuing their objectives. Yet, as we will see, the Bucktail Republicans were not all of one mind on the complete disenfranchisement of blacks. And, hence, a compromise would have to be struck.

The bill to revise the New York State constitution became law on March 13, 1821. Delegates to the convention were elected a month later, on June 13. A majority of the delegates to the convention were members of the Bucktail Republicans.[82] When the Constitutional Convention assembled in late August, four issues for consideration appeared to take precedent among the delegates: an alteration of the judiciary system, the abolition of the Council of Revision, a change in the appointment power (i.e., the Council of Appointment), and an extension of the right of suffrage.

On September 19, the delegates turned their attention to the elective franchise. For two weeks straight, the delegates engaged in a spirited debate over the qualifications for suffrage and the dangers inherent in expanding it. According to Alexander, three views predominated on the question of the suffrage: those who favored some type of freehold qualification, those who advocated universal suffrage, and those who sought a compromise between the two and favored abolition of a freehold qualification but opposed universal suffrage.[83] Federalists were staunchly in the first group, many Bucktail Republicans were in the second group, whereas Van Buren represented the third group. Eventually, a version of the position advocated by Van Buren would prevail. But race would cut across all three positions and quickly became one of the biggest sticking points. Notwithstanding the restrictive laws concerning the certificates of freedom passed several years earlier, blacks were allowed to vote alongside whites just as long as they met the same property qualifications. However, the gradual abolition of all slavery in New York was to take effect within a few years, and delegates were faced with the prospect that tens of thousands of blacks might be eligible for the franchise by the end of the decade. By contrast, many delegates had made the expansion of the suffrage a theme in their calls for a constitutional convention. Thus, the question of the suffrage soon turned on whether or not an expansion of the suffrage was to include whites and blacks, or just whites.

Bucktail Republicans knew the black vote went overwhelmingly to the old Federalists, and they looked to the convention as their chance to finally diminish the impact of this loyal voting block. Interests and political expediency were at stake here. But there was also an ideological component to the Bucktails' position when it came to the question of race and citizenship. As Peterson explains: "That the free Negroes had, as far as they could be qualified, generally voted the Federalist ticket of their former masters contributed to the hostility [Bucktail] Republicans like [Samuel] Young and Van Buren felt for the Negro franchise. Underlying this political motive, however, was the conviction that democracy was for whites only."[84] Not all agreed with the likes of Young. Martin Van Buren would come to play a central role in bringing the divergent views of the Bucktails together behind one compromise. On the other side, the Federalists walked their own fine line between ideology and expediency, arguing, on the one hand, that voting was a natural right and could not be abridged on the basis of race, and asserting, on the other, that there should be some type of property qualification that would no doubt serve to disenfranchise a large portion of the Republican base.

The main ideological divide between the two sides was made abundantly clear on the first day that the franchise was debated. Stephen Ross was one of the first Republicans to rise to argue against the enfranchisement of blacks. He began by stating that the concept of "natural rights" only applied to the state of nature and not to the institutions of a civil government that are formed after. Other qualifications for full citizenship had to be considered. Thus, although blacks may be considered "free and equal" theoretically in the state of nature, they were not truly citizens of New York because "they are seldom, if ever, required to share in the common burdens or defence of the state."[85] Ross then proceeded to argue against black enfranchisement on ascriptive grounds:

They are a peculiar people, incapable, in my judgment, of exercising that privilege with any sort of discretion, prudence, or independence. They have no just conceptions of civil liberty. They know not how to appreciate it and are consequently indifferent to its preservations. Under such circumstances, it would hardly be compatible with the safety of the state, to entrust such a people with this right … the truth is, this exclusion invades no inherent rights.[86]

He concluded by arguing that, in granting blacks the right to vote in New York, political leaders run the risk of inviting blacks from other parts of the country to the state. The inference is clear: for Ross New York was to be a "white man's" Republic, devoid both of black citizens and representatives. "I fear that an extension to the blacks would serve to invite that kind of population to this state, an occurrence which I should most sincerely deplore … next blacks will claim to be represented by persons of their own colour, in your halls of legislation. And can you consistently refuse them? It would be well to be prepared for such a claim."[87]

Soon thereafter, Federalist leader Peter Jay rose to counter Ross's argument. He appealed to the principles on which Jefferson had based his ideas in the Declaration.[88] Jay argued that this basic right of citizenship was inalienable to anyone born in the state of New York. But going further, he revived the natural rights, environmentalist argument made by his father's generation of political leaders that held at its core that any inferiority due to race could be conquered through civic education:

Why, sir, are [black males] to be excluded from rights which they possess in common with their countrymen? What crimes have they committed for which they are to be punished? Why are they, who were born free as ourselves, natives of the same country, and deriving from nature and our political institutions, the same rights and privileges which we have, now to be deprived of all those rights, and doomed to remain forever as aliens among us? … It is true that that some philosophers have held that the intellect of a black man, is naturally inferior to that of a white one; but this idea has been so completely refuted, and is now so universally exploded, that I did not expect to have heard it in an assembly so enlightened as this. … That in general the people of color are inferior to whites in knowledge and industry, I shall not deny. You made them slaves, and nothing is more true than the ancient saying, "The day you make a man a slave takes half his worth away." Unaccustomed to provide for themselves, and habituated to regard labor as an evil, it is no wonder that when set free, they should be improvident and idle, and that their children should be brought up without education, and without prudence and forethought. But will you punish the children for your crimes; for the injuries which you have inflicted upon their parents? Besides, sir, this state of things is fast passing away. Schools have been opened for them, and it will, I am sure, give pleasure to this committee to know, that in these schools there is discovered a thirst for instruction, and a progress in learning, seldom to be seen in other schools of the state. They have also churches of their own, and clergymen of their own colour, who conduct their public worship with perfect decency and order, and not without ability.[89]

After making his case on moral grounds, Jay turned to questions of political expediency. He anticipated the argument that the black vote was beholden to Federalists leaders and argued instead that their numbers were significantly small such that no mischief could come from granting them the franchise. "The whole number of coloured people in the state … amounts to less than a fortieth part of the whole population. When your numbers are to theirs as forty to one, do you still fear them?" He then concluded by urging the delegates not to "stain" the constitution with "unreasonable prejudices" that were in "direct violation of the principles you profess."[90]

Bucktail Republican Erastus Root then rose to make the case that blacks, although afforded certain rights, have no real "anchorage" in the country because they are not called on to defend it in times of war. Thus, they were not true citizens in every sense of the word and should not be granted the right to vote. To Root, it was clear that citizenship rested on at least three aspects: property rights, voting rights, and the duty to defend the borders of the country. And citizenship was akin to a family of which persons of African descent could never be part. In Root's view, blacks could not be allowed "to disturb our political family" by being given the chance to change the nature of the government through elections. Taking a swipe at both the Federalists and the inability of blacks to vote independently, Root asserted:

> I should suppose there was some cause for alarm—when a few hundred negroes of the city of New York, following the train of those who ride in their coaches, and whose shoes and boots they had so often blacked, shall go to the polls of the election, and change the political condition of the whole state. A change in the representation of that city may cause a change in your assembly, by giving a majority to a particular party, which would vary your council of appointment who make the highest officers of your government—Thus would the whole state be controlled by a few hundred of this species of population in the city of New York.[91]

The heated back and forth between proponents and opponents of black suffrage continued on the first day the convention focused on the elective franchise. Yet it was clear from the outset that even within the Bucktail Republican camp there was not a consensus on this issue. Young's fellow Bucktail delegate from Delaware County Robert Clarke rose after Root to counter what he had argued. With some embarrassment, Clarke claimed that the "elocution" arrayed against him was formidable. Perhaps to the surprise of many of his Bucktail Republican colleagues, he then proceeded to give one of the more impassioned speeches on the rights of blacks and the suffrage. Clarke began by reminding the delegates of the principles laid out in the Declaration and the natural rights it protected. "I am unwilling to retain the word *white* because its detention is repugnant to all the principles and notions of liberty, to which we have heretofore professed to adhere, and to our declaration of independence, which is a concise and just expose of those principles."[92] Clarke then recited the Declaration. Continuing on this theme, Clarke admonished his colleagues:

> I think you cannot exclude them without being guilty of a palpable violation of every principle of justice. We are usurping to ourselves a power which we do not possess, and by so doing, deprive them of a privilege to which they are, and always have been, justly entitled—an invaluable right—a right in which we have prided ourselves as constituting our superiority over every other people on earth—a right which they have enjoyed ever since the formation of our government—the right of suffrage.[93]

Clarke then questioned his colleagues who asserted that blacks had no stake in American society because they were not called on to defend its borders during war. "In your late war," he shot back at Republicans, "they contributed largely toward some of your most splendid victories. On Lakes Erie and Champlain, where your fleets triumphed over a foe of superior in numbers, and engines of death, they were manned in a large proportion with men of colour." He went on to refute the argument that blacks were the only ones who did not exercise the right of suffrage judiciously, imploring Republicans to "go on and exclude also the many thousands of whites fawning, cringing sycophants, who look up their more wealthy and more ambitious neighbors for direction at the polls, as they look up to them for bread." Clarke then concluded with an admission that he looked upon blacks in similarly to his opponents. But he sketched out the fundamental differences between his ideological views on race and those other Bucktail Republicans. The latter viewed blacks with contempt, whereas Clarke and certainly a majority of the Federalists in the hall looked on the same group of humans with pity and even guilt.

I lament as much as any gentleman, that we have this species of population among us. But we have them here without any fault of theirs.
They were brought here and enslaved by the arm of violence and
oppression. We have heaped upon them every indignity, every injustice; and in restoring them at this late day (as far as practicable) to
their natural rights and privileges, we must make but a very partial
atonement for the many wrongs which we have heaped upon them.
… I admit that the blacks are a peculiarly unfortunate people, and I
wish that such inducements may be held out as shall induce them to
become a sober and industrious class of community, and raise them
to the high standard of independent electors.[94]

Toward the end of the day, another Bucktail Republican and staunch ally
of Martin Van Buren, Colonel Samuel Young, rose to speak. He began by
echoing his colleagues and discounted the notion that voting was a "natural right." He then appealed to his colleagues to consider public opinion in
making their decision on the question of black suffrage. He began:

In forming a constitution, we should have reference to the feelings,
habits, and modes of thinking of the people. The gentleman last up
has alluded to the importance of regarding public sentiment. And
what is the public sentiment in relation to this subject? Are the
Negroes permitted to a participation in social intercourse with the
whites! Are they elevated to public office! No Sir—public sentiment
forbids it. This they know; and hence they are prepared to sell their
votes to the highest bidder. In this manner you introduce corruption
into the very vitals of the government. … This distinction of colour
is well understood. It is unnecessary to disguise it, and we ought to
shape our constitution so as to meet the public sentiment.[95]

Young then reaffirmed the ascriptive ideology to which he and his Bucktail colleagues adhered in his concluding remarks. He stated flatly:

The minds of blacks are not competent to vote. They are too degraded
to estimate the value, or exercise with fidelity and discretion this
important right. It would be unsafe in their hands. *Their vote would
be at the call of the richest purchaser.* If this class of people should
hereafter arrive at such a degree of intelligence and virtue, as to
inspire confidence, then it will be proper to confer this privilege
upon them. At present emancipate and protect them; but withhold
that privilege which they will inevitably abuse. Look to your jails and
penitentiaries. By whom are they filled? By the very race, whom it is
now proposed to clothe with the power of deciding upon your political rights.[96]

The debate over black suffrage raged on the next day. The two views heretofore presented—complete enfranchisement, on the one hand, complete disenfranchisement, on the other—were not favored by a majority of the delegates. But, quite simply, there was no other alternative at that point. By contrast, the delegation as a whole was leaning toward some type of black voting rights. On September 20, a vote was taken on whether to restrict the franchise solely to whites; it failed by a vote of sixty-three to fifty-nine. Martin Van Buren originally voted to do away with the racial classification because allowing blacks to vote would mean tax revenue from blacks; disenfranchising them meant not taxing them.[97] But he realized that the potential danger a potential large black voting block in New York City presented to his political aspirations and began to seek another solution.

Over the next several days, delegates turned to a more general discussion about citizenship and property rights. Federalists had long been in favor of a property qualification for voting, and by September 24, the suffrage committee had moved to consider a $250 qualification for some elections. Most Bucktail Republicans were opposed to it. Although Van Buren began the convention favoring some type of property qualification for voting, he changed his position—at least when it came to the white laborers in the state. On September 25, Van Buren rose to decry the more restrictive franchise on the basis that it would effectively disenfranchise "this class of men, composed of mechanics, professional men, and small landholders, and constituting the bone, pith, and muscle of the population of the state."[98] Van Buren then went on to criticize conservative Federalists who had supported black suffrage but who would impose property qualifications on the white yeoman workers of the state. Taking up the mantle of Jefferson, Van Buren made an impassioned argument against the property qualification:

> It was ... but yesterday, that [Federalists] afforded the strongest evidence of their continued hold upon our feelings and our judgments, by the triumph they effected, over the strongest aversions and prejudices of our nature—on the question of continuing the right of suffrage to the poor, degraded blacks. Apply ... for a moment, the principles they inculcate to the question under consideration, and let its merits be thereby tested. Are those of your citizens represented, whose voices are never heard in your senate. ... Who had hitherto constituted a majority of the voters of the state? The *farmers*—who had called for, and insisted upon the Convention. *Farmers and freeholders!* Who passed the law admitting those, who were not electors, to a free participation in the decision of the question of *Convention or No Convention,* and also in the choice of delegates to that body ... the farmers of this state had by an overwhelming majority admitted

those who were not freeholders, to a full participation with themselves in every stage of this great effort to amend our constitution, and to ameliorate the condition of the people.[99]

The convention returned to race and the suffrage on September 29. That day, a new committee was convened to specifically formulate language on black suffrage to be embodied in the draft Constitution. The body consisted of thirteen members; Samuel Young and eight other members had originally been opposed to any black suffrage, whereas four members of the committee were in support.[100] Young immediately announced his plans to insert the word "white" into the suffrage clause. On October 4, his committee did so. Two days later, the debate resumed over black suffrage. But by October 6, Van Buren had come to realize the futility in completely disenfranchising blacks. That day, he rose to object to the insertion of the word "white" in the suffrage article. At the same time, he endorsed a provision that would place a $250 property qualification on blacks. Other Bucktail Republicans fell in line. As the body began to consider this provision, Federalist Asa Eastwood made one more attempt at a more lenient compromise by putting forth a motion to lower the property qualification on blacks to $100. The motion failed. Late in the day on October 6, the body voted as a whole solely on the black suffrage provision. It passed by a vote of 72–30.[101]

On October 8, the committee presented the entire section of the document pertaining to property qualification for a full vote. Judge Platt, a Federalist on the suffrage committee, made one last plea against the racial restriction. He said that Colonel Young had previously delivered a "eulogium on liberty and equality, in our happy state" and then concluded by "moving a resolution, in substance, that thirty seven thousand of our free black citizens, and their posterity, for ever, shall be degraded by our constitution below the common rank of freeman."[102] In short, Platt accused Young of being hypocritical. In actuality, Young had been quite consistent throughout: his argument all along had been along the lines of racial ascriptivism and citizenship manifested in the white man's republic. Van Buren's compromise was in direct opposition to Young's views, but realizing few alternatives he supported it. Platt then argued once more on natural rights grounds, mixed with racial paternalism:

> Our Republican text is, that all men are born equal, in civil and political rights; and if this proviso be ingrafted into our constitution, the practical commentary will be, that a portion of our free citizens shall not enjoy equal rights with their fellow citizens. All freemen of African parentage, are to be constitutionally degraded: no matter how virtuous or intelligent. … Before we adopt this proviso, I hope

gentlemen will take a retrospect of the last fifty years. Consider the astonishing progress of the human mind, in regard to religious toleration; the various plans of enlightened benevolence; and especially the mighty efforts of the wise and the good throughout Christendom, in favour of the benighted and oppressed children of Africa.[103]

One last time, Platt brought to the floor of the convention for a vote that would again strike the word "white" from the provision. It failed overwhelmingly: seventy-one delegates voted against it, thirty-three voted for it. Soon, a second vote was taken on the entire section with the language included on the $250 property qualification for blacks. It passed 74–38. The entire article on the suffrage provision was passed by the convention overwhelmingly on October 29. And, in January 1822, New York voters approved the new constitution by a margin of 74,732 to 41,402.

Conclusions on Race Formation and Voting Rights in New York

It is telling that, despite their majority numbers in the convention, Bucktail Republicans could not get the word "white" inserted in the final draft of the constitution. Yet, the $250 property qualification for blacks passed by a more than 2–1 majority. The votes were not there for the former; they were for the latter. Why?

Let me conclude this chapter on New York by coming back to the dynamic of race formation for an explanation. We have seen that the demographic and socioeconomic changes in New York over the course of the opening decades of the nineteenth century had real political consequences. In searching for a majority coalition, Republican leaders played the race card against Federalists as they sought to incorporate poor white farmers and laborers into their political camp. The bond between Federalists and black New Yorkers was cemented in the Revolutionary period. But Republican politicians represented a new generation of leadership with different views on race. I have argued that the old guard Federalists were for the most part racial paternalists, whereas the emerging Republican coalition was built largely on racial ascriptivism. In the decades before the Constitutional Convention, Federalists responded to Republican racial threats—sometimes forcefully, sometimes halfheartedly. Yet, it was clear from the actions of the much of the Federalist leadership that blacks were indeed part of the Federalist coalition.

Thus, leading up to the constitutional convention of 1821, two of the three conditions for racial disenfranchisement that I outlined in Chapter 1 were present: (1) racial conflict had indeed taken place as an outgrowth of rapid economic and demographic change, and (2) political actors (Republicans) seeking electoral advantage placed themselves in a position to successfully prey on this racial conflict by arousing poorer whites who became part of their coalition. And, yet, only a partial disenfranchisement of blacks was effected. If we look at the vote in the convention, the evidence suggests that there was a large block of swing votes, roughly two dozen or so, comprised mostly of Bucktail Republicans who voted no on the insertion of the word "white" in the suffrage article but yes on the $250 property qualification. Indeed, this was the compromise crafted by Martin Van Buren after it was clear that complete racial disenfranchisement would fail. Bucktail Republicans followed Van Buren's lead. This leads me to suggest that the third requirement of the changing structure of race formation—an ascriptive racial belief system—had become the paradigm of a majority of the Bucktail Republicans, but not the entire delegation. As such, its dominance had not been *fully* realized. As we saw, some Bucktail Republicans argued passionately for black suffrage, even though many more voted against black disenfranchisement.

Article II Section 1 of the Constitution of 1821 read:

> But no man of color, unless he shall have for three years [the residence qualification for whites was one year] a citizen of this state, and for one year preceding any election, shall be seized and possessed of a freehold estate of the value of two hundred and fifty dollars, over and above all debts and encumbrances charged thereon; and shall have been actually rated, and paid a tax thereon, shall be entitled to vote at such an election.

While the property qualification on blacks was more restrictive, it should be noted that blacks were not required to perform military service. In addition, blacks who did not meet the $250 freehold qualification were not required to pay taxes.

In the end, most of the compromises crafted by the convention delegates on black suffrage were positions advocated by Martin Van Buren. To a large extent he got exactly what he wanted. Van Buren and his allies supported the clause on the grounds of long-run incentive—he believed, in other words, that a property qualification of $250 placed upon blacks would lead to the self-improvement of the Negro in New York. Individual black men would become more industrious and less idle, according to this line of thinking, and hence effect an amelioration of the economic condition of blacks as a class. Perhaps what the Bucktails knew but did not outwardly acknowledge was that blacks were doomed at this time to toil in the lowest stations in New York society. The Bucktail Republican party that advocated for hard work and industry on the part of blacks was the same party that drew much of its support from white laborers hostile to the upward social mobility of blacks. A black man could work all his life and not acquire this much property. And even though New York was inundated with poor white immigrants during this period, within five years all restrictions save for a taxpaying qualification were dropped on whites.

In the short run, however, Van Buren and the Bucktails achieved specific goals they had set out to accomplish. First, they were able to secure a restricted franchise that essentially disqualified nearly 15,000 potential black voters across the state—including a heavily concentrated black population in New York City that predominantly voted the Federalist ticket. The restrictive access to the ballot remained in place for the rest of the antebellum period in New York. For example, in the thirty-year period between 1825 and 1855, the number of free blacks eligible to vote in New York City remained quite small. In 1825 for example, only 68 of the 12,559 blacks in the city were qualified to vote. Ten years later only 255 of the 12,913 black residents met the property qualifications. And in 1855, only 100 of the 11,840 black inhabitants cast a vote.[104]

The second goal Van Buren and his allies accomplished was an expanded franchise for what was the base of his party in New York—propertyless but taxpaying white laborers. Thus, by 1821 the "white man's democracy" we equate the Jacksonian era with was already in place. Martin Van Buren played a crucial role in this transformation—at the very least he helped to shape racial ascriptivism and use it for political gain that would help keep the Democratic Party in power for the next several decades.

Blacks continued to agitate for the franchise in New York after 1821 as the Democratic Party took hold of state politics. Blacks first sought to align themselves with the emergent Whig Party in the 1830s. But when the Whigs failed to push for black suffrage, they turned to the Liberty Party and the Free Soil Party in the 1840s. The rise of the Republican Party in New York in the late 1850s still did not serve the interest of the black population in New York. Even though New York helped to elect Abraham Lincoln to the White House in 1860, that same year New York voters overwhelmingly turned down a proposal for equal suffrage for blacks; the same occurred as late as 1869, one year before the Fifteenth Amendment was ratified. Thus, similar to Pennsylvania, black New Yorkers were forced to wait until federal intervention for the franchise. But the seeds of the Republican-black relationship in New York were sown in Old New York in the days of Federalist dominance.

CHAPTER 3

"An Asylum for the Oppressed Injured Sons of Europe"

The Disenfranchisement of Blacks in Pennsylvania

The Creation of the White Republic of Pennsylvania

The *herrenvolk* ideology of the white republic reached its apex when the Supreme Court handed down the *Dred Scott* decision in 1857. Chief Justice Roger Taney's long and rambling opinion rested firmly on two arguments but went on to imply a third. First, Taney asserted that blacks were not citizens under the proper meaning of the Constitution, leaving Dred Scott without redress in an American court of law. Second, he argued that the federal government did not have the power to regulate slavery in the territories, thus rendering the Missouri Compromise of 1820 null and void. Finally, and perhaps most bizarrely, Taney intimated that states did not even have the power to abolish slavery, as doing so amounted to a violation of the constitutional right to private property. All of these conclusions flowed from one ostensibly basic question: "The question is simply this," Taney asked. "Can a negro, whose ancestors were imported into this country, and sold as slaves, become a member of the political community formed and brought into existence by the Constitution of the United States, and as such become entitled to all the rights, and privileges, and immunities, guaranteed by that instrument to the citizen?"[1] Taney responded in the negative: "We think that [blacks] are not, and that they are not included, and were not intended to be included under the word 'citizens' in the Constitution, and can therefore claim none of the rights and privileges which that instrument provides for and secures to citizens of the United States."[2] He continued:

> On the contrary, they were at that time considered as a subordinate and inferior class of beings, who had been subjugated by the dominant race, and, whether emancipated or not, remained subject to their authority, and had no rights or privileges but such as those who held the power and the Government might choose to grant them. … They had for more than a century before been regarded as beings of an inferior order, and altogether unfit to associate with the white race, either in social or political relations; and so far inferior, that they had no rights which the white man was bound to respect.[3]

To render these conclusions about race, citizenship, and the Constitution, Justice Taney claimed to engage in the judicial practice of original intent—that is, he sought to understand the words and the meaning of the Constitution as the framers had intended them some seventy years earlier. But his method and the findings it uncovered amounted to no more than an act of historical erasure: in his dissent in *Dred Scott,* Justice Curtis reminds us that "as free colored persons were then citizens of at least five States, and so in every sense part of the people of the United States, they were among those for whom and whose posterity the Constitution was ordained and established."[4] The historical record was essentially ignored by Taney because it could not be squared with the racial ascriptivist views that had been on the rise throughout the first half of the nineteenth century. In order to make the case that Dred Scott was not a citizen, Taney first had lay claim to the fact that the United States had *always* been a white man's republic, and that the framers had *never* intended to grant blacks those rights afforded to whites. By the time the *Dred Scott* case made its way to the Supreme Court for oral arguments in 1854, ascriptivism had become firmly embedded as the dominant racial belief system of the country. And with Taney's decision it became constitutionally protected.

Taney's decision was not the first time a court in the United States had based its decision on racial ascriptivism. Some twenty years before *Dred Scott,* the Pennsylvania courts were asked to settle two similar cases concerning the question of citizenship for blacks. Whereas in *Dred Scott* the issue turned simply on a man's right to freedom, both of the Pennsylvania cases dealt with the issue of voting rights, and whether or not the Pennsylvania constitution granted blacks that privilege. One originated in 1835 in Luzerne County; the other in Bucks County in 1837. In the former, a black man was denied the right to vote and petitioned the court for redress. In the latter, two Democratic officials sued, claiming that the illegal votes of several dozen blacks tilted the election to their Whig rivals. Ultimately, both cases were decided against the black voters. And, in both decisions, the Pennsylvania courts employed the same argument that would form the backbone to Taney's opinion in *Dred Scott* two decades later: blacks were not granted the right to vote in Pennsylvania because they had *never* been considered part of the political compact formed under the Pennsylvania Constitution. It mattered little that blacks had actually been voting in Pennsylvania for nearly half a century; what mattered was that the words "citizen" and "freeman" were never meant to include blacks in the first place. Twenty years before the Supreme Court determined that the United States was exclusively a white man's republic, the Pennsylvania courts had practiced their own version of historical erasure in coming to the same conclusion about the Keystone State.[5]

The *Dred Scott* case cannot be divorced from the explosive national debate over the issue of slavery in the 1850s. Similarly, the Pennsylvania court cases originating in the mid-to-late 1830s also must be placed within the context of race relations in the state and the depths to which they had plummeted at that point. The 1830s were marked by heightened racial conflict across much of Pennsylvania as the state found itself both geographically and politically on the front lines of the simmering national battle over slavery and freedom. Philadelphia, more than any of the major cities of the North—more than Boston, Providence, and even New York—quickly became the major focal point. W. E. B. DuBois put it this way in his excellent but somewhat neglected study on blacks in Philadelphia in the late nineteenth century: "Philadelphia was the natural gateway between the North and the South, and for a long time there passed through it a stream of free Negroes and fugitive slaves toward the North, and of recaptured Negroes and kidnapped colored persons toward the South."[6] This stream of black bodies moving back and forth across the Mason-Dixon Line and in and out of the streets of Philadelphia provoked a tension with a white population comprised mainly of unskilled immigrants. Throughout the decade, race riots took place with increasing frequency amid a growing backlash against the efforts of the burgeoning abolitionist movement. Philadelphia thus at once became ground zero of the antislavery movement and anti-black sentiment. The first riot took place in late 1829 after Fanny Wright Darusmont had given a number of addresses advocating the emancipation of slaves and social equality between the races. In 1831, not far to the south in Southampton, Virginia, the Nat Turner insurrection occurred, sending fugitives streaming into Philadelphia with horror stories about the possibility of slave revolts spreading throughout the South and spilling over into northern urban centers where most free blacks lived. The response of political leaders in the Pennsylvania legislature was to propose by statute that free blacks carry passes as proof of their free status; all other blacks would be excluded from the state. Abolitionists were successful in preventing its passage, but the inexorable slide toward further racial restrictions in Pennsylvania had begun. More race riots occurred in 1834 and 1835. When delegates convened in 1837–1838 to draft a new constitution for the state, voting rights for blacks became one of the most heated issues under debate—especially after it appeared that blacks had determined the outcome of local elections in favor of the Whig candidates in Bucks County that year. In the end, Democratic delegates were successful in placing a racial voting restriction in the new constitution, disenfranchising tens of thousands of black Pennsylvanians until the Fifteenth Amendment was ratified in 1870.

The disenfranchisement of blacks in antebellum Pennsylvania has been explored in the past by several scholars. Roy Akari's early work on the Constitutional Convention of 1837–1838 mentions the disenfranchisement of blacks in passing without going into much detail.[7] Lyle Rosenberger's excellent analysis of the election of 1837 in Bucks County emphasizes local partisan competition and the threat that the black vote posed to the Democratic Party in the county.[8] Julie Winch and, most recently, Eric Ledell Smith both focus on the role of blacks in the fight against disenfranchisement, but Smith goes beyond Winch's work to explain disenfranchisement by looking at state partisanship (rather than local partisanship as Rosenberger's analysis does) and the "social factors and motives ... within a historical narrative."[9]

Although all of these works paint a fairly clear picture of the events leading up to black disenfranchisement in antebellum Pennsylvania, none of them seek explicitly to link the issue of black voting rights to the larger development of race formation in the state from colonial times to the mid-nineteenth century or, for that matter, the more general the racial dynamic of the North as a whole in the same time period. As we saw with the case of New York, black disenfranchisement in Pennsylvania needs to be situated within these larger concerns that were operating both at the state and national levels.

The road that Pennsylvania traveled to become one of the most racially restrictive states in the North by 1838 is rather extraordinary if we consider its history from colonial times, through the Revolutionary era, and up to the drafting and ratification of the Constitution. In 1681, Charles II had granted a colonial charter for the land west of the Delaware River, known then as West Jersey, to William Penn, who in turn sought to create a "wilderness Utopia" in the new world for his Quaker brethren.[10] The prospect of escaping both the political and religious corruption of England appealed to Penn as he looked, in the words of Gary Nash, to "serve at once, God, personal fortune, and fellow Quakers."[11] Although indentured servitude for persons of African descent had been introduced previously in the region under Dutch rule, the practice of slavery in Pennsylvania during colonial times was not without controversy, for several reasons that range from the moral to the economic. For one, the Quaker leaders of the colony from the late seventeenth century to the middle of the eighteenth century were unsure that the Golden Rule—"to do as they would be done by"—could be reconciled with the practice of holding other human beings in slavery for life. Even before the Pennsylvania colony was founded, members of the Society of Friends traveled throughout the West Indies advising brethren to treat their slaves mildly and manumit them after a few years of servitude. But even under such moral pressure, the fact remains that most of the slaveholders in Pennsylvania in the first half of the eighteenth century were English Quakers.[12] In this instance, economic considerations trumped moral ones. By the 1750s, however, this would change as Quaker leaders pressed the Assembly to pass legislation ending the importation of slaves in to the colony. Society of Friends leaders such as Ralph Sandiford, Benjamin Lay, and Anthony Benezet then turned their attention to fellow Quakers who owned slaves, pressuring them to manumit their slaves or else face the risk of being banned from the affairs of the Society. By 1758, the Society had made manumission mandatory for its members.[13]

Moreover, from its origin Pennsylvania was populated by Germans who had always been opposed to slavery and consequently refused to own slaves. Germans constituted as much as one-third of the overall population of Pennsylvania as late as 1790, exerting a good deal of political and moral influence over its political leaders.[14] Aligned religiously with the Friends, they were shocked to find slavery in Penn's colony and issued the first formal protest against slavery in the New World in Germantown, Pennsylvania, in 1688.

There also was an economic dimension to the problem of slavery in Pennsylvania. From the opening of the eighteenth century, white workers in Pennsylvania objected to the importation of slaves on the grounds that black slaves lowered their wages by taking potential job opportunities. On several occasions, the Pennsylvania Assembly moved to raise the duty charged on slaves to restrict their numbers in the colony. Each time, the British crown repealed the laws and lowered the duties. This continued throughout the first half of the eighteenth century until Quaker leaders were finally successful in doing away with importation altogether. Although Quakers objected to the importation of slaves on moral grounds, poorer whites gladly went along with the same policies because they promoted and protected their economic interests.

Whether the spread of slavery was opposed for moral or economic reasons, the evidence suggests that, by the middle of the eighteenth century, the dominant political culture of Pennsylvania—rooted in the stark ways of Quakerism—made it one of the more racially lenient colonies in the years leading up to the Revolutionary War and the period immediately following it. Under Quaker influence, Pennsylvania was the first colony to set up schools for black children (1750s) and the first state to pass an abolition law (1780). The constitutions drafted in 1776 and 1790 made no mention of race in the qualification for the suffrage, which lent legitimacy to the argument that blacks were granted the right to vote by those two documents.

The aim of this chapter is to offer an explanation for the disenfranchisement of blacks in Pennsylvania in 1838. As I have done previously, I suggest here that we need to look at black disenfranchisement through the lens of race formation, and first take into account the social and economic transformation of the state from the Founding through the first half of the nineteenth century. DuBois understood the importance of these socioeconomic factors in the political development of Pennsylvania when he wrote in *The Philadelphia Negro*:

> A curious comment on human nature is this change in public opinion [in Pennsylvania] between 1790 and 1837. No one thing explains it—it arose from a combination of circumstances. If, as in 1790, the new freedmen had been given peace and quiet and abundant work to develop sensible and aspiring leaders, the end would have been different; but a mass of poverty-stricken, ignorant fugitives and ill-trained freedmen had rushed to [Philadelphia], swarmed in the vile slums which the rapidly growing city furnished, and met in social and economic competition equally ignorant but more vigorous foreigners. These foreigners outbid them at work, beat them on the streets, and were enabled to do this by the prejudice which Negro crime and the anti-slavery sentiment had aroused in the city.[15]

DuBois's analysis implies that a certain set of political outcomes resulted from the socioeconomic changes during these fifty years. By and large, that is an accurate assessment: blacks just up from slavery in and around Pennsylvania and fugitives from the South flooded Philadelphia in the opening decades of the nineteenth century at the very moment waves of European immigrants (particularly Irish) were arriving. These forces combined to change the racial and ethnic makeup of Philadelphia, as well as the state. But, by themselves, these changes alone do not fully explain the *political* transformation that took place. Thus, I think we need to flesh out the political dynamic implied in DuBois's sociological explanation, and analyze how political actors responded to the changing demographics.

Once we do, we shall see that, first, partisan conflict and party competition played a significant role in the disenfranchisement of blacks in 1838. Smith and Rosenberger's respective works make clear the role which partisan conflict and party competition played in black disenfranchisement. Yet, we need to approach the issue of partisanship from a much broader historical perspective than either Bucks County as Rosenberger does, or the entire state as Smith suggests. Black communities were under increasing attack in the two decades before the Constitutional Convention of 1837–1838. Legally, they were allowed to vote across most of the state; by the 1830s, many were nonetheless being intimidated from the polls by hostile whites. But it was not until the reemergence of party competition after roughly forty years of one-party politics in Pennsylvania that the legal disenfranchisement of blacks was enacted. When actual black votes decided a local election in favor of the ascending Whig Party in 1837, the once-indestructible Democratic Party quickly sought a more permanent political solution to the problem of black voter influence than mere random acts of violence and intimidation.

Second, we will also see that the racial conflicts of Pennsylvania in the years between the 1770s and the 1840s were undergirded by a racialized discourse framed on two sides by competing racial belief systems. If the dominant view of Pennsylvania's leaders was paternalistic in its outlook toward blacks during the Revolutionary period, this view lost out to the dominant ascriptive ideology of the state's leaders by the 1830s. In short, the "white republic" of Pennsylvania, far from a forgone conclusion during this period, was created discursively by Pennsylvania's political leaders in the opening decades of the nineteenth century. Although contested by a small but ardent group of political leaders and abolitionists espousing their paternalistic views, the white republic of Pennsylvania was finally institutionalized with the ratification of the Constitution in 1838.

The creation of the white republic of Pennsylvania was foreshadowed as early as 1805 when Thomas Branagan, an Irish immigrant who took up residence in Philadelphia at the turn of the century, wrote that the United States was "appropriated by the Lord of the Universe to be an Asylum for the Oppressed, Injured Sons of Europe."[16] Although Branagan had the United States in mind when he wrote these words, he was actually looking at the racial dynamic of Philadelphia as a prime example of what the United States *might* look like if the white republic was *not* institutionalized and brought into existence. We shall return a bit later to Branagan's writings and the role they played in the discursive development of Pennsylvania politics. What is important to understand for now is that his vision of a white republic, put forth in the opening decade of the nineteenth century, was institutionalized nearly forty years later when blacks were written out of the electorate.

I first analyze the demographic changes of Pennsylvania in the period between the Founding and the late 1830s, paying particular attention to changes wrought by gradual abolition in the state and its peculiar relationship to slavery in the neighboring South. Next, I situate racial conflict within the context of party competition in Pennsylvania from the Revolutionary Period to the late 1830s. There I argue that one-party politics from 1800 to the mid-1830s, rather than facilitating the disenfranchisement of blacks in the state, served to prevent the issue from becoming salient. Only when the Whig-Anti-Mason coalition begins to compete for power in the state do Democratic leaders seek the disenfranchisement of blacks. Third, I seek to place both socioeconomic and partisan concerns within the context of a racial discourse framed by two competing ideologies, with a particular emphasis on the heated debates surrounding racial disenfranchisement that occurred on the floor of the Constitutional Convention of 1837–1838.

Under Increasing Attack: Gradual Abolition of African Americans and Social Change in Pennsylvania, 1780–1838

Indentured servants of African descent had been in the region around the Delaware River as early as the 1640s, some forty years before Pennsylvania existed as a colony under the British crown. By the time William Penn was granted the charter by Charles II, hereditary, lifetime slavery had become common practice throughout the colonies. In Pennsylvania, the active demand for blacks increased as both the British crown and merchants operating out of the port of Philadelphia found trafficking in slavery to be profitable. The earliest estimate on record for the number of slaves in the colony appears in 1721, which placed the number of blacks somewhere between twenty-five hundred and five thousand.[17] Over the next thirty years, the black population of Pennsylvania swelled to eleven thousand, with as many as six thousand blacks residing in Philadelphia alone.

The 1750–1760s mark the beginning of the end to slavery in Pennsylvania. As mentioned earlier, two forces mitigated the spread of slavery over the course of the first half of the eighteenth century: the first was moral in origin, the second economic. There existed in Pennsylvania since its founding a strong antislavery sentiment among members of the Society of Friends, particularly those of German descent. Although most of the slaveholders in the early years of the colony were Quakers, leaders urged their Friends at Society meetings to end the wretched and un-Christian like practice of slavery. As early as 1712, Quakers were petitioning the

Provincial Assembly to end slavery.[18] Although the legislature refused to abolish the practice of slavery, slaveholding Quakers complied with the calls for voluntary manumission. Gary Nash asserts that, by the 1740s, one out of every three Quakers had released their slaves by will.[19] By 1760, Quaker leaders were successful in getting all their brethren to manumit their slaves or else face expulsion from the Society. Manumission of slaves by Quakers continued to increase in the years leading up to the Revolutionary War as the rhetoric of freedom and slavery forced slave owners in Pennsylvania to reassess their own practices in light of the perceived oppression by the British crown.

By contrast, the practice of slavery had been a cause of economic concern to leaders of the Pennsylvania colony from the opening of the eighteenth century. It should be kept in mind that indentured servitude included both whites and blacks in the seventeenth century. Although indentured, workers of either race did not have to compete with slave labor for employment. However, once free, laborers found themselves shut out of many opportunities by masters using their own slave labor. By 1708, the economic conflict had taken on an explicitly racial complexion as free white mechanics protested to the state legislature against this custom. In 1712—the same year Quaker William Southeby petitioned the Assembly to abolish slavery—the duty on slave importation was raised from 20 shillings to 20 pounds. The British crown objected because the slave trade had become a lucrative business for companies operating out of the West Indies. It was consequently reduced to 5 pounds. When the number of slaves increased again in the early 1720s, whites protested against the "employment of blacks," and the legislature responded by declaring that the custom of employing *any* black laborer was "dangerous and injurious to the republic." The Assembly also sought to restrict emancipation in 1726 on the grounds that "free negroes [were] an idle and slothful people."[20] Over the course of the next several decades, Pennsylvania authorities would pass many acts and ordinances criminalizing behavior based mainly on skin color.

Thus, from the colony's origins, we see two conflicting views on race in Pennsylvania that nevertheless lead to the same conclusions on the issue of slavery. On the one hand, slavery was perceived by Quakers as a moral evil to be exterminated because it did not coincide with the Golden Rule of Christianity. On the other, slavery was perceived as an economic threat by unskilled free white laborers seeking only to carve out a meager existence for themselves. The logic of the Quaker disposition would lead to a paternalistic uplift ideology whereby blacks, once freed, needed to be given religious and educational instruction. By contrast, the logic employed by the white laboring classes would lead to the ideology of the "white republic," whereby blacks, as a result of their inherent inferiority, needed to be kept separate in every way—politically, socially, and economically—from white society. As we shall see, these two conflicting views on race formed the backdrop to the political development of Pennsylvania throughout the rest of the eighteenth century and into the nineteenth, ebbing and flowing with historical events and the demographic changes sweeping across the state.

By the 1760s and 1770s, the cultural logic of Quakerism predominated as Pennsylvania leaders incorporated the natural rights philosophy of Revolutionary rhetoric into critiques against slavery. Calls for abolition had reached a feverish pitch, and on March 1, 1780, in the midst of the Revolutionary War, Pennsylvania passed the first abolition law in the United States.[21] It provided that no child born in Pennsylvania after that date would be a slave; but any child (negro or mulatto) born to a slave mother would be held in service until he/she reached twenty-eight years of age. Furthermore, the bill required that all slaveholders register their slaves with state authorities by no later than November 1, 1780. During roughly the same time, manumission of slaves proceeded apace. Nash asserts that, between 1767 and 1775, the slave population of Philadelphia was halved.[22] Part of the decrease was a result of high black mortality rates, low black fertility rates, and slaves being sold out of the city. Nonetheless, manumission played a significant role in the decline of slavery as the number of free blacks in the state increased during these years.

But although the free black population of Pennsylvania was on the rise by the 1780s, the *overall* population of blacks declined in Pennsylvania in the forty years between 1750 and 1790. According to the first national census taken in 1790, there were a total of 10,274 blacks in the state, or about 1,000 fewer than in the middle decades of the eighteenth century.[23] Of these, roughly two-thirds were free. Much of the decline came amid the Revolutionary War as the black population in the state, much like in other states, was scattered and decimated by death and flight in the fighting.

The 1790s signal a drastic turning point in the racial makeup in the city of Philadelphia. In the years between the Revolutionary War and the end of the War of 1812, Philadelphia became a refuge for blacks of all backgrounds—for those freed in the state and in the rest of the North, on the one hand, and for those escaping the chains of slavery in the South, on the other. By the opening decades of the nineteenth century, Philadelphia had become the "gateway" between North and South described by DuBois in *The Philadelphia Negro*. As Table 3.1 shows, the black population of the city underwent a fivefold increase in the years between 1790 and 1810. Whereas blacks made up roughly 4 percent of the population in 1780, by 1820 that figure had tripled to 12 percent. Black density in Philadelphia declined somewhat in the years after that, but remained around 9 percent for most of the antebellum period.

Table 3.1 White and Black Population and Density in Philadelphia, 1780–1830[24]

Year	White Population	Percent White	Black Population	Percent Black	Total Population
1780	30,900	96	1,100	4	32,000
1790	42,018	95	2,078	5	44,096
1800	63,242	90	6,436	10	69,678
1810	82,221	89	9,656	11	91,877
1820	100,662	88	12,110	12	112,772
1830	149,140	91	14,554	9	163,694

Two reasons seem to account for the rapid increase in the black population of Philadelphia. First, blacks residing in other parts of the state and the immediate regions in the North, once freed, were flocking to Philadelphia looking for employment. Second, blacks freed or escaping from slavery south of Pennsylvania also migrated to the city. Nash estimates that two-thirds of all blacks living in Philadelphia and working in the maritime industry during this period came from within a one hundred-mile radius of the city. This area would include not only Pennsylvania, New Jersey, and New York but also the slave states of Maryland, Delaware, and Virginia.[25] Indeed, Pennsylvania was at the geographical crossroads in the ongoing development of slavery in the United States in the opening decades of the nineteenth century, and Philadelphia was its portal. Table 3.2 shows the population of whites and blacks in Philadelphia as a percentage of the overall population of the state. By 1800, nearly half of all blacks in the state resided in Philadelphia. By contrast, only 10 percent of all whites living in the state resided in Philadelphia, making black Pennsylvanians four times as likely to reside in the city than whites.

Although both the black population and black density in the population of Philadelphia increased dramatically during this period, the black density in the overall population of Pennsylvania nudged up only slightly throughout the antebellum period. As Table 3.3 shows, blacks made up

TABLE 3.2 Black and White Population in Philadelphia as Percent of Pennsylvania Population[26]

Year	Percent of Pennsylvania Population	
	Black	White
1790	20.3	9.5
1800	43.8	10.9
1810	41.7	10.6
1820	35.5	9.9

TABLE 3.3 Black Density in Pennsylvania
Population, 1790–1850[27]

Year	Percent Black
1790	2.4
1800	2.7
1810	2.9
1820	2.9
1830	2.8
1840	2.8
1850	2.8

no more than 3 percent of the population of the state at any point in the period between 1790 and 1850. Black density peaked in the 1810s and then proceeded to decline for the rest of the antebellum years. At no point did the black density increase by more than half a percentage point in a ten-year period. Thus, although blacks were flooding to the city of Philadelphia in the opening decades of the nineteenth century, the migration of whites into the rest of the state during the same period offset many of these increases (see Table 3.2). White ethnics were moving to Philadelphia, but they also were settling in other parts of the state—particularly in the region west of the Allegheny Mountains.

As mentioned earlier, the gradual abolition law passed by the Pennsylvania Assembly in 1780 stipulated that any child born to a mother held in slavery would be freed on reaching the age of twenty-eight. Thus, by 1808, manumission was taking place all across the state. Gradual abolition no doubt played a large role in both the increase in number of free blacks in the state and the black migration to Philadelphia. By 1810, there were only 795 slaves and 22,493 free blacks in Pennsylvania.[28]

What social and economic circumstances were associated with these demographics changes in the years preceding the state Constitutional Convention in 1837–1838 when blacks were disenfranchised? Turner, DuBois, and Nash all paint for us a stark picture of the black community in and around Philadelphia struggling for survival in the years spanning 1800 to 1840. Despite an emphasis on religious and educational instruction by the Quaker elite and the Pennsylvania Abolition Society from the 1770s through the opening decades of the nineteenth century, the public records indicate a large wave of black vagrancy and crime in the city in the years that followed. The 1810 census showed that 45 percent of the 365 prisoners at the Walnut Street Prison in Philadelphia were black. By contrast, only 3.5 percent of the cases presented for trial in the city between the years 1798 and 1802 involved black defendants.[29] The increase in crime coincided with the transition blacks made from living in white households to living on their own. In 1800, 56 percent of all Philadelphia blacks lived in white households; by 1810, that number had dropped to 39 percent. Ten years later, only 27 percent of blacks resided in white households.[30] Blacks were forging their own communities in Philadelphia, but were doing so in the face of increasing political and economic discrimination, on the one hand, and residential segregation, on the other. A good indicator as to how drastically race relations had changed in the city as early as 1805 is exemplified by an incident at the Independence Day festivities of that year. In previous years, residents of the city from all racial and economic backgrounds had gathered in front of Independence Hall to commemorate the signing of the Declaration of the Independence and the drafting of the Constitution. However, in 1805, dozens of white citizens turned the festivities into a racial pogrom and attacked numerous free blacks, chasing them from the square. Nash states that the Independence Day celebration in the years following this incident became primarily a white working-class festival, "and black citizens could enter the socially redefined public space in front of Independence Hall only at their peril."[31] The practice continued well into the 1830s. Well-meaning, upper-class whites of Philadelphia also stayed away from Independence Hall on Fourth of July after 1805, imbuing the Independence Day festivities with both a racial and class bias.

Both white and black leaders were also frustrated in their attempts to provide black children educational instruction during this period. The Quaker abolitionist Anthony Benezet had established the first school for black children in Pennsylvania in the 1750s. In the 1790s, the Pennsylvania Abolition Society continued to provide schooling for black children, but with limited success. The Cherry Street School had merely twenty students enrolled in 1799. Black leaders such as Absalom Jones and Richard Allen established their own schools through black churches, but these, too, met with limited success. An 1805 survey found that the seven schools operating in Philadelphia had enrolled merely 556 students (both children and adults) of the thousands of blacks in the city. By 1813, the number of students had actually decreased to 414.[32]

The upshot is that in the years before the War of 1812 we begin to see the establishment of a distinct color-line for black residents just emerging from slavery who were migrating to Philadelphia from across the state or from the South. In the years following the war, social conditions worsened for blacks as crime and vagrancy became a major concern throughout the city. It brought further recriminations against the black community by white leaders. In 1821 and 1822, the *Philadelphia Gazette* ran a series of articles depicting the city as dangerous and unsafe.[33] A year later, the governor of the state announced in his message to the state that crime among blacks over the previous five years had increased faster than their numbers; in 1821, there were 113 blacks and 197 whites sent to the penitentiary, an astoundingly high figure for a city whose black population was roughly 12 percent.[34]

The rising racial hostility in Philadelphia came amid the emergence of two movements that swept across both North and South on the heels of one another in the period between 1817 and 1838. The first of these was the colonization movement, the second the abolitionist movement. In 1816, a Federalist legislator from Virginia named Charles Fenton Mercer proposed that the federal government colonize all free blacks from the United States on the West Coast of Africa. Mercer believed, like many whites and blacks at the time, that growing white prejudice would prevent free blacks from gaining any type of social or political equality in the United States. In December 1816, with the backing of notable political leaders of the country such as Thomas Jefferson and James Madison, the American Colonization Society was formed. Philadelphia became one of the major focal points of its activities. Initially, the Society held much appeal for black leaders in Pennsylvania such as Richard Allen, Absalom Jones, and James Forten—who all saw the rising racial animosity in Philadelphia and concluded that migration to Africa was the only solution. Moreover, Forten was close friends with black Bostonian Paul Cuffe who had envisioned a similar solution for all black Americans. On January 15, 1817, black religious leaders called a meeting attended by three thousand black Philadelphians at the Bethel church to discuss the colonization efforts. After the meeting adjourned, Forten reported back to Paul Cuffe that "not a soul" of the three thousand assembled expressed support for the Society's activity. Forten asserted that blacks "were very much frightened" that "colonization" amounted to nothing more than "deportation."[35] Moreover, blacks distrusted whites who had proposed and supported colonization, arguing that removing all free blacks from the United States only facilitated the perpetuation of slavery in the South. In the end, Forten and the rest of the black leaders of Philadelphia were shocked to find that the black masses at the meeting that evening unanimously rejected colonization. Black Philadelphians at once resolved to stay and fight for abolition of slavery throughout the United States.

Several attempts were made by white and black leaders across the country to initiate colonization to Africa in the 1820s, all with very little success. In Philadelphia, the American Colonization Society persuaded only a handful of blacks to board ships headed to the West Coast of Africa. In 1824, with conditions deteriorating for blacks throughout the North, the Haitian Emigration Society was formed. This latest attempt at colonization was met with more enthusiasm in black communities in urban centers such as Baltimore, Boston, Philadelphia, and New York. By 1825, some seven thousand emigrants had left for the island of St. Domingue. Yet, within two years, most blacks had returned to their homes in the North, disillusioned by the relatively wretched conditions in Haiti and by their own unrealistic expectations.

Colonization efforts continued well into the 1830s but never amounted to the mass black exodus that its founders had envisioned. Nonetheless, the rise and fall of the American Colonization Society is a curious chapter in United States history. It is the first organized attempt to make the United States a white republic. It did not succeed. But what is perhaps overlooked in the historical record is the role the Society and its progeny played in the emergence of the abolitionist movement. The efforts by the proponents of the American Colonization Society galvanized free blacks all across the North against slavery in the 1820s. Without black abolitionism, we are left wondering how fervent white abolitionism would have been, as James Brewer Stewart made clear in *Holy Warriors: The Abolitionists and American Slavery*:

> When identifying the precipitating causes of the white abolitionist commitment, one must instead emphasize the interaction between the spiritual stirrings of these particular young New Englanders and the unprecedented slavery-related crises which opened [the 1830s]. In the early 1830s, well-organized African Americans suddenly began espousing violence in the cause of emancipation. ... In this respect, black abolitionism was the parent of the white crusade.[36]

As the 1830s opened, Philadelphia found itself at the crossroads of the increasingly shrill debate over slavery. The black community was caught between the emerging abolitionist movement on one side and the rising hostility of poor white immigrants on the other. In effect, every move on the part of the abolitionist movement was met with a backlash directed largely at the black community. Beginning in 1829, a series of race riots ensued that spanned the next decade. In 1833 a demonstration of mainly working-class Irish took place against abolitionism at the very first meeting of the American Anti-Slavery Society. In the summer of 1834, blacks and whites clashed for two nights in a riot that involved upward of five hundred men. Whites stormed through the black districts of the city burning and looting black homes and churches. Well-to-do blacks such as the son of James Forten were especially targeted. One black man was killed and the property damage was tremendous. DuBois points out that the assault on the black community of Philadelphia was well organized: whites who lived in and around the targeted areas placed lights in their windows, signaling to the marauding crowd not to attack that particular dwelling.[37] A year later, in a scene resembling the Boston Tea Party sixty years before, an angry group of whites hurled abolitionist literature into the Delaware River while the mayor of the city stood by and watched. And, in 1838, just before the convention that disenfranchised blacks in Pennsylvania adjourned, thousands of whites gathered at the newly constructed Pennsylvania Hall built by abolitionist supporters and burned it to the ground as prominent abolitionists such as William Lloyd Garrison and the Grimke sisters looked on in horror. Apparently the mob had become overly agitated when blacks and whites walked arm in arm into the hall and sat together without any distinction.[38] The next night, whites moved on to burn down both the Society Friends' Shelter for Colored Orphans and a black church in another part of the city.

It is against this backdrop of social unrest and racial conflict that the debates concerning black suffrage took place in the Constitutional Convention of 1837–1838. A period in Pennsylvania history that had begun, in the words of Gary Nash, in an "optimistic spirit of racial harmony" fifty years before had by that time descended into the vilest form of race prejudice and a never-ending spiral of race wars.[39] Pennsylvania had been at the forefront of the early abolitionist movement and was instrumental in espousing the natural rights philosophy of the Revolutionary era. It was the first state to pass an abolition bill, of which the leaders at the time were fiercely proud. By the 1830s, however, it had become one of the most racially intolerant states in the North. Traveling across the North in 1831, Alexis de Tocqueville wrote:

> Race prejudice seems stronger in those states that have abolished slavery than those where it still exists … the Negro is free, but he cannot share the rights, pleasures, labors, griefs, or even the tomb of him whose equal he has been declared; there is nowhere where he can meet with him, neither in life or in death.[40]

By the late 1830s, the racial intolerance Tocqueville witnessed across the North had become manifested most strongly in Philadelphia.

Partisanship in the Democratic Arch, 1770s–1838

That the changing demographics of Pennsylvania in the opening decades of the nineteenth century precipitated much of the backlash against blacks is clear. In his thorough study of the Negro in Pennsylvania from Colonial times to the Civil War, Edward Turner argues, similarly to DuBois, that the influx of blacks into the state hastened the rising racial hostility in the years between the Revolutionary War and the Civil War. Turner explains that:

In the background there was always that essential, primitive aversion which the race of one color seems to feel for the race of another, and which during the last thirty years before the Civil War was increased by the fury against "abolitionism" and fear of disunion. Yet the two most real and specific causes which any white man living in Pennsylvania between 1800 and 1861 would have advanced to explain his prejudice, were the immigration of negroes, and the increase of negroes' crime.[41]

For the most part, Turner's assessment is accurate: Pennsylvania's geographical position made the issue of slavery palpable to all Pennsylvanians. Blacks were streaming into Philadelphia around the turn of the nineteenth century from all directions. Many were destitute and illiterate fugitive slaves with no ties to the white elite of the city and little possibility of finding work. Some had come from as far away as St. Domingue in the wake of the Haitian slave revolt of the late eighteenth century. With little or no alternative, they turned to theft merely to survive. On the other side, this foreign group of blacks frightened many well-meaning whites who had wholeheartedly supported abolition and the protection of fugitives from slave owners and bounty hunters. Different speech patterns and a more militant attitude toward whites helped to break the bonds of paternalistic duty that had been reinforced under the doctrine of Quakerism.

But, as important as these factors were, I suggest here that there is more to consider in the transformation of Pennsylvania and the concomitant disenfranchisement of blacks than merely their influx into the state or the behaviors they displayed once they arrived. For one, we also need to inquire into the shifts in the white population in Pennsylvania in the same period. More important, however, we want to understand how political actors interpreted these demographic changes, and how they used them for partisan advantage or political gain. In this section I want to inquire into the relationship between the demographic shifts and partisanship in Pennsylvania during this period: how did the shifting social and economic conditions of the state affect party formation, on the one hand, and how did Pennsylvania's political leaders respond and seek to shape political reality in the face of such changes, on the other?

At the same time that blacks were coming to Philadelphia in the 1790s, Irish immigrants were arriving in numbers that offset the black migration by as much as seven to one. Edward Carter estimates that nearly thirty thousand Irish arrived in Philadelphia between 1790 and 1800.[42] Many quickly moved on to other parts of the state and country, but one could nonetheless conclude that Irish migration to Pennsylvania held the black density of the state steady in the opening decades of the nineteenth century (see Table 3.3). Moreover, most of the Irish immediately gravitated to the Republican Party in the 1790s; they remained as one of the most loyal voting blocks of the Jeffersonian Republicans in the first party period and the Jacksonian Democrats in the second. One need not look very far for the reason: Federalists abhorred Irish migration and sought to put an end to it through the infamous Naturalization Act in 1797 and the Alien and Sedition Acts of 1798. On July 1, 1797, Federalist Congressmen Harrison Gray Otis gave his "Wild Irishmen" speech on the floor of the House where he warned against the possibility of these radicals disturbing "our tranquility, after having succeeded in the overthrow of their own government."[43]

As was the case in New York, poor Irish immigrants in Pennsylvania responded to Federalist political leaders by flocking to the ascendant Republican Party. There they found a home; but it is also there that, in the words of Noel Ignatiev, they learned to become "white." According to Ignatiev, Pennsylvania's Irish population took the lead in the rising wave of racial hostilities, playing major roles in the conflicts that began in the first decades of the nineteenth century and lasted through the 1830s.[44] Ignatiev impressively documents the origins of the link between Irish incorporation into the Democratic fold and the latter's white supremacist ideology all across the North in the middle decades of the nineteenth century. He goes on to argue that the creation of Irish "whiteness" played the biggest role in the Democratic Party's continual rejection of nativism from the Jeffersonian Revolution of 1801 through the end of Reconstruction.

But the comparisons between Pennsylvania and New York end there. For, throughout all of the first party period, and part of the second, partisanship in the Keystone state operated in a drastically different fashion than in New York or anywhere else for that matter. In *The Second American Party System*, Richard McCormick explained partisanship in Pennsylvania this way:

> In no state, surely, did political parties present such indistinct outlines as in Pennsylvania. Although politics was conducted on a partisan basis from a very early date, the parties were loosely organized, rarely reflected sectional or ideological cleavages, and lacked effective state-wide leadership. ... Political alignments in state elections were often markedly different from those that prevailed in national elections. ... The manifestations of instability persisted until 1840. Party formation in Pennsylvania, then, cannot be portrayed in terms of sharp and durable alignments, nor can transitions in political patterns be dated with precision.[45]

McCormick is correct with one exception: the only date that can be marked with precision in the early history of party formation in

Pennsylvania is 1799—the year that the Jeffersonian Republicans seized power once and for all from the weakening Federalists. Carter suggests that the Republican victory that year was ignited in large part by the Irish vote.[46] One year later, Pennsylvania politicians gladly took partial credit for the triumph of Jefferson in the presidential election and boasted that the state led the way. For them, Pennsylvania was his "keystone in the democratic arch." From that point until 1840, the party of Jefferson and the party of Jackson held power continuously in the Keystone state. Whereas the Federalist Party remained relatively competitive in other northern states until the War of 1812, Pennsylvania Federalists were in disarray soon after Jefferson ascended to power. As early as 1802, Federalist James Ross, who had lost a bid for governor three years earlier, looked at the partisan arrangement in the state and lamented: "No possible exertion, nor any grade of talents infinitely beyond mine, can stop the wild career which our affairs are destined to run for a long time to come, and there is nothing to soften the melancholy scenes every day exhibited, of the wanton destruction of that fair fabric of social happiness and serenity which had been reared with so much toil and Wisdom."[47]

If Jeffersonian and Jacksonian democracy held sway in Pennsylvania continually from 1800 to 1840, the question of the type of "democracy" it was becomes an issue. That question has been recently analyzed by Andrew Shankman in his excellent book *Crucible of American Democracy: The Struggle to Fuse Egalitarianism and Capitalism in Jeffersonian Pennsylvania.*[48] Shankman contends that, while Jeffersonianism and Jacksonianism dominated Pennsylvania politics for the first four decades of the nineteenth century, that period was nonetheless characterized by deep ideological battles over the fundamental concepts of democracy and "the people." "[Pennsylvania Jeffersonians] understood that democracy could work only if virtually all citizens were free of dependence on resources controlled by their fellow citizens. But they disagreed about how best to ensure that happy condition."[49] Shankman's point is that "Democratic" politics up until the 1830s were at once consensual and factious—consensual in that all political leaders claimed to be heirs of "Jeffersonianism," factious because the same political leaders could not agree on what that meant.

The Democratic Republicans and the Democrats were hard to define in Pennsylvania politics simply because there was not a continuing set of policies to give the party a durable structure. Furthermore, the history of Pennsylvania politics from the Revolutionary War to 1800 reveals similar characteristics. When the first constitution of Pennsylvania was drafted in 1776, it was put forth and supported by the Radical Constitutionalists. They were opposed by the more conservative propertied men, referred to as Republicans. Thus, in 1776 the Constitutional Party consisted of the radical democratic element of the state, while the Republicans were the aristocrats of Pennsylvania society. After nearly a decade of stiff partisanship, the Republicans succeeded in ushering in what Brunhouse calls a conservative "counterrevolution" when they pushed through the constitution of 1790.[50] These same Republicans also supported the federal constitution, hence aligning themselves with the Federalists on the national level. By 1790, there was little in the way of an "Antifederalist" faction to speak of in Pennsylvania.[51] That year, Thomas Mifflin was elected governor unanimously and did not take a party label for his entire nine-year tenure. But when the names "Federalists" and "Republicans" took on national significance in the 1790s, much of the propertied, conservative group merely took over the leadership of the Republican Party in Pennsylvania. The rest retired from politics. This explains to a large extent the weakness of Federalism in the state in the 1790s and thereafter. Thus, when immigrants such as the Irish poured in to the state during that decade, there was nowhere else to go, politically speaking. When the Federalists made issue of the naturalization question on the national level, the choice was made all the easier. According to Klein, "The mass of the people cast their ballots for a mere word which they vaguely associated with their personal welfare but which they never were able to clearly define ... [therefore] the only concrete evidence of the [Democratic Republican] party was the voters themselves who upheld the name regardless of what it meant."[52] In Pennsylvania in the 1790s, the name meant anything but the hated policies of Federalism.

Much as Shankman and Ireland argue that the concept of "democracy" was at the center of partisan politics in the state, Sanford Higginbotham's *The Keystone in the Democratic Arch* argues similarly that the one principle which guided politics in Pennsylvania before, during, and after the advent of Jeffersonianism was the notion of popular rule.[53] Certainly, Pennsylvania boasted one of the most democratic constitutions of the Revolutionary era, as it granted the suffrage to all taxpaying males without regard to property qualifications. Beyond this, however, party politics in the first- and second-party periods were characterized by the incessant creation and dissolution of rival factions under the Democratic Republican banner that were based more on personality and patronage than on principle. In fact, Shankman does a masterful job at documenting the evolution of the Philadelphia Democrats, the Quids, and the Snyderites—though his claim is that there were principles and ideology involved in the factional splits. According to both Higginbotham and Shankman, at times strict adherence to the party principles of Republicanism was abandoned. During the War of 1812, for instance, Pennsylvania Republicans came to advocate the Hamiltonian policies of the protective tariff, internal improvements, and the chartering of the Second Bank of the United States. The first protected the burgeoning industrial base of the state, the second helped to connect the western part of the state to the east and to upstate New York, and the third was housed in Philadelphia. In 1816, the Federalist *Lancaster Weekly Journal* pointed out the contradiction when it bellowed: "These [Democratic Republicans] are now in one breath commending the measures formerly abused, and in the next vilifying the men who taught them those measures. They do not even acknowledge that they have changed their ground!"[54] Democratic Republicans in Pennsylvania were the heirs of Jefferson, but astonishingly they were advocating the policies of Hamilton.

A decade later, Pennsylvania was one of the first states to jump on the Jacksonian bandwagon, having preferred him for president in the 1824 election by a margin of six to one over his nearest opponent, John Quincy Adams. In 1828, the state rallied behind Old Hickory again when it chose his slate of electors by a two-to-one margin.[55] Personally, Jackson remained very popular in his first term as president. But his policies were detrimental to the interests of the state—particularly with respect to those that the Jeffersonians had adopted in the wake of the War of 1812: the tariff, internal improvements, and the Second Bank. The fact is that Jackson opposed all three vehemently, vetoing bills on the first two and draining the funds from the third. As popular as he was, his stance on these issues was not lost on Pennsylvanians. In March 1831, the *Crawford Messenger* bluntly stated: "Pennsylvania stands diametrically opposed to Andrew Jackson."[56] When he stood for reelection in 1832, Jackson won by a margin of only 20,000 votes out of 180,000 cast, mainly on the sheer force of his personality. The Anti-Mason candidate for governor lost that year by only three thousand votes. The Democrats continued to dominate state politics in national elections, but their power was waning on the state level.

Throughout the rise of Jacksonianism, then, Pennsylvania operated under a dual system of politics: in national elections, the state was pro-Jackson, whereas on the state level the Democrats were consistently pressed by the Anti-Masons.[57] After 1832, the divide deepened. And the state Democratic Party strained to express continual support for Andrew Jackson on the one side and play down the effects of his unpopular policies on the other. But in Jackson's second term the state parties of Pennsylvania began to come into rough congruity with the parties on the national level as the Anti-Masons and Whigs entered into an uneasy coalition and exploited the blatant contradictions in the state Democratic Party ideology. How could Democrats retain power on the state level while the national party proposed policies unpopular in the state? In effect, the politics of Pennsylvania were at last becoming nationalized, just as elsewhere in the country in the second party period, and it was placing strains on the once-indestructible pillars of Jacksonian Democracy.

In 1835, the Anti-Mason-Whig coalition won the governorship and the House in the Assembly; it moved closer to taking the Senate as well. The next year, that hated New York politician and Jackson's hand-picked successor Martin Van Buren narrowly squeaked out a victory in the presidential race by just 3,000 votes out of 176,000 cast.[58] But four years later, William Henry Harrison would beat Van Buren in Pennsylvania in a rematch by just four votes out of nearly three hundred thousand cast. After nearly a half-century, party competition had finally been restored to the Keystone state.

Thus, one could argue that the advent of Jacksonian Democracy in Pennsylvania really did two things at once, one reinforcing the other. First, rather than establishing Democratic dominance in the state, Jacksonian Democracy helped to break one-party politics and *reintroduce* party competition in the state after forty years of indistinct and loosely organized partisan arrangements. It did so by forcing the political parties to focus on a set of issues rather than on personalities and patronage. Second, Jacksonian Democracy assisted in doing away with that "dual system" of politics McCormick speaks of that had emerged in the state over the previous two decades by bringing the state parties in line with the national parties on these issues. Once it did, the cleavages between the state Democratic Party and the national Democratic Party were exposed, giving the Anti-Masons and the Whigs the opening they needed in order to ascend.

At this point we need to return to the question at hand to ask once again: what impact did racial conflict in the state have on partisanship, and what impact did partisanship have on racial conflict? Put another way, if the "Democratic" Party had been in power, albeit nominally, since 1799 with the Jeffersonian-Republican victory of that year, and it had gained victory on the wave of immigrant support that tilted the party toward a more ascriptive racial ideology, why were blacks not legally disenfranchised until 1838?

The answer to this question is twofold. First, the Democratic Republicans were not fully committed to the racial ascriptivism in the opening decades of the nineteenth century, just as the party of Jefferson in the state was not wholly committed to a Jeffersonian vision of an agrarian society of yeoman farmers operating with little intrusion by the national government. Although politically dominant in state politics, the Democratic Republicans were not altogether of one mind on the issue of race. Second, and more important, the Democrats finally became the party of the white man's republic only after party competition was reintroduced in the state in the mid-1830s. Race and the question of black suffrage became significant when and only when blacks not only were loyally voting for the Whig Party, and could also actually affect the outcome of elections such as in Bucks County. Party competition not only revealed the cleavage on the issue of race between the parties, it actually forced members of the party to choose on the issue of race. Racial ascriptivism became the discursive tool by which the Democrats blocked black suffrage. The (re)aligning of the parties that had begun in Jackson's first term over issues such as internal improvements, the Second Bank, and the tariff culminated in 1838 when the word "white" was placed in the qualification for the suffrage. In a word, the Democratic Party at that point became the party of white supremacy in Pennsylvania.

Given the dominance and the ethnic makeup of the Democratic Republican Party in the early 1800s, we would be led to assume that racial disenfranchisement would have been one of the first moves the party would make. Furthermore, with no Federalist Party to either contend for black voters or to protect their rights, the situation would have been made that much easier. It should be recalled that, in New York, the old Federalist aristocracy was instrumental in protecting blacks' rights in the opening decades of the nineteenth century against increasing attacks by the Republicans. As I pointed out in Chapter 2, it was the party of the Livingstons, the Jays, the Hamiltons, and the Morrises that kept a paternalistic watch out for blacks and argued that they were by nature "probably" (in the words of Alexander Hamilton) equal in faculties to whites. By contrast, Pennsylvania had no old aristocratic families that inhabited the world of politics to cast their long shadows over the Revolutionary era the way that New York did. The greatest Pennsylvania politician, Benjamin Franklin, lived long enough only to see the constitution of the state revamped in 1790. But what Pennsylvania did have was what might be described as an early form of a single-issue interest group, or a quasi-political party focused solely on this one issue of race. Imbued with the doctrine of Quakerism, the early abolitionists fought valiantly for the rights of blacks throughout the period under consideration here. Thus, the leaders of the early abolitionist movement and their successors cast, in their own way, a long shadow across Pennsylvania politics.

Founded in 1775 and reorganized in 1784, the Pennsylvania Abolition Society's (PAS) complete name was "The Pennsylvania Society for Promoting the Abolition of Slavery, for the Relief of Free Negroes, Unlawfully Held in Bondage, and for the Improvement of the African Race." It did work in each of these areas, but perhaps it was most successful in helping free blacks. The Society assisted blacks in purchasing their freedom, gave them recommendations for employment, provided education, and generally tried to ensure that free blacks were well treated. In 1789, the PAS organized what it called visiting committees to inquire into problems blacks faced. The PAS was not only the first abolition society founded in the United States, it also was called on time and again by abolition societies in other states to assist in their particular fight against slavery. Several southern slaveholders intent on freeing their slaves even sent them to Pennsylvania to receive religious and educational instruction from the organization's leaders. The PAS was more effective on the protection of blacks in many ways than the Federalists had been in other states. Despite the dramatic demographic shifts that the state underwent, they dutifully filled a void left there by the absence of a viable opposition Federalist Party such as in New York.

As racial hostilities surged in the state in the opening decades of the nineteenth century, the PAS sought to block any policy that was detrimental to blacks. It used the tactics of moral suasion and political pressure by petitioning political leaders and increasing public awareness. An example of this is the question of fugitive slaves and kidnapping. The kidnapping of free blacks and fugitive slaves was a concern in Pennsylvania as early as the 1780s and would continue to be an issue well past the 1830s. The first act against kidnapping passed by the Pennsylvania legislature was in 1788, when imprisonment and a fine of 100 pounds were imposed.[59] In 1791, Governor Mifflin publicly chastised two white men indicted for the crime in Washington County. After the Fugitive Slave Act of 1793 was passed, questions were raised as to whether or not the federal government would protect blacks in the state. The PAS soon pressed for legislation guarding against the kidnapping of free blacks. Several kidnapping incidents in the state that had occurred around the turn of the century received much publicity. The legislature considered strengthening the kidnapping laws several times between 1803 and 1807. In 1812, the PAS once again petitioned the legislature for a stronger penalty but concluded four years later at its annual meeting that little had been done to rectify the problem.[60] Despite their pessimism, their efforts met with success. In 1818, a white man from Philadelphia was sentenced to three years in prison and a 300 pound fine for luring three blacks to Delaware who were never seen again. Finally, public sentiment against kidnapping forced stronger action, and in 1820 Governor Findlay pressed the legislature to pass a tough anti-kidnapping bill. Entitled "An Act to Prevent Kidnapping," it provided for a penalty of not less than $500 or more than $2000, one half of which was to go to the prosecutor. It forbade justices of the peace or aldermen to involve themselves in any fugitive slave case, bringing the law into conflict with the provisions of the Fugitive Slave Act of 1793. A kidnapper could be imprisoned anywhere from seven to twenty-one years. If a fugitive slave was remanded to the South under the Fugitive Slave Act, the judge was required to file a description and report with the clerk of the Quarter Sessions.[61]

As a result of increasing pressure from southern states and over the objections of the PAS, Pennsylvania was forced to comply with the national laws. In 1826, after a Maryland delegation had traveled to Harrisburg to meet with Pennsylvania legislators, the state passed a law allowing a claimant to imprison an alleged fugitive slave pending a trial. However, the law strengthened the penalties against kidnapping.[62] It was this piece of legislation that placed the issue of slavery before the Supreme Court for the first time. In *Prigg v. Pennsylvania,* decided in 1842, the Court held that Pennsylvania had no say whatsoever in the issue of fugitive slaves—in other words, the return of slaves was a federal question that did not concern the states.[63] In 1847, the legislature redoubled its efforts against the kidnapping of fugitive slaves when it passed a law forbidding any state official to issue a warrant for the return of a fugitive slave.

The constant presence of a strong abolitionist movement in Pennsylvania thus restricted the effects of racial animosity that had been on the rise since the beginning of the nineteenth century. Contempt was heaped on blacks during this period; in response, the PAS preached an ethic of moral uplift and compassion. On many occasions political leaders responded positively, with the backing of public opinion. This in part explains why Pennsylvania appears as a bundle of contradictions during this period. To return once again to the astute observations of Edward Turner:

> In the treatment of the Pennsylvania Negro after 1800 there is seemingly a strange contradiction, for he was the victim of violent prejudice and at the same time received the liveliest sympathy and aid. During the whole period, while funds were being raised to ship Negroes to Africa, while the Legislature was overwhelmed with petitions for their exclusion, while one race riot followed another, and while everything was done to convince the world that Pennsylvania desired no negroes, or at least no more of them, there was witnessed the curious spectacle of action on the part of the state, which betrayed an apparent desire to have them after all. From 1830 to 1860, almost never was assistance refused to a fugitive slave from the South, even when he was known to be such; and during this time with what was the greatest difficulty a master could recover his property. In the course of this conduct men and women of Pennsylvania went any length of risk and self-sacrifice to assist runaways. Toward the end of the period the state was brought to the threshold of nullification. All this was for the most part the outcome of the abolitionist and antislavery movements, which at last overran the state.[64]

In short, Pennsylvania was caught between the racial ideology of paternalism, propounded mainly by the members of the PAS on one side, and the racial ideology of ascriptivism, put forth by proponents of the white man's republic, on the other. Ironically, although the Democrats held complete power in the state, this battle was fought to a political standstill. It is no coincidence that the issue of black suffrage came to the fore at the very moment party competition resurfaced in Pennsylvania—simply because now blacks posed a real threat to the proponents of the white republic in the Democratic Party. With the racial cleavages between the parties visible, each side would have to make their appeals for and against the suffrage based upon these competing racial ideologies. It is to these competing racial ideologies that I now return in order to investigate the role they played in the development of state politics. I do this with an eye turned toward the outcomes of the Constitutional Convention of 1837–1838, which shall follow.

Race and Racial Discourse in Pennsylvania from Colonial Times to 1837

As I intimated at the outset, the competing racial ideologies are as old as the Pennsylvania colony itself.

In 1686, a ship carrying Quakers from the Palatine region in Germany sailed into the port on the Delaware River at Philadelphia. It had been pursued over the high seas by another vessel filled with Turkish pirates, intent on capturing the Quakers and selling them into slavery. The German and Dutch Quakers had been invited to Pennsylvania by William Penn personally on his missionary journeys to Germany and through his reports of Pennsylvania that were translated into German and circulated widely. They had arrived in the colony and the New World safe and sound. But what they found there shocked them.

The leader of the new settlers was Francis Daniel Pastorius. What Pastorius and his followers found was slavery—moreover, slavery that was being perpetuated by their Quaker brethren. After settling in what became known as "Germantown" just outside of Philadelphia, Pastorius finally spoke out on the practice of slavery. On April 18, 1688, he scribbled down a letter denouncing slavery and presented it at the meeting of the entire community that evening. In it, Pastorius asserted that slavery violated the fundamental laws of Christianity, as the difficult but nonetheless unyielding creed of "do unto others as ye would that they should do unto you" was utterly disregarded by anyone engaged in the practice. Such conduct may have been expected by the Turkish barbarians who chased them across the Atlantic—but to see Christians steal and traffic human bodies across the Atlantic was unacceptable. Moreover, Pastorius chastised his fellow Quakers for violating the Seventh Commandment by breaking up black families and bringing together those already married in new combinations. Finally, he said that slavery violated the natural laws of humanity that Penn's colony was created to uphold:

> There is a liberty of conscience here which is right and reasonable, and there ought to be likewise a liberty of the body, except for evil doers, which is another cause. But to bring men hither, or to rob and sell them against their will, we stand against.[65]

Pastorius's admonition was the first call to end slavery in the New World and began a long debate among Quakers that would not be resolved for nearly a century. When the letter was forwarded to the Annual Meeting of the Friends that same year, the Quaker leadership was slow to respond; Quakers were in fact profiting from the slave trade and would continue to do so. By the opening decades of the eighteenth century, most of the slave holders in the colony were in fact Quakers.

The letter also reveals at an early stage the onset of racial paternalism in Pennsylvania. Rooted in the Quaker views of Christianity and humanity, it would evolve over the course of the next century as Quaker leaders such as John Woolman, Ralph Sandiford, Benjamin Lay, and Anthony Benezet modified it by adding particular aspects of the natural rights philosophy of eighteenth-century Enlightenment thought. Benezet was one of the first to argue consistently that the degraded condition of blacks was a result of the evils of slavery and not of the color of their skin or mental capabilities. He also was one of the first to advocate for the educational instruction of blacks to prepare them for society after slavery. On the eve of the Revolution, Benezet expressed his racial paternalism most clearly when he wrote concerning slavery:

> I can truly and with sincerity declare that I have found among the negroes as great variety of talents as among the like number of whites; and I am bold to assert that the notion, entertained by some, that blacks are inferior in their capabilities, is a vulgar prejudice, founded on the pride or ignorance of their lordly masters, who have kept their slaves at such a distance as to be unable to form a right judgment of them.[66]

Benezet played a large role in combating notions of black inferiority of the middle decades of eighteenth century in Pennsylvania. He greatly influenced the leaders of the Revolutionary generation in their thinking about slavery with his educational work. On the eve of the Revolutionary War, Dr. Benjamin Rush published a pamphlet entitled *An Address to the Inhabitants of the British Settlements on the Slavery of Negroes in America* at Benezet's urging. There Rush argued:

I need hardly say any thing in favour of the Intellects of the Negro, or their capacities for virtue and happiness, although these have been supposed, by some, to be inferior to those of the inhabitants of Europe. The accounts which travelers give us of their ingenuity, humanity, and strong attachment to their parents, relations, friends and country, show us that they are equal to the Europeans. … Slavery is so foreign to the human mind, that the moral faculties, as well as those of the understanding are debased, and rendered torpid by it. *All the vices which are charged upon the Negroes in the southern colonies and the West-Indies, such as Idleness, Treachery, Theft, and the like, are the genuine offspring of slavery, and serve as an argument to prove that they were not intended for it.*[67]

Even toward the end of his life, a no less complex figure than Benjamin Franklin came to embrace racial paternalism. As Nash and Soderlund point out in their *Freedom by Degrees: Emancipation in Pennsylvania and its Aftermath,* Franklin's views on slavery throughout the eighteenth century served as a microcosm of the history of the slavery in and around Philadelphia.[68] For most of his life, he was a buyer and seller of slaves. From his earliest writings in the 1720s and 1730s, Franklin believed those with African ancestry to be inferior to Europeans. By the 1740s, the Anglican evangelical minister George Whitefield was visiting Pennsylvania and promoting educational instruction for black children—an act that was met with considerable ridicule among most whites (even Quakers) in the colony who believed that slaves were savages and did not have the moral capacity that whites possessed. Through the 1740s and 1750s, Franklin resisted the growing calls for abolition among the Society of Friends' faithful. But, in 1758, Franklin enrolled one of his own slaves, Othello, in a school run by a group affiliated with the Anglican Church called the Bray Associates. After visiting the Bray Associates School in 1762, Franklin wrote to his friend John Waring:

I was on the whole much pleas'd, and from what I then saw, have conceiv'd a higher Opinion of natural Capacities of the black Race, than I had ever before entertained. Their Apprehension seems as quick, their Memory as strong, and their Docility in every Respect equal that of white Children.[69]

During the Revolutionary War years and amid increasing calls for abolition across the newly formed states, Franklin refused to free his slaves. Slowly, however, his views on the capabilities of blacks were evolving. By 1787, Franklin had become an abolitionist. The last public office he held was the presidency of the Pennsylvania Abolition Society. A year before his death in 1790, Franklin issued a public statement on slavery on behalf of the PAS. In it, he stated:

> Slavery is such an atrocious debasement of human nature, that its very extirpation, if not performed with solicitous care, may open a source of serious evils. The unhappy man who has long been treated as a brute animal, too frequently sinks beneath the common standard of the human species. The galling chains, that bind his body, do also fetter his intellectual faculties, and impair the social affections of his heart. ... To instruct, to advise, to qualify those, who have been restored to freedom, for the exercise and enjoyment of civil liberty, to promote in them habits of industry, to furnish them with employments suited to their age, sex, talents, and other circumstances, and to procure their children an education calculated for their future situation in life; these are the great outlines of the annexed plan, which we have adopted, and which we conceive will essentially promote the public good, and the happiness of these our hitherto too much neglected fellow-creatures.[70]

The views expressed by these political and religious leaders in Pennsylvania, by the 1770s, had begun to dominate the thinking on race throughout the Pennsylvania colony. At the same time, a democratic impulse had swept over the colony amid revolutionary fervor. In 1776, Pennsylvania drafted a constitution on the heels of the publication of Jefferson's Declaration of Independence. It provided for the most liberal suffrage clause of any of the new state constitutions, stating that "every freeman of the full age of twenty one years, having resided in this state for the space of one whole year next before the day of election for representatives, and paid taxes during that time, shall enjoy the right of an elector." Any male could vote as long as he met the residence and tax-paying requirement. The constitution also made no mention of race, a point that both opponents and proponents of black suffrage argued in the Constitutional Convention of 1837–1838 reinforced their views on the subject.

Four years later, Pennsylvania became the first state to enact a gradual abolition law. The influence of the natural rights philosophy of the Revolutionary era was made evident in the preamble to the Abolition Act of 1780. In Section II, it stated that:

> And whereas the condition of those persons, who have heretofore been denominated negro and mulatto slaves, has been attended with circumstances, which not only deprived them of the common blessings that they were by nature entitled to, but has cast them into the deepest afflictions, by an unnatural separation and sale of husband

and wife, from each other and from their children, an injury, the greatness of which can only be conceived by supposing that we were in the same unhappy cause.

Furthermore, the Abolition Act of 1780 went on to declare that free blacks were in all respects to be treated as free men and free women.[71] Even as partisan conflict heated up between the Constitutionalists and the Republicans during the latter years of the Confederation, the political leadership of Pennsylvania nonetheless remained dedicated to the abolitionist cause and its underlying beliefs in racial paternalism. Republicans were successful in ushering in the "counterrevolution" in 1790 by drafting a new constitution that modified some of the democratic impulses institutionalized in the previous document. Yet, the suffrage qualification remained the same; what is more, it did not explicitly exclude blacks from voting. Albert Gallatin, who later would become the staunch Republican ally of Thomas Jefferson, was successful in the constitutional convention held in 1789 in getting the word "white" stricken from the suffrage clause. Even as he became an avid defender of Republicanism, Gallatin remained sympathetic to the plight of blacks. Several years after the ratification of the Pennsylvania constitution, Gallatin reflected on the recent slave revolt in Haiti in a letter to his friend. There he wrote:

> Who has been right or wrong in the lamentable scene of Hispaniola nobody can tell; but to view the subject independently of the motives and conduct of the Agents who may have brought on the present crisis, I see nothing but the natural consequences of slavery. For the whites to expect mercy either from mulattoes or negroes is absurd and whilst we may pity the misfortunes of the present generation of the whites of that island, in which, undoubtedly, many innocent victims have been involved, can we help acknowledging that calamity to be the just punishment of the crimes of so many generations of slave traders ...[72]

What is made plain by the discursive record of the pre- and post-Revolutionary years is that racial paternalism had in fact become the dominant racial paradigm of the political leaders of Pennsylvania. It formed the normative arguments underlying the calls for abolition and went so far as to provide equal citizenship for blacks. Yet, racial ascriptivism would soon emerge—or, rather, reemerge—as the nineteenth century commenced.

Racial ascriptivism also had its origins in the early colonial period in Pennsylvania. As mentioned at the outset, slavery was opposed in the early eighteenth century on both moral and economic grounds. Whereas German Quakers provided the initial impetus for the moral objections to slavery, it was the poor white laborers of the state who provided the impetus for the economic objection.[73] In the opening decades of the eighteenth century, the provincial assembly began passing laws differentiating between slaves and servants. The assembly also passed legislation restricting the interaction between whites and blacks. In 1712, whites began petitioning the assembly to restrict the importation of slavery because slave labor was beginning to severely limit the economic prospects of poor free whites. The assembly responded by increasing the duty imposed on each slave, but the British crown soon repealed the law and reinstated a significantly smaller duty. In 1725–1726, an important colonial law was passed that forbade the mixture of the two races. No black was to be joined in marriage with any white. Furthermore, the law sought to regulate the movement, actions, and behaviors of both slaves and free blacks. No black slave was to go farther than ten miles from home without written leave from his master; nor could he be caught from his master's house after nine o'clock p.m. without permission. Whites were severely restricted in employing free blacks, and free blacks were not allowed to meet in company of more than four together. The preamble to the law provided the justification for the racially restrictive elements to the law when it began: "free negroes are an idle, slothful people, and often burdensome to the neighborhood and afford ill examples to other negroes …"[74]

Thus, racial ascriptivism had its origins in a conflict that from the beginning had both economic and racial dimensions. Blacks—both slave and free—posed a threat to the economic well-being of lower-strata whites from the earliest days of the colony's existence, and attempts were made on the part of colonial leaders to respond to the pressure by limiting the number of slaves brought in to the colony. In other words, we see traces of the white republic ideology from the opening of the eighteenth century in Pennsylvania. As Nash asserts, this thinking formed the "majority" opinion on race for most of the middle decades of the century: blacks were seen as slothful, idle, vagrant, and inherently inferior.[75] Consequently, they were unwelcome. No amount of religious or educational instruction could change these ascriptive characteristics. Pushed to the background during the Revolutionary era, racial ascriptivism resurfaced in the opening decade of the nineteenth century in Pennsylvania as the free black population increased substantially in Philadelphia.

The first individuals to draw on these ascriptive views on race in the early 1800s were Pennsylvanians of Irish descent. One such figure was Thomas Branagan. Both Noel Ignatiev and Gary Nash point to the extraordinary writings of Branagan and the influence they had on the perceptions of political leaders and the white masses in the state.[76] Branagan was born in Dublin in 1774. In 1790, he sailed to Africa from Liverpool on a slave ship, where he remained for several months among the African natives. From there, he traveled to the West Indies and stayed in Antigua for four years. Watching the slave trade firsthand for over five years, Branagan began having serious moral doubts about slavery. He returned to Dublin within a year to settle his father's estate, but then like so many of his countrymen, he set sail for Philadelphia, arriving there in 1799.

In 1804, Branagan published a blistering attack on slavery entitled *Preliminary Essay on the Oppression of the Exiled Sons of Africa.* In keeping with the natural rights rhetoric of the Revolutionary era, he based his attack on the natural equality of all human beings, asking whether or not blacks:

> Possess the same specific nature, the same faculties and powers, corporal and mental, the same attachments and aversions, sensations, and feelings with the inhabitants of Asia, Europe, and America? Is it not a prevailing sentiment among all the nations of mankind, that all men, as they come into the world, are equal. ... Are not the innumerable millions of mankind, members of one family and children of one father?[77]

However, the very next year, Branagan published another work on race that moved in an entirely different direction. Entitled *Serious Remonstrances Addressed to the Citizens of Northern States, and Their Representatives,* the work expressed alarm at what Branagan saw in the North as gradual abolition was taking hold and fugitives were migrating from the South. *Serious Remonstrances* began by denouncing slavery because it "destroys moral rectitude and natural justice."[78] He thereby renewed his calls for moral instruction of blacks by whites. But about halfway through the one-hundred-plus page pamphlet, the argument shifted from a denouncement of slavery to the impact the black population was having on the North. Everywhere Branagan looked, he saw an amalgamation of the races wreaking havoc upon the morals and economic possibilities of whites—particularly the Irish and the Germans. He argued that America was "appropriated by the Lord of the Universe to be an Asylum for the Oppressed, Injured Sons of Europe."[79] Furthermore, the recent slave uprising in Hispaniola should give white northerners pause not only in their treatment of blacks but also the extent to which they should want to continue to accept them in northern cities. At the current pace of migration, Branagan contended, there may be as many as fifty thousand blacks in the city of Brotherly Love by the year 1865.[80] This would have had disastrous consequences for the North:

> On they come with all the accumulated depravity which they have been long accustomed to; such as lying, pilfering, stealing, swearing,

deceit; and a thousand meaner vices, the fruits of slavery. When they arrive, they almost generally abandon themselves to all manner of debauchery and dissipation, to the great annoyance of many of our citizens. Indeed, the depredations many of them commit on society, is too tragical to mention ...[81]

For Branagan, Blacks posed both a threat to both the economic well-being and the "purity" of the white republic. He continued:

I would again ask such: would thee be very contented for to have a negro for thy daughter's husband, a negress for thy son's wife, and in short have them assimilated into the family as well as the general and state governments, and methinks I hear a negative answer to this question. ... I solemnly declare I have seen more white women married to, and deluded through the art of seduction by negroes in one year in Philadelphia, than for 8 years I was visiting [Africa and the West Indies] ...[82]

Branagan concluded his rant by arguing that the "co-mingling" of servants in the well-to-do homes of whites had further caused the low morale of poorer whites.

Branagan's solution to having lascivious and ignorant blacks overrun America was to colonize them in the recently purchased territories of Louisiana, paralleling Jefferson's "civilization" program to use the Louisiana territory for Native Americans. "If slaves were sent to that fertile country of Louisiana, the climate of which is particularly congenial to their natures, I am confident not only thousands in the South, but numbers of Africans in these states would rejoice if my plan was adopted by congress, or one similar to it instituted."[83] Hence, a dozen years before the American Colonization Society was founded in 1817, Thomas Branagan proposed his own version of the white republic ideology.

Branagan had fully shifted his attention to the dangers of black citizenship in the United States. There was no call here for continued religious and educational instruction that would provide blacks with a hand up and out of slavery and into the ranks of the citizenry. On the contrary, the emphasis was on the debauchery and idleness of blacks. And while Branagan did indeed assert that these behavioral characteristics are a result of the pathologies of slavery, it was not a far jump from this assertion to the conclusion that *blackness* as such was equated with idleness and debauchery. The transformation from racial paternalism to racial ascriptivism in Pennsylvania was underway. As we shall see, it became full-blown in the debates surrounding black voting rights in the Constitutional Convention of 1837–1838. In Branagan's view, citizenship for blacks in the United States was simply out of the question. Such an attempt would have led to an amalgamation of the races. And here we come to the central idea that underwrites Branagan's ascriptive views: the United States in general, and Pennsylvania in particular, was intended to be an "Asylum for the Oppressed, Injured Sons of Europe"—or, in other words, a white man's republic.

Branagan's *Serious Remonstrances* marks the reemergence of racial ascriptivism in the discursive development of Pennsylvania. All Branagan did was take a look around Philadelphia and bear witness to the changes it had undergone: if current trends held up his vision of a white republic would be swept away in the tide of black bodies streaming into the city. He thus made an appeal to ascriptivism to make his case. Other Irish Philadelphians with influence over public opinion also would come to make similar ascriptive arguments. The Irish publisher of the newspaper *Democratic Press* John Binns is another case in point. An early and fervent supporter of Jeffersonianism, Binns was a fierce defender of the ideology of the white republic. In articles in his paper, he consistently argued against the rights of citizenship for blacks. During the War of 1812, he called the free black people of Philadelphia "a very numerous and useless class" which "could be better spared [for the war] than any other."[84] For Binns, not even military service provided blacks with the rights of citizenship. In the wake of the Missouri crisis, he was one of the first to argue that Congress did not have the right to regulate slavery in the territories. As he ascended the Republican ladder and became one of the main power brokers in state politics, Binns remained a fervent supporter of the white republic ideology.

Political leaders were faced with the fundamental question of black citizenship as gradual abolition took effect and migration continued. In 1807, the first motion was made in the state legislature to exclude blacks from the electorate. It was denied. In 1826, Governor Shulze asked the legislature if the definition of "freeman" should include "persons of colour." Calls to disenfranchise blacks were consistently spurned by leaders who argued against racial disenfranchisement, mostly at the behest of the Pennsylvania Abolition Society. But amid the race riots of the 1830s, the right to vote for blacks came under heavy attack. Evidence suggests that blacks had been voting in the state since the Revolutionary years in at least seven counties in the state.[85] But blacks were increasingly intimidated from the polls in other regions. In 1837, an English traveler in Pennsylvania inquired of a white citizen about black suffrage. "Just let them try [to vote]!" was the response he received.[86]

In 1835, a black man by the name of William Fogg was denied the right to vote in Luzerne County on account of his race. He sued Hiram Hobbs, the election inspector in Greenfield who had turned him away from the polls, on the grounds that his vote was "fraudulently and maliciously refused."[87] Judge Scott of the county court was asked to decide whether or not the Pennsylvania constitutions of either 1776 or 1790 or any state laws passed had explicitly or implicitly granted blacks the right to vote. Fogg argued that the constitution granted him such a right, while Hobbs countered that "a free negro or mulatto is not a citizen, within the meaning of the law of the constitution and the laws of the United States and the state of Pennsylvania, and therefore is not entitled to the right of suffrage."[88] In his opinion, Judge Scott concluded that blacks did in fact have the right to vote under Pennsylvania law. He wrote:

> We know of no such expression in the constitution or laws of the United States, nor in the constitution or laws of the state of Pennsylvania, which can legally be construed to prohibit free negroes and mulattoes, who are otherwise qualified, from exercising the rights of an elector. The preamble to the act for the gradual abolition of slavery, passed on the 1st of March 1780, breathes a spirit of piety and patriotism, and fully indicates an intention in the legislature to make the man of color a *freeman*.[89]

Hobbs immediately appealed the case to the Supreme Court of Pennsylvania. But although Scott's decision was the first shot fired in the debate that would grow in intensity for the next three years, the case itself received relatively little attention. As the spring of 1837 and the Convention neared, the *Fogg* case awaited a hearing from the state Supreme Court. But the Supreme Court made the cautious choice of not ruling on the case until the Constitutional Convention revised the suffrage article.

The Constitutional Convention of 1837–1838

Racial disenfranchisement was the outcome of the Constitutional Convention of 1837–1838, as other studies have shown. But curiously none of these studies have actually analyzed the words of the delegates themselves—neither for what they say about the racial beliefs of the delegates, nor for what they indicate about the delegates' partisanship. This section looks at these debates carefully with the intention of showing, first, how racial ascriptivism had become the dominant view on race matters within the convention, and, second, how partisanship coupled with these ascriptivist views played the key role in the vote to disenfranchise blacks.

One hundred thirty-three delegates convened at Harrisburg on May 2, 1837. On May 17, the committee on the suffrage article presented its report to the whole delegation. It contained no mention of the question of suffrage for blacks. Furthermore, the "minority" report of the committee also ignored the question. The entire convention considered the suffrage article as it was presented out of committee on June 19. Democratic delegate John Sterigere rose and moved to add a racial restriction in the suffrage article. He argued that most other states in the union had adopted such a provision, most recently Tennessee and North Carolina. Phineas Jenks of Bucks County opposed Sterigere's motion, countering that no one in Bucks County opposed the right of blacks to vote. Furthermore, he contended that there were many blacks in Bucks County who had large property holdings and thus a vested interest in government. Consequently, they should retain the right. Benjamin Martin of Philadelphia County then took the floor to passionately defend Sterigere's position. Martin argued that blacks were not capable of voting responsibly; furthermore, granting blacks the right to vote would essentially grant the black man the same prestige as the white man in what was intended to be a white republic. Drawing on the ideas first spelled out by Branagan some thirty years before, he asserted that:

> It is in vain to tell me, that these individuals are on the same scale in society, and gifted with the same intelligence, as ourselves ... when I look at them, and then at myself, and what the world is composed of, I cannot but see a vast difference. ... We are the descendents of Europe ... we have been in advance, and have given a tone to civilization throughout the world, and why are we now to think of retrograding and going down?[90]

After Martin yielded, several other delegates rose to voice their objections to the motion put forth by Sterigere. At this very early point in the debate, it was not clear that the antiblack suffrage delegates had enough votes to pass the racial restriction. Consequently, at the behest of his political allies, Sterigere withdrew his motion from the floor.

On Friday, June 23, Benjamin Martin once again took up the case of the racial restriction. He appealed to ascriptive notions of race and made the case that black suffrage was a violation of the laws of nature. Other delegates countered that adding the word "white" was too vague and requested that Martin yield until a later date while the convention attended to other business. This time Martin called for a vote, and in an extraordinary move the motion was defeated by a vote of 61–49.[91] A majority of the Coalition was joined by twelve Democrats in opposing the motion. The suffrage article was consequently dropped and the convention moved on to other matters until it reconvened on July 14. Black suffrage would not be raised until the convention reconvened on October 17 later that year.

When the convention adjourned in the summer of 1837, few Pennsylvanians were deeply concerned over the issue of black suffrage. Yet all of this was to change within a few months. The local elections held on the eve of the convention's reconvening caused an uproar around the question of black suffrage. That October, two Democratic officials in Bucks County filed suit in county court arguing that they had lost election because dozens of blacks had voted illegally, thus throwing the election to their Whig counterparts. Democrat Jacob Kachline lost the election for commissioner by twenty-five votes, whereas Democrat F. L. Boder lost the election of auditor by a mere two votes. Newspapers across the state picked up on the story and fanned the flames of racial hostility. The *Bedford Gazette* claimed that blacks had come to the polls with guns and forced their way to the ballot box, threatening to shoot anyone who stopped them.[92] It also accused abolitionist Thaddeus Stevens of inciting blacks to violence in their attempts to vote. The *Pennsylvanian* made much of the fact that blacks had changed the outcome of elections elsewhere because they were allowed to vote in many localities all over the state—though it proudly pointed out that blacks were not allowed to vote in Philadelphia because they were not assessed taxes.[93] By the time that the delegates reconvened, the question of black suffrage had become the major constitutional issue with which they were confronted.

Delegates cautioned against deciding the issue until Judge John Fox in Bucks County and the Supreme Court had handed down their respective decisions in the two cases involving black voting rights. The Supreme Court sat on its hands and awaited the outcome of the convention; however, in December 1837, Fox assertively took the issue head on and handed down a decision.

The central question that Judge John Fox contended with was, once again, whether or not blacks were considered "citizens" or "freemen" under the meaning of the previous Pennsylvania constitutions or state laws. Displaying his impressive knowledge of the history of Pennsylvania, Fox went all the way back to the original charter granted to William Penn to discern whether at any point blacks were meant to be considered "freemen" like their white counterparts. Fox concluded that at no point did the previous political leaders of Pennsylvania ever intend to include blacks in the status of "freemen" or "citizen" as the terms were defined—not the constitution of 1776, not the gradual abolition law of 1780, and not the constitution of 1790. Predating Justice Taney's argument by twenty years, Fox argued that "the negro race was then, and still is, a degraded caste, and inferior in rank to the white."[94] He continued by inquiring:

What white man would not feel himself insulted by a serious imputation that he was a negro, and who, having believed himself to be of the white race, if he should be found so strongly tainted with black blood, would not feel and experience, that he had fallen greatly in social scale? What white parent, if he had any affection for them, could contemplate without deep grief and mortification the probable social condition of his mulatto children. … Is it possible that an inferior and degraded race were called in to take part in these high function [of voting]?[95]

Fox went further to argue that the U.S. Constitution also did not bestow citizenship on blacks. His legal reasoning predated that of Justice Taney's by asserting that the word "people" in the preamble of the Constitution is equated with "citizen;" furthermore, "citizen" under the original meaning of the Constitution was equated with "white." Fox concluded by saying that:

The people of Pennsylvania, who framed the present constitution were a political community of white men exclusively, and that colored persons of African blood, were not contemplated by that constitution. That the latter have not, and never had, any *chartered* or constitutional rights, but have always been, and still are, subject to such laws as the sovereign power may make for their government.[96]

Essentially, Judge John Fox reaffirmed the ascriptive views underpinning the white republic. His opinion was published immediately and distributed to every member of the delegation, as well as all through the state. Now armed with Fox's decision and the support of the public that had been whipped up into a frenzy over the issue, Democratic delegates in the convention moved immediately to place a racial voting restriction in the suffrage clause.

On January 17, 1838, the convention turned its attention back to the suffrage article. Benjamin Martin rose to make a motion adding the word "white" in the article. This time, he pressed his case harder on ascriptive grounds:

I would preserve [blacks] and theirs, by the laws, and by the constitution; but to hold out to them social rights, or to incorporate them with ourselves in the exercise of the right of franchise, is a violation of the law of nature, and would lead to an amalgamation in the exercise thereof, that must bring down upon them, the resentment of the white population. Sir, the divisionary line between the races, is so strongly marked by the Creator, that it is unwise and cruelly unjust, in any way, to amalgamate them, for it must be apparent to every well judging person, that the elevation of the black, is the degradation of the white man.[97]

The debate on the suffrage article quickly became heated as delegate after delegate expressed interest in the "excitement" over the issue and rose to either defend the motion or argue against it. Whig delegate William

Maclay of Mifflin County rose to counter Martin's argument. Maclay reminded the delegation of the paternalistic views that had predominated during the Revolutionary Era and countered that disenfranchisement would stigmatize blacks rather than secure prestige for whites:

> I feel altogether averse to the proposition now before us. ... No such proposition, as the one now made, could have passed in any law of Pennsylvania in the time of the revolution, or during the time that the men of the revolution held the government of the commonwealth in their hands. ... I do not, however, oppose the present motion so much on the ground that it could not have been passed in former times in Pennsylvania, as on the ground that it is unjust at any time ... [disenfranchisement] is calculated to fix a stigma upon the people on whom it is intended to operate. It is throwing an obstacle in the way of their improvement. It is, in fact, adding another item to the long catalogue of wrongs which these people have endured. It should be recollected that the coloured people among us are a poor and helpless race; they are entirely in our power; we may pass such laws as we please respecting them; and if we do them an injustice they have no redress.[98]

Thomas Earle of Philadelphia County reverted back to the Golden Rule in Christianity and then picked up on Maclay's point by sarcastically mocking the other side in their "wisdom" about the founders: "What did the Declaration of Independence of the United States say? Did it mean what it said? Did the gentleman from Luzerne [George Woodward] mean to assert, that Jefferson, Madison, Franklin, Patrick Henry, Hancock, Judge Marshall, and in short, all the patriots and wise men of the former and present age, did not mean what they have said?"[99] Soon thereafter, the convention was adjourned, but debate resumed the very next morning in the same spirited manner.

John Sterigere of Montgomery County rose on the morning of the 18th and contended that the great majority of the public was against black enfranchisement. He then argued on partisan grounds by contending that the masses of black voters would be swept up into one of the political parties by a demagogue or "abolitionist" and fundamentally alter the balance of power in the state between the competing parties. The notion of a black electoral constituency was wholly unacceptable:

> It is an insult to the white man to propose this association, and ask him to go to the polls, and exercise the right of a freeman with negroes. ... This number would produce 10,000 voters. These will, in the mass, join one of the greatest political parties, or be controlled by

some political demagogue, or modern abolitionist, and must become the umpire between the two great political parties in the state ... reject this amendment, and we shall have tens and hundreds of thousands of this base and degraded caste, vomited upon us.[100]

Supporters of black suffrage could only counter the vitriol of Sterigere and his antiblack enfranchisement colleagues by arguing from a paternalistic perspective and pointing out that blacks had worked their way up to respectability despite all the obstacles thrown in front of them. Walter Forward of Allegheny County rose to make the case for black suffrage: "I find that they are regarded as morally responsible beings," he began, "and that we never excuse them for any offence they may have committed against the laws of the land, on the ground that they are an inferior race of beings." He continued:

> I find this to be the case, and I infer from this, that the rights of the coloured man are as precious as my own, and that the government under which he lives may influence his happiness as much as it may influence my own; and that therefore if he has equal intelligence, virtue, patriotism, he has the same right to vote as I myself possess. I set up no claim to superiority in the eye of Him who created both, and I dare not place my vote on that ground.[101]

Each delegate who now rose to speak was met with an uproar by the other delegates. At several points in the convention record, the reporter explains that the noise in the hall was too loud to record accurately everything each speaker was saying. Each side dug in and made their points by mocking the other side's position. William Darlington from Chester County rose to speak out on behalf of black suffrage and forcefully chastised opponents who argued that the framers of the constitution of 1790 did not intend to include blacks in the political community. He took out a letter written to him on December 21, 1837, by seventy-seven-year-old Albert Gallatin. In it, Gallatin recollects that the word "white" was struck from constitution in 1790 at his urging. "It was no part of their plan to exclude coloured persons from the right of suffrage, and hence it is, that they so framed the provision as to suffer 'every freeman' to vote in the choice of those who should represent him."[102] Darlington then mocked Sterigere and his fellow Democratic delegates by reading a proclamation issued by their leader Andrew Jackson addressed to free blacks in Louisiana during the War of 1812. In it, Jackson urged blacks to defend New Orleans:

"I expected much from you; for I was not ignorant that you possessed qualities most formidable to an invading enemy," the letter stated. Darlington then concluded passionately:

I ask in the name of God and of our common country, is this the age—is this the time—is this the day in which we, the people of Pennsylvania, having gone so far in the glorious march of civilization, improvement, and *christianity*—is this the time in which we will take away from any portion of our fellow citizens, the rights which they have enjoyed for a period of fifty years?[103]

Soon the tone reached a breaking point. The animosity between the sides was so intense that at one point the convention doorkeeper, Thomas Jefferson Becket, became overzealous and ejected three prominent blacks from the spectators' gallery. Amid the growing rancor most speakers appealed to the same principles in varying ways: opponents of black suffrage argued that blacks were inferior, that they were never intended to be part of the political community, and that to grant them the vote would not only debase the white man but also would lead to a flood of blacks into the state. Supporters of black suffrage countered that blacks had made substantial moral and economic progress since the abolition of slavery, that the Golden Rule forbade treating blacks differently, and that the men of the Revolutionary Era had intended to include blacks under the term "citizen" or "freemen."

When a vote was finally called on the suffrage question on January 20, 1838, the motion to insert the word "white" in to the new constitution was approved by a 77–45 margin.[104] The vote was not completely decided along party lines: only three Democrats voted against the suffrage restriction, but nineteen members of the Whig-Anti-Mason coalition defected to vote with the Democrats. In his unpublished doctoral dissertation, Edward Price argued that the absence of the staunch abolitionist Thaddeus Stevens proved to be a serious blow to the cohesiveness of the coalition. Stevens left earlier that month to return to the legislature in Harrisburg to fight for the Gettysburg Railroad and bank reform. He had been instrumental in securing the right to have blacks read their petitions before the delegates at the convention; he also worked hard behind the scenes to block the first attempt to disenfranchise blacks before the convention adjourned for the summer.[105] Without his leadership on the suffrage question, rank-and-file members of the Whig-Anti-Mason coalition voted to amend the suffrage article.

After the Pennsylvania State constitutional convention adjourned in the late winter of 1838, the Pennsylvania Supreme Court finally moved to settle the *Hobbs v. Fogg* case that had been pending for nearly three years. The court reversed the ruling from the Luzerne County court and held that William Fogg's rights were not violated when election commissioner Hiram Hobbs turned him away from the polls. Judge Gibson delivered the decision for the court. In his opinion, Gibson asserted once and for all that Pennsylvania indeed had been a white republic since its creation. He referred to "antecedent legislation" that furnished "other proofs that no colored race was party to our social compact." Gibson continued:

> As was justly remarked by [Judge John] Fox, in the matter of the late contested election, our ancestors settled the province as a community of white men, and the blacks were introduced into it as a race of slaves; when an unconquerable prejudice of caste, which has come down to our day, insomuch that a suspicion of taint still has the unjust effect of sinking the subject of it below the common level. Consistently with this prejudice, is it to be credited that parity of rank would be allowed to such a race?[106]

Gibson concluded by pronouncing "that men of color are destitute of title of the elective franchise." In fact, the issue had already been settled by the delegation at the constitutional convention: Gibson's opinion only served to make the creation of the white republic of Pennsylvania more complete by stamping the seal of the Pennsylvania Supreme Court on it.

Like Judge John Fox before him and Chief Justice Roger Taney after him, Gibson claimed only to base his ruling on the original intent of the founders of the commonwealth of Pennsylvania. And, like his fellow jurists, Gibson had to engage in an act of historical erasure in order to make his ascriptive ideology plausible. By 1838, Pennsylvania had become what Judge Gibson, Judge John Fox, Thomas Branagan, John Binns, and the members of the Democratic Party that pushed for black disenfranchisement in the constitutional convention had always thought it *ought* to be: a white republic.

Conclusion

The transformation in the racial politics of Pennsylvania from the latter decades of the eighteenth century to the mid-nineteenth century was indeed quite extraordinary. It was not lost on W. E. B. DuBois, who wrote in *The Philadelphia Negro*:

> A curious comment on human nature is this change in public opinion [in Pennsylvania] between 1790 and 1837. No one thing explains it—it arose from a combination of circumstances. If, as in 1790, the new freedmen had been given peace and quiet and abundant work to develop sensible and aspiring leaders, the end would have been different; but a mass of poverty-stricken, ignorant fugitives and ill-trained freedmen had rushed to [Philadelphia], swarmed in the vile slums which the rapidly growing city furnished, and met in social

and economic competition equally ignorant but more vigorous foreigners. These foreigners outbid them at work, beat them on the streets, and were enabled to do this by the prejudice which Negro crime and the anti-slavery sentiment had aroused in the city.[107]

The transformation of Pennsylvania during this period from a state of racial leniency to the "white republic" was largely a result of the changing dynamics of race formation: a fundamental change in the social and economic conditions in the state, the rise of partisanship in the state that brought the state parties into alignment with the national parties on the major issues of the day, and the shift in the racial belief system of Pennsylvania political leaders during this period from paternalism to ascriptvism. The white republic of Pennsylvania emerged at that point—and it could only emerge when these three factors came together by the time the convention of 1838 conducted its business.

The leaders of Revolutionary Pennsylvania were racial paternalists at heart. They argued that blacks could be lifted from their degraded condition and taught the virtues of citizenship. By contrast, the leaders of the Keystone State in the 1830s believed no amount of moral and mental uplift could remove blacks from their state of worthlessness. They were racial ascriptivists—and they were successful in integrating their white republic ideology into the fundamental laws of the state. Blacks in Pennsylvania sought mightily to keep the suffrage question alive for the remainder of the antebellum period, sending petition after petition to the state assembly in those years. When the state house failed to act, blacks sought the assistance of the federal government. In 1855, a petition entitled *Memorial of Thirty Thousand Disenfranchised Citizens of Philadelphia to the Honorable Senate and House of Representatives* was sent to Washington. In it, black Philadelphians asked Congress to get involved on their behalf in the struggle for the franchise. The public conscience of Pennsylvania was against them, and they therefore turned to the national government for help. But the federal government was incapable of handling the race issue decisively at that time: the Kansas-Nebraska Act had been passed the year before, superseding the Missouri Compromise and allowing for "popular sovereignty" in those states carved out of the territories. Also, the previous year, oral arguments in the *Dred Scott* case were heard. One year later, in 1856, the Republican Party ran its first candidate for President as the Whigs disintegrated over the slavery issue. And, as the country slid toward Civil War, black Pennsylvanians remained second-class citizens in the white republic of Pennsylvania.

CHAPTER 4

"Servility Is not Confined to Color"

The Disenfranchisement and Reenfranchisement
of Blacks in Rhode Island

Race, Class, and Black Reenfranchisement Amid the Dorr War

Late on the evening of May 6, 1844, Thomas Wilson Dorr delivered his closing argument before a jury that would ultimately find him guilty of treason against the state of Rhode Island. For the duration of the two-week trial, Dorr acted as his own counsel because his principal attorney, Samuel Atwell, had taken ill. The trial had not gone well; at every turn, Chief Justice Job Durfee disallowed Dorr's principal line of defense, which, simply put, was that treason against an individual state in the Union was altogether impossible. Unbowed and unapologetic, Dorr launched into a three-hour monologue outlining why he believed the armed insurrection he led in the spring and summer of 1842 to capture the state government was justified. "What I did I had a right to do," Dorr stated emphatically. He declared that he had "been duly elected governor of this state under a rightfully adopted and valid republican state constitution, which I took an oath to support to the best of the means placed within my power." Dorr then compared his own plight to the persecution experienced by Galileo over two centuries earlier and an ocean away, implying that his accusers were no different from a band of Inquisitors:

> Some ages ago, a natural philosopher was accused and silenced before the inquisition for teaching that the earth turned on its axis.

As he retired, after his forced confession to the contrary, from the presence of the officers of the justice that day, he exclaimed, "Still it turns!" and in spite of all the opposition of false philosophy, it has turned ever since.[1]

Returning to the American context, Dorr concluded by cloaking himself in the natural rights rhetoric of the Revolutionary era, which formed the philosophical basis of his suffrage movement.

There are other immutable doctrines, and other honest convictions, which cannot be forced out of a man by any human process. The sun will not rise upon any recantation by me of the truths of '76, or of any one of the sound principles of American freedom. The servants of a righteous cause may fail or fall in the defence [sic] of it. It may go down; but all the truth that it contains is indestructible, and will be treasured up by the great mass of our countrymen. If I have erred in this Rhode Island question, I have the satisfaction of having erred with the greatest statesmen and the highest authorities, and with the great majority of the people of the United States.[2]

By 11 p.m. on that evening, Dorr had fallen silent and the jury had been given final instructions from Justice Durfee. In the early morning hours of May 7, it returned with a guilty verdict. Thomas Dorr was sentenced to life in prison for the act of treason against the state of Rhode Island.

To be sure, not all who witnessed what is commonly known as the Dorr War thought Dorr's actions as noble as Dorr himself imagined. In fact, many considered him merely to be the leader of a lawless, propertyless band of rogues hell bent on seizing the government. Dr. Francis Wayland, president of Brown University at the time, compared Dorr to the Roman tyrant Tiberius Gracchus. Congregationalist minister Mark Tucker called him talented and mad, and likened him instead to that troublemaking abolitionist "William Lloyd Garrison ... propagating errors of the worst character, assailing all government, the Holy Sabbath, and the Christian Ministry."[3] Dorr's name continued to be linked to roguery and anarchy long after he entered prison on June 27, 1844, and was unconditionally released just a year later. In 1848, the Supreme Court heard oral arguments in *Luther v. Borden,* in which the home of one of Dorr's lieutenants Martin Luther was entered and searched under the draconian "Alergine Law" passed by the landholding General Assembly during the crisis. Whig Senator Daniel Webster was called on to defend both Borden and the actions taken by the "legal" government of Rhode Island at the time. Webster seemed to be responding directly to Dorr himself when he summed up before the Court:

The long seeing sagacity of our fathers enables us to know, equally well, where we are, when we hear the voices of tumultuary assemblies, and see the turbulence created by numbers, meeting and acting without the restraints of law; and has most wisely provided constitutional means of escape and security. When established authority of government is openly contemned [sic]; when due deference is not paid to the regular and authentic declarations of the public will; when assembled masses put themselves above the law, and calling themselves the people, attempt by force to seize on the Government; when social and political order of the State is thus threatened with overthrow, and the spray of the waves of violent popular commotion lashes the stars, our political pilots may well cry out; "nimirum haec illa Charybdis!"[4]

On the face of it, *Luther v. Borden* was merely a case about an illegal trespass. In actuality, it became a second indictment of the Dorr insurgency. With Chief Justice Roger Taney presiding, the Supreme Court accepted Webster's argument and held that the Court had no jurisdiction to rule on the legitimacy of the "People's Constitution" drafted by Dorr's followers and approved by a larger portion of the Rhode Island electorate than had ever participated in previous elections. In the Court's view, that was a political question to be decided by the "political" branches of government. But given that the legal government of Rhode Island at the time possessed legitimate sovereignty, it had every right not only to search Martin Luther's home, but also to smash all aspects of Dorr's extralegal maneuvers.

Such were the conflicting views of the legacy of Thomas Dorr, most of which remain to this day. To some, he is a radical democrat who fought vigorously for the cause of expanded suffrage, and hence for human freedom; yet to others, his is a liberty, in the words of Webster, "supported by arms to-day, crushed by arms tomorrow"—a liberty "without power except in spasms." Although Dorr's legacy continues to be the subject of spirited debate, the causes of the Dorr War are rather straightforward and clear. So, too, are the outcomes: regardless of one's views of Dorr's actions, it is hard to escape the conclusion that the extension of the suffrage that resulted from the conflict was wrung from a reluctant legislature that acted in response to the agitation Dorr had instigated. Less clear, however, is why—in the middle of all the turmoil—black Rhode Islanders were granted the right to vote. That question demands an explanation, which is the subject of this chapter.

To be sure, volumes have been dedicated to a study of the Dorr War and its aftermath. Yet comparatively little has centered directly on the struggle of blacks for reenfranchisement that came to play a significant role in the outcomes.[5] Black Rhode Islanders were first disenfranchised by state stat-ute in 1822 and then reenfranchised in wake of the Dorr War in 1843. It was the only state in antebellum America that blacks won back the right to vote after losing it. From the late eighteenth century to that victorious point for black Rhode Islanders, the state underwent its own peculiar dynamic of race formation, as I will show in this chapter. Using the framework laid out here, my aim is to explain how and why blacks were able to regain the right to vote. At first glance, one could easily make the case that the franchise was a fortunate by-product of the chaotic and contingent set of events that comprised the Dorr conflict—that black Rhode Islanders were simply "in the right place at the right time." I will not argue against that point: to an extent blacks in Rhode Island did find themselves in a fortuitous situa-tion aligned with the Law and Order Party against the Dorrites. Yet, to let the issue rest there would be missing the social, economic, and political undercurrents that brought blacks to the very opportunity that the Dorr War presented to them.

As with the other states at which I have looked, I assume that black disenfranchisement would have occurred in Rhode Island if three condi-tions had been met: (1) if racial conflict took place as an outgrowth of rapid economic and demographic change; (2) if political actors seeking electoral advantage were in a position to successfully prey on this racial conflict by arousing poor white immigrants; and (3) if an ascriptive racial belief system became the dominant racial paradigm for understanding citizen-ship rights for blacks. These conditions were met by the 1820s when blacks were disenfranchised. But by the 1840s and the onset of the Dorr War, all three conditions were no longer satisfied in Rhode Island. We will see that blacks were forced out of the coalition with Dorr's suffrage followers largely because of conditions 1 and 2. Blacks then aligned themselves with the Law and Order (or Whig) Party during the Dorr War; in the eyes of Law and Order party leaders foreign-born whites were to be feared more than Rhode Island's blacks. They were racial paternalists who were willing to bring blacks into their coalition during the strife. When the new con-stitution was drafted, blacks were repaid for their loyalty with the elective franchise. Hence, condition 3 was not met in Rhode Island, which is why I argue that blacks regained the franchise.

I will begin by briefly tracing the socioeconomic and demographic changes in the state from the Revolutionary War to the Dorr War. Simi-lar to other northern states, Rhode Island underwent a rapid economic transformation in the opening decades of the nineteenth century. The state economy expanded from simply a maritime/agrarian one to include manufacturing during this period. The shifting economic base was accom-panied by a demographic shift: as the nineteenth century unfolded, the industrialized northern part of the small state began to dominate the agrarian southern and western sections. The change brought property-less migrant and immigrant workers to the counties in and around Providence. At the same time, blacks in the state were emerging from slavery and migrating toward Providence where they would carve out a meager existence. Not surprisingly, ethnic and racial conflict ensued as poor whites and blacks competed for the same economic opportunities.

Political change did not keep pace with the new environment wrought by the socioeconomic changes that had developed by the 1830s. The failure on the part of political actors to enact constitutional reform becomes crucial in the runup to the Dorr conflict. As we shall see, partisans on all sides consistently refused to enact constitutional reform that would greatly expand the suffrage. From 1800 to 1840, agitation for constitutional reform intermittently flared up and never completely died out. During the election of 1840, when nearly four-fifths of the eligible electorate across the country cast their votes, Rhode Island sent only about a third of all males over the age of twenty-one to the polls.[6] As Conley points out, the stage was set for a "showdown between the immoveable object and the irresistible force."[7] On one side of the conflict, the landholding Anglo elite; on the other, a cadre of reformers leading the propertyless, mostly white ethnic masses. Interestingly enough, this economic conflict did not materialize into a partisan conflict until the election of 1840.

Up to that point, race played a relatively minor role in the overall dynamic of state politics. Once up from slavery, blacks were disenfranchised and subsequently retreated to the protection of their own communities as they constantly faced physical intimidation and assault. By the early 1830s, as the black community—mostly centered in a section of Providence—showed economic and social progress, black leaders began agitating on their own behalf for political rights. They would continue to do so for the next decade, but with no success.

All of this would change amid the Dorr conflict. By 1840, which is where I train the brunt of my narrative, a well-organized black community saw its political opportunity in the fluid situation. In late 1840 and early 1841, blacks joined—and were invited to join—with the "suffragists," that is, Dorr's movement, which consisted of propertyless, white ethnic laborers. But two developments would later split this biracial coalition: first, the growing presence of the abolitionist movement in the state of Rhode Island, which was despised by white ethnics that comprised the mass of the suffrage movement (particularly the Irish), and the successful nativist appeals by the landholder's party that served to instill fear in citizens that the state was being overrun, not by blacks, but by white Catholic immigrants.

In order to pursue their objective of the elective franchise—an objective that by the late 1830s had caught the attention of national abolitionist leaders such as Frederick Douglass and William Lloyd Garrison—black Rhode Islanders were forced to side with the Law and Order Party. The switch in allegiances occurred in 1842 after the Suffrage Party broke with Thomas Dorr's promise of racial inclusion and placed a racial voting restriction in the People's Constitution drafted in late 1841. To be sure, Whig politicians accepted black support only reluctantly, but did so after blacks displayed their loyalty by raising a military regiment and patrolling the streets of Providence amid the Dorr War in the summer of 1842. Rhode Island blacks would remain in alliance with the Whigs during the remainder of the second-party era and, despite dissatisfaction with the Whigs, voted consistently for the Whig ticket.

Partisanship was both a precursor to, and a result of, the Dorr conflict; it was rooted in socioeconomic developments, specifically the impact of industrialization and immigration in creating a propertyless working class. By the early 1840s, this partisanship had structured racial political opportunity. At the same time, racial tensions shaped partisan coalition formation. In Rhode Island as elsewhere, the racial tensions on display during the Dorr War were articulated through a competing set of racial discourses that had been in existence since the Revolutionary period but came to the foreground as fundamental questions of citizenship were raised. Not surprisingly, the rank and file of the suffrage movement employed ascriptive rhetoric in arguing against the enfranchisement of blacks. Dorr himself resisted ascriptivism, but to no avail. In response, Whigs countered that blacks had earned the rights of citizenship during the Dorr conflict by displaying their patriotism and loyalty. The paternalism on the part of the Whigs was apparent, as we will see. Here I will just offer the words of Dorr sympathizer William Goodell, who wrote concerning the role of blacks in the conflict that:

> The admission of the dependent colored people to vote, as well as to fight, and to *boast of their support,* answers their selfish purposes, and is impudently trumpeted to their praise. That such facts should occur, only proves what everybody should have known before, *viz.*: that servility is not confined to color, and that aristocracy under heaven will as soon wield the power of the colored people to suppress the liberty of the whites, as the power of the whites to hold the colored people in bondage, whenever it suits their convenience.[8]

For Goodell and the rest of the rank-and-file suffragists, blacks were used as a tool by the aristocratic landholders to suppress the rights of the white masses. No doubt, this alliance was made out of "convenience"—but the alliance was only formed after the suffrage association had succumbed to racial ascriptivism. If blacks came to play a significant role in the successful bid on the part of the landholders to suppress the Dorr insurgency, the suffragists really had no one to blame but themselves.

Up from Slavery: Blacks in Rhode Island and Socioeconomic Change, 1770s–1840

A black population existed in the tiny Providence Plantation colony from its origins in 1647. Although slavery was never legally institutionalized in Rhode Island, it nonetheless proliferated until it was abolished in the wake of the Revolutionary War.[9] By the early years of the eighteenth century, Newport, located along the southern coast, had become a major slave-trading center of New England—second in importance only to Boston. In 1708, the colony imposed a 3 pound tax on each slave imported, partially out of the financial benefits to be gained and partially out of the fear of having the colony overrun by blacks. But in 1732, the British Crown objected on grounds that the tax was harming the slave trade. It subsequently repealed the import duty. Tax or no tax, the number of slaves in Rhode Island increased over the first half of the eighteenth century, and the growth rate in the black population outpaced that of the white population. In the years leading up to the Revolution, however, the black population declined considerably while the white population continued to increase, as Table 4.1 indicates.

As in most of the rest of New England, slavery in Rhode Island took on a dual character. On the one hand, slaves toiled in the fields of the coastal Narragansett plantations surrounding Newport alongside indentured whites and Narragansett Indians to produce wool, dairy, products, corn, and tobacco. On the other hand, slaves were found in the households of commercial Newport and in the small urban shops of shoemakers, blacksmiths, carpenters, and fisherman in Providence.[10] And as in much of New England, slavery, although integral to the economy of Rhode

TABLE 4.1 White and Black Population Growth in Rhode Island, 1708–1774[11]

Year	White	Black	Percent Black
1708	7,181	425	5.6
1730	17,935	1,648	8.4
1749	32, 773	3,077	8.6
1756	35,939	4,697	11.6
1774	59,707	3,668	5.8

TABLE 4.2 White and Black Population Growth in Rhode Island, 1790–1820[12]

Year	White	Black	Percent Black
1790	64,470	4,335	6.7
1800	65,438	3,684	5.6
1810	73,214	3,717	5.0
1820	79,457	3,602	4.5

Island in many ways,[13] never took hold to the extent that large populations of slaves were imported to work the plantation fields that dotted the coastline. In the waning days of slavery, both the black population and the density of blacks in the overall population declined. It continued to decline as the eighteenth century drew to a close and the nineteenth century opened (see Table 4.2).

As in other colonies during the pre-Revolutionary era, attacks on slavery in Rhode Island were promulgated by a Quaker community that had been awakened to its cruel realities. As early as 1760, Quaker elder John Woolman visited the colony and acknowledged that the number of slaves on the coastal plantations "made deep impressions on me."[14] By 1770, Quaker preacher Samuel Hopkins of Newport had become a leading critic of the slave trade and lost no opportunity to denounce the practice in his sermons. But Newport, which was the commercial and political center of the colony at the time, was unlike other northern cities in the pre-Revolutionary era in one important respect: it was dominated by both slave traders and Quaker merchants, the latter of whom had struggled for years to balance their moral obligations with their economic interests. In response to the clash between morality and economy, the colonial legislature passed a weak bill in 1774 that prohibited the importation of slaves into the colony. The preamble drew on the natural rights rhetoric of the times and stated that "those who are desirous of enjoying all the Advantages of Liberty themselves, should be willing to extend personal liberty to others." However, the bill subsequently included many exemptions to the ban on the importation of slaves, thus gutting it considerably.[15] In effect, the attempt at banning the slave trade in Rhode Island was half-hearted.

With the onset of the Revolutionary War, emancipation in Rhode Island took hold as many blacks were first freed and then conscripted into the Rhode Island militia. By most accounts, the black soldiers of Rhode Island performed valiantly during the war. John Eustis of Massachusetts, who argued passionately for the rights of blacks on the floor of Congress during the Missouri Compromise debate, singled out black Rhode Islanders as a prime example of black citizenship and patriotism during the Revolution when he contended that "they discharged their duty with zeal and fidelity. The gallant defence [*sic*] of Red Bank, in which the black regiment bore a part, is among the proofs of their valor."[16] In the wake of the Revolution, white Rhode Islanders repaid the debt owed to blacks by passing a gradual abolition law in March 1784.[17]

For the next several decades, the free black population increased substantially in the state. Under the gradual abolition law, any black child born to a slave after March 4, 1784, was freed on reaching the age of majority—eighteen for females, twenty-one for males. Such children were bound to their masters until that time, and the slave owner was responsible for the child's "education" until the age of majority was reached. By 1820, the slave population in Rhode Island had dwindled down to a mere several dozen; in Newport, the foothold of plantation slavery in the state, the number of slaves had declined to seventeen, and the census of the same year recorded only four slaves in Providence.[18] In 1774, there had been a total of 1,246 blacks in Newport and only 303 living in Providence. By 1825, the free black population in Providence had increased to 1,414—over four times the amount of blacks in the city fifty years before. As Rhode Island entered an era of industrial expansion between 1800 and 1830, manumitted blacks were moving from south to north, converging mainly on Providence where a burgeoning if small black community began to thrive. Furthermore, the newly freed class eventually possessed and maintained some modicum of economic independence from the white majority.

By the second decade of the nineteenth century, nearly two-thirds of all blacks lived in black-headed households. Most of those living outside black households were children who remained in white households as apprenticed house servants placed there by their black parents; in return for their services, black children received educational instruction from whites.[19] The patron-client relationship between upper-class whites of Rhode Island society and blacks that had been formed first in slavery and then subsequently in the Revolutionary era remained residually well into the 1820s. The white elite of Rhode Island society promoted an uplift ideology whereby blacks were to be acculturated to a white society largely through educational instruction and religious teaching. These ties were formed in the days of slavery and took the shape, specifically in Rhode Island, of whites allowing blacks into their churches and, to a lesser extent, their schools. However, the removal of blacks from white households coincided with an attempt at racial separation through the creation of wholly black institutions. Although black groups such as the Free African Union Society and the African Benevolent Society had been in existence in Newport since the 1790s, by 1820 there was a concerted effort on the part of both paternalistic whites and black leaders to establish separate schools and churches for blacks.

By 1822, blacks had begun to live lives separated from their former slaveholders and abolitionist patrons. Many had migrated to the northwest part of Providence and had begun to thrive under dire conditions in a ramshackle part of town populated by the more rowdy elements of the city—including criminals, fugitives, wayward sailors, and prostitutes.[20] Removed from white households, blacks experienced the earliest versions of *de facto* housing segregation that characterized life for Northern blacks for much of the twentieth century. The degraded conditions of this part of town appalled many whites, but, unlike Quaker leaders, whites began to rethink the causes of those conditions. Increasingly, the black community became a target of attack for white citizens of Providence. During this period, two race riots ensued in the black sections of town.

The first one, known as the Hard Scrabble Riot, began on October 18, 1824, when a white mob formed in North Providence after blacks in the area refused to get off the sidewalk when approached by a group of whites. Forty members of the white mob converged on the house of one of the more respectable black men in the community, Henry T. Wheeler. Wheeler ran a dance hall downstairs, and immediately the mob began destroying his property as nearly one thousand spectators looked on. Throughout the night, the mob destroyed some twenty more houses of black residents. After they had leveled the dwellings, rioters then went to the household goods that remained and carted them off to Pawtucket just down the road from the predominantly black neighborhood and sold them at auction.[21] Amid the riot, a white Providence man, Oliver Cummins, was grazed in the mouth with a bullet from the gun of a black resident of Hard Scrabble. He was guarding the mob against attack. Cummins and three other whites were brought to trial for their part in the riot—although none were jailed. A privately published report called the *Hard Scrabble Calendar* commented on the riot and intimated that the actions of the white mob were justified given the depravity of conditions among Providence's black population. It said:

> Here were held the revels and midnight orgies of the worst part of this class of the population of Providence. Owing to the differences in the severity of our Police and that of the neighboring cities in relation to the blacks, the number had increased in this town, as ascertained by a recent enumeration, to upwards of 1200 persons ... the mass, as it might be inferred, can hardly be considered a valuable acquisition to any community, and their return to the respective places from whence they came, probably would not be considered a public calamity.[22]

At the trial of the four white men, the defense attorney made it clear that the black population of Providence was unwelcome in the fair city of Providence. In arguments reminiscent of the vigilante justice of mob lynchings in the opening decades of the twentieth-century South, the defense attorney Joseph L. Tillinghast stated that, "it was the resort of the most corrupt of the black population, who supported their debaucheries and riots by carrying thither the plunder of their masters and pawning it for a participation in these disgusting scenes ..." Because the town leaders refused to clean up—and clean out—Hard Scrabble, "the populace at length took it into their hands and destroyed this sink of vice: and there was not a sober citizen in the town who could regret it."[23] Tillinghast closed his arguments by mocking the Hard Scrabble section of town and its black residents:

> Gentleman of the jury—the renowned city of Hard Scrabble lies buried in its magnificent ruins! Like the ancient Babylon it has fallen with all its graven images, its tables of impure oblation, its idolatrous rights and sacrifices, and my client stands here charged with having invaded this classic ground and torn down its altars and its beautiful temples. ... It is much to be regretted that among the thirty or forty witnesses the Attorney General has examined, some of them have not explained the etymology of this name. Perhaps after all it is only meant as the descriptive of the *shuffling* which is practiced there in the graceful evolutions of the dance, or the zig-zag movements of Pomp and Phyllis, when engaged in treading the *minuet de la couer.* But be that as it may, we must all agree that the destruction of this place is a benefit to the morals of the community.[24]

In the wake of the Hard Scrabble riot, the black residents of Providence were faced with an increasingly hostile living environment. They were under attack politically, physically, and verbally. Broadsides began to appear that predated the minstrel show ventriloquism elsewhere in the 1830s and 1840s. This one, for instance, insinuated that the good behavior of blacks in Providence could win over a suspicious white population and thereby help to keep other blacks from migrating to the city:

> I guess it best now for us brack folk be easy,
> And no longer lives immoral and lazy,
> But gain honest living by sweat ob our brow;
> Depend on't de white folk won't den trouble or 'tack us,
> But de good people of Providence will always respec us,
> As they are won't to respec all good people now ...
> So Miss Boston keep home your lazy black rabble.
> Nor compel them seek shelter again at Hard Scrabble,

For every maggot should stick to he core;
For should they visit us gain they may find it foul whether
We've plenty of Tar and de ground cover'd wid Fether
And we've Pitch to pitch you all out door.[25]

By the mid-1820s, Providence became the focal point of racial conflict, as it was there that over half of the entire black population in the state resided. Blacks in the city endured another race riot, in 1831, begun when a group of black seamen brawled with a group of white seamen in the seedy section of town known as Snow Town. After an initial night of rioting on September 21 in which the black seamen chased the white seamen from Olney Street, a white mob assembled the next night to avenge the previous evening's episode. A small militia and the governor of the state met them there; neither was able to quell the mob. The conflict continued for roughly two more days, until finally two militia companies were called out to restore peace. In the ensuing conflict, four members of the mob were killed. But once again, the prevailing view of the time was that the destruction of black property was warranted given the degraded conditions of the neighborhood. Editorials appeared that placed blame, not on the white mob, but on the actions and behaviors of blacks. No mention was made that blacks were not allowed to live anywhere else but in the seediest sections of town. As one facetiously said, "The mob made but little noise and were expeditious and scientific in the performance of their arduous duties. Not one reputable dwelling was attacked."[26]

Against these rising hostilities, the black community of Rhode Island nonetheless persevered and continued to practice a form of self-help. Educational instruction and religious teaching were the forms it took. Few blacks attended the churches of whites before 1820. When the African Union Meeting House was established that year, one in twelve blacks were estimated to be churchgoers. Over the next two decades, several other black churches cropped up, and by 1840 one in six blacks were going to church regularly.[27] Blacks also continued to petition city leaders for educational assistance throughout this period. In 1838, the city of Providence funded the construction of a public school solely for black children. Whereas illiteracy had been nearly universal in 1822, Bartlett estimates that by 1840 about half of all Providence blacks could read.[28]

Despite discrimination in employment, the economic fortunes of the black community also improved throughout the period of racial disenfranchisement. Rammelkamp points out that by 1830 the net wealth of the black community nearly doubled over the previous ten years to $18,000. On the eve of the Dorr War, the estimates range from $35,000 to $50,000.[29] Thus, in two decades, the wealth of the black community increased anywhere from four to five times. Some in the black community owned as much as $4,000 in real estate. Blacks had become owners of groceries, shoe repair shops, clothing stores, and candy stores.

The economic and social advances were accompanied by an increase in the sphere of political activism. Black leaders such as the young preachers Alexander Crummell and Jeremiah Asher, the clothier James Hazard, and the teacher Ransom Parker advanced their arguments before the white population. White political leaders took notice of black economic advances and pressed for the taxation of the black community. Beginning 1829, the Providence black community petitioned the state's General Assembly each year for the elective franchise, arguing along the same rhetorical lines of the Revolutionary period that "taxation without representation" was akin to slavery. In 1841, this plea was partially if not rather oddly addressed. After community leader Alfred Niger presented a remonstrance that argued for the right to the suffrage, the General Assembly responded by passing a law that retained the color qualification for voting but exempted men of color from taxes on real and personal property. It retained the taxation on all whites—even those unable to vote. This was seen as a rather bizarre move by the Assembly and helped to fuel the growing racial conflict between poor disenfranchised whites and blacks. But members of the General Assembly were not willing to consider the alternative of allowing blacks to vote. As one member put it, "Shall a Nigger be allowed to go to the polls and tie my vote? No, Mr. Speaker, it can't be."[30]

At the same time as blacks were moving up from slavery, Rhode Island was in the midst of wrenching economic change. In *The Transformation of Rhode Island, 1790–1860,* Peter Coleman traces that economic transformation. He contends that Rhode Island moved through three economic phases of development: (1) an economy based on maritime activity (pre–Revolutionary War to 1800); (2) an era of industrialized experimentation (1800 to 1830); and (3) an era of industrialized expansion (1830 to 1860).[31] By 1790, when a state convention debated the ratification of the U.S. Constitution, Rhode Island's mercantilist economy was entirely dependent upon activity in and around the mouth of Narragansett Bay. "Even in the most remote hamlets of the western hill country, the affairs of farmers, mechanics, craftsmen, and storekeepers were touched by the ocean."[32] Trade with Europe and other parts of the world fueled Rhode Island's economy, as Newport and the surrounding bay towns thrived on maritime-based but largely agricultural economic activity. From Northern Europe came naval stores such as tarrow, iron, steel, and glass; from England and France came wines, liquors, and cheeses; from the Mediterranean came spices, cork, currants, and merino sheep. In return, Rhode Island merchants exported staves, tobacco, sugar, rum, and coffee—all crops grown in the southern and western fields of the state.[33] European trade peaked in the opening decade of the nineteenth century, as collected duties went from $39,000 in 1800 to $108,000 in 1806. Even after the normalization of trade with Europe in the wake of the Jeffersonian Embargo of 1808 and the War of 1812, Rhode Island's maritime activity never reached the same lucrative levels.[34]

By the turn of the nineteenth century, Rhode Island's economy was ripe for industrial transformation, particularly in cotton manufacture. In 1789, the Quaker merchant Moses Brown and his assistant Samuel Slater converted a Pawtucket Mill in North Providence into a cotton mill and, for the first time in America, spun cotton by waterpower. Within the next two decades, and particularly during the War of 1812 amid economic embargoes, Rhode Island's cotton industry expanded greatly. By 1815, three-fifths of southern New England's cotton factories were in Rhode Island.[35] Furthermore, most of these factories were located in what Coleman describes as "expanding towns" in the state—Cranston, Johnston, Providence, and North Providence, to name a few, all in the northern portion of the state.[36] By contrast, the once-thriving agricultural and maritime towns in the south and west of the state began to lag behind in industrial development. Coleman classifies these as either "static" or "declining." By 1832, the cotton industry had become the dominant economic engine of the state. And two-thirds of all the capital, employees, and cotton spindles were concentrated in these northern expanding towns.[37]

The economic changes wrought by the growing industrialization of the state in the opening decades of the nineteenth century are significant because of the political pressures and racial and ethnic tensions to which they eventually gave rise. As the major engine of the state economy moved to the industrialized north of Rhode Island, so, too, did workers seeking employment in the cotton mills. Many of these workers were Irish immigrants. As Gilkeson points out, the Irish began to arrive in and around Newport in the mid-1820s to help build the Blackstone Canal, which linked Providence to Worcester, Massachusetts.[38] Their numbers in 1828 were a scant two hundred. But by 1855, ten thousand Irish resided in Providence, comprising almost a quarter of the population of the city. The stark increase in the number of Irish immigrants served to fuel nativist sentiments that lay at the foundation of the class, racial, and ethnic tensions that sparked the Dorr War. As these immigrants arrived in the industrialized towns of Warwick, Providence, Smithfield, Cranston, and the like, workers were immediately disqualified from the franchise because of the $134 freehold qualification enacted just before the turn of the century. In addition, the original apportionment scheme under the Charter gave more representation to the southern towns around Newport, as from its earliest days the latter had been the most populous region of the state.[39] Thus, economic and demographic shifts were catalysts for the agitation around the franchise and the system of representation that ensued. As we shall see, the simmering conflict over constitutional reform was fueled mainly by a growing propertyless working class, on the one hand, and a resistant, landholding elite, on the other.

Constitutional Development and Partisan Conflict, from Colonial Times to 1840

The Charter of Rhode Island was drafted in 1663 at the time of the colony's founding under Charles II of England. The document was one of the more remarkable charters formed during the colonial period in that it allowed Rhode Island to retain an extraordinary amount of autonomy from the British crown while providing protection from the other larger colonies. It granted Rhode Island's legislature the authority to make or repeal any laws, as long as those laws were not repugnant to the laws of England. It also mandated annual elections for all at large officers of the colony, and stated that the inhabitants of the colony "shall have and enjoy all liberties and immunities of free and natural subjects" as if they were born in the realm of England. Finally, it provided for "Full liberty in religious concernments." Rhode Island's charter was so progressive for the times that citizens were unwilling to scrap it once they declared independence in mid 1776. The charter was not replaced until 1843—making Rhode Island the last of the original colonies to adopt a new constitution.

This is rather extraordinary considering Rhode Island's radical commitment to the revolutionary cause of overthrowing the British crown. On June 15, 1774, less than one month after news of the Boston Port Bill arrived in Massachusetts, the Rhode Island General Assembly appointed delegates to the anticipated Continental Congress. Rhode Island was the first colony to do so. Yet, although every other state beside Connecticut[40] drafted a constitution in the Revolutionary period/Confederation years, Rhode Islanders clung vociferously to the Charter and made no revisions to it except on July 18, 1776, when the legislature passed a resolution providing that "the style and title of this government, in all acts and instruments, whether of public or private nature, shall be the State of Rhode Island and Providence Plantations."[41]

The franchise laws of the state were revised several times in the period leading up to the Revolutionary War and in the years immediately following it. A property qualification had been required for electors since the Charter was granted in 1663. In March of that year, all persons (males) were required to be "of competent estates" in order to be admitted into the ranks of the freemen.[42] No amount of property was placed in the original

Charter, as relatively few colonists held land at that time. However, in the eighteenth century, the franchise laws were altered no less than five times as property qualifications were refined. In 1723–1724, the General Assembly set the real estate value for electors at 100 pounds, or 40 shillings rent per annum. In addition, the Assembly admitted the eldest son, in accordance with English laws. In the 1729–1730 session, the qualification was fixed at 200 pounds real estate or 10 pounds per annum rent. In 1746, the qualification was raised to 400 pounds real estate or 20 pounds per annum rent. In August 1760, however, the Assembly eased the property qualification considerably when it lowered it to a freehold requirement worth 40 pounds or a rent of 40 shillings per year.[43] This qualification remained until well after independence, when in 1798 the Assembly fixed the property qualification of electors at $134 or a rent of $7 per year.[44]

Although Rhode Island maintained a property qualification throughout the eighteenth century, these franchise laws were in many ways at once more liberal and more restrictive than those in other colonies. On the one hand, owning a freehold did not automatically entitle a male to the franchise—he had to pass admission by the existing freemen of the town, who might in fact reject him without regard to his freehold.[45] On the other hand, the agrarian-based economy and the comparatively low property requirement allowed many freeholders to become eligible for the vote. By 1746, the colonial statutes had described the real estate qualification as "low" and the method for admitting freeman as "lax." During this period, roughly 75 percent of all white males were able to meet the suffrage qualifications—although far fewer actually voted.[46] Formally, however, Rhode Island was by far one of the most democratic colonies of the period; it would remain so in statehood, as long as the economic base of the state remained agricultural in nature and the majority of its citizenry consisted of small landholding farmers. But political reform did not keep pace with these socioeconomic changes, and "democracy" in Rhode Island declined precipitously as the nineteenth century opened.[47]

Chilton Williamson has argued that Rhode Island "was becoming a Britain in miniature" during the first half of the nineteenth century.[48] By this, he means that a Jeffersonian-style, agricultural community quickly became an urban, industrial society, but that this transformation occurred *before* an expansion of the suffrage was granted. The Rhode Island experience stands in stark contrast to many states that expanded the suffrage well before industrialization of the economy and immigration occurred. The $134 freehold qualification for voting in the state was relatively easy to meet in a society of farmers and townspeople, and in fact half to three-fourths of all white males did meet the freehold qualification up to the end of the eighteenth century. But workers flooded to the urban centers of the state as cotton manufacturing developed. Thus, economic changes forced political pressure upon the shrinking landholding elite of the state to ease suffrage qualifications. At the same time, dramatic shifts in the population base of the state forced the same leaders to reconsider the apportionment scheme set out for the state General Assembly in the original Charter. As the economy became more industrialized the northern towns surrounding Providence began to expand, while the southern towns surrounding the port at Newport declined. By the early 1830s, only a third of all white males met the freehold qualification. In the great democratic era of the expansion of the suffrage, Rhode Island was not only undemocratic, but it also was moving in the opposite direction as propertyless laborers increasingly populated the state's manufacturing centers.

Far from serving the great cause of "expanding democracy," partisan competition in Rhode Island in the opening decades of the nineteenth actually limited the possibilities for constitutional reform. Although the parties competed vigorously for office, they colluded in ensuring that nonproperty holders remained out of the electorate. Since pre-Revolutionary times, Rhode Island had always experienced an unusually mature level of partisan conflict.[49] During the Revolution, partisanship declined, but the state found itself at the vanguard of the Jeffersonian, democratic impulses circulating, especially in the wake of the Declaration of Independence. This is one reason why Rhode Island was unwilling to scrap its Charter after independence—the Charter had established a form of government dominated by a popularly elected legislative branch with annual elections, along with a weak executive and a judiciary dependent on the General Assembly. Many state constitutions drafted in the Revolutionary period resembled Rhode Island's democratic charter. In 1786, partisan conflict was revived as the "Country" party was pitted against the "Minority" party over the issue of paper money. This conflict resembled the emerging national concern between Federalists and Antifederalists, that is, between an urban merchant class and a rural agrarian class. The Country party was comprised of farmers and advocated the issuance of paper money; the Minority party opposed it. When the Constitutional Convention was called in the summer of 1787, the farmers prevailed and Rhode Island chose not to send a delegation to Philadelphia. The state's agricultural interest opposed the creation of a stronger federal government, while the townspeople argued that a stronger central government could effectively control the poor.[50] However, in 1789, the Antifederalists lost control of the General Assembly, which subsequently allowed the Federalists to call a convention to ratify the Constitution.[51] One year later, Rhode Island ratified the Constitution, making it the last of the original colonies to do so.

From 1789 to 1800, the state's congressional representatives were predominantly proponents of the Federalist agenda.[52] However, Thomas Jefferson's victory swept Republicans into congressional office in Rhode Island. About the same time, the first calls were being made to address the structure of the state government. These questions simmered during the first two decades of the nineteenth century but emerged full blown by 1820. Federalist reformer George Burrill made the earliest calls for constitutional reform in 1797, when he argued for the principle of "one man one vote" in the General Assembly.[53] He advocated for a constitutional convention to replace the venerated Charter and create more just political institutions for Rhode Island. This was the opening salvo in a debate over the constitution that ebbed and flowed continually for the next forty years. Burrill revived his calls for constitutional reform a decade later in a pamphlet entitled *A Few Observations on the Government of the State of Rhode Island*. In it, he contended that the Revolutionary War had validated the concept of popular sovereignty, and that any changes in the state's constitution had to come from the people themselves—not the legislative authority.[54] Burrill's Jeffersonian rhetoric would be revived and repeated many times by Dorr supporters amid the conflict in the early 1840s.

On the eve of the War of 1812, the issue of constitutional reform was rekindled, this time by Democratic Republicans in the wake of Federalist victories in the congressional elections of 1808 and 1810, and the gubernatorial election of 1811. Amid the Jeffersonian Embargo, both farmers and merchants opposed the Republican agenda, and as the country moved closer to war, Federalists were successful in placing the state Republicans on the defensive.[55] Democratic Republicans claimed the Federalists had stolen these elections because Federalist freeholders had subdivided their lands and issued lifelong leases to Federalist sympathizers—thus ensuring that the tenants were able to meet suffrage qualifications. In January 1811, Democratic Republicans introduced for the first time a petition to remove all suffrage qualifications for voting. It passed the Republican controlled Senate, but failed in the Federalist controlled House. While Democratic Republicans made rhetorical statements about freedom and the expansion of the suffrage, one commentator at the time contended it was a political maneuver, and that "many of the senators were zealously opposed to free suffrage."[56]

The debate over constitutional reform predictably died down, but it was revived immediately in its wake as Federalists found themselves on the wrong side of the war effort. By 1818, the Federalist Party was all but defunct in the state, and was reduced to a small minority all across the country. But the state's Republicans soon divided over intrastate issues, specifically the constitutional questions of the apportionment scheme for representation in the General Assembly and the suffrage qualification. By

1820, with Providence quickly becoming the industrial center of the state, the city's press began clamoring for constitutional reform. That year, the newly published *Manufacturers' and Farmers' Journal* insisted that "the glaring defects of our miserable system, and its utter inconsistency in principle with all our received notions of republican government should be fully laid before the people."[57] The reformers behind the publication asserted that the government of Rhode Island was neither established by the people of the state nor amenable to them. Yet a General Assembly consisting largely of Anglo-American landholders from the agricultural towns surrounding Newport continually rebuffed calls for a constitutional convention. The constitutional conflict suddenly became a partisan one and was turning on North/South, industrial/agricultural axes, with the press in Providence generally pushing for constitutional reforms and Newport landholders generally opposing them. In February 1821, a resolution was finally passed authorizing the freemen of the state to decide on the desirability of convening a constitutional convention later that spring. In April, the question was defeated by a vote of 1905 to 1619. The counties of Newport, Washington, and Kent voted against it, whereas the counties of Providence and Bristol voted for it.[58]

That same year, the Republicans nominated William Gibbs for governor. The choice was important because, for the first time in thirty years, the party in power nominated a candidate who was *not* from Providence. This move infuriated Providence Republicans and, in a move to challenge the power of the southern wing of the party, joined with remaining Federalists to nominate a Providence candidate, Samuel Bridgham. The electoral returns show that Gibbs received his support from the same block of voters that defeated the referendum on the constitutional convention. Moreover, the conflict realigned partisan interests sectionally—Newport Federalists deserted their Providence allies and helped elect Gibbs by a majority of one thousand votes. This coalition of southern and western landholders would form the base of the Jacksonian party in the state a decade later—but, ironically, alongside Bridgham and the other Providence landholders they were opposed to in 1821.[59] The following year another referendum calling for a constitutional convention was defeated, but this time the reformers opposed it as well. The referendum of 1822 provided for a constitutional conclave apportioned in the same manner as the legislature. In the words of reformers, little change on the extension of the franchise was expected to come from a "convention composed of delegates distributed in the same manner as the lower house."[60]

By 1822, the Republicans had once again solidified their dominance in state party politics. But a latent conflict boiled just beneath the surface between the agricultural interests and the urban interests of the state.

With the Federalist Party all but dissipated, the "era of good feeling" meant the collapse in importance of national issues and the return of intrastate partisanship in Rhode Island. Yet, that same year and with little public debate, blacks were disenfranchised in Rhode Island. In its January session of 1822, the Rhode Island legislature moved to exclude blacks from the electorate but retained the property qualification on all white males. The statute read: "Be it enacted by the General Assembly, and by the authority thereof it is enacted, that the freeman of each town in this State, at any of their town-meetings, shall and they hereby have full power granted them, to admit so many white persons, inhabitants of their respective towns, freemen thereof, as shall be qualified, according to this act."[61] The act kept the freehold qualification for whites at $134 and $7 rent per year.

Two years later, the first constitutional convention in the state's history was convened. Under the provisions of the convention, the constitution could only be ratified with a vote of three-fifths of all eligible voters. It was not even close: The proposed constitution of 1824 was defeated by nearly a 2–1 majority (3,206 to 1,668). The only towns that approved of the constitution were those described by Coleman as "expanding"—which included the northern belt of Providence, North Providence, Smithfield, Warwick, and Bristol. The static and declining towns of the south and west rejected the constitution by a margin of nearly seven to one.[62] The vote is telling, for it shows that the freemen of Providence who voted were willing to forego their concerns about universal white male suffrage in order to secure a constitution that reformed the basic structure of government and reapportionment schemes of the General Assembly. In other words, in the mid-1820s the suffrage question still took a backseat to other pressing issues of constitutional reform. Within a decade, the suffrage question would lie at the heart of the constitutional debate.

The first attempt at constitutional reform thus failed miserably. Amid the wave of democratic changes sweeping across the United States, and the concomitant expansion of the suffrage to most white males, Rhode Island was lagging further behind. The same year that the proposed constitution went down, only 12.4 percent of the state's total white male population voted for president. In 1828, as voter turnout levels were nearing 70 percent across the country, 18 percent of the state's total white male population voted in the Adams-Jackson election. Through the 1830s, voter turnout for presidential elections in Rhode Island did not reach 25 percent of the total white male population. By 1840, when the national average soared to nearly 80 percent, about a third of the white male population voted in Rhode Island.[63] In short, the "Age of the Common Man" had not extended to Rhode Island; or, more accurately, the age of the common man had ostensibly come and gone in the state, as a higher percentage of the white male population had voted before the War of 1812 than in the period of Jacksonian Democracy.

Constitutional reform receded for several years after the debacle of 1824, resurfaced briefly in 1829, then remained dormant until after the presidential election of 1832. That year, Anti-Jackson candidate Henry Clay won a plurality of the popular vote in Rhode Island.[64] A list of Providence freemen compiled in 1832 tallied only 1,216 eligible voters—roughly 32 percent of the white male population in the city.[65] Although Andrew Jackson was returned to the White House with a self-proclaimed mandate to be the "tribune of the people," the Jacksonian Democrats of Rhode Island—comprised mainly agrarian interests to the south and west of the state—were staunchly opposed to any suffrage extension or reapportionment scheme in the General Assembly. Once again, Providence became the hotbed of agitation. In 1833, a radical group of workers began a push for constitutional reform that centered on the question of the restricted suffrage. Seth Luther, a carpenter and labor spokesman, led the charge as he taunted and ridiculed the propertied classes of the state in a speech delivered on April 19 that was later printed as *An Address on the Right of Free Suffrage*.[66] In it, Luther reminded his audience that he was merely a poor journeyman carpenter, but that the "small potato aristocrats" in Rhode Island had perpetuated a freehold system that was "contrary to the Declaration of Independence, the Constitution of the United States, the Bill of Rights of the State of Rhode Island, and the dictates of common sense." As Gettleman has pointed out, Luther's rousing speech drew upon a Jeffersonian communitarianism that accepted economic inequalities but rested on political equality and mutual respect.[67] Furthermore, he revived the natural rights philosophy of the Revolutionary Era—also found in Burrill's orations at the turn of the century—to argue that government is created by the people to protect inalienable rights, and that a republican form of government renders to the people the right to change their government when it violates those inalienable rights:

> [The people] … have a right to assemble in primary meetings, and appoint delegates to the Convention. That convention have [sic] a right to form a Constitution, and to submit it to the people. If they adopt it, it is the law of the land.[68]

Luther's call for a constitutional convention operated on two levels at once. On the one hand, his was a tactical decision meant to overcome the experiences of the early 1820s, when the General Assembly had arranged for only freemen of the state to attend the convention. In 1822, reformers rejected the idea; in 1824, the convention produced a document that was voted down. Claiming that the people themselves had the right to appoint delegates, Luther and his followers hoped to do an end run around the reactionary Assembly. On the other hand, Luther's call was a powerful rhetorical device in the debate over the suffrage that linked the struggles of the Revolutionary period to the contemporary struggle for the franchise. By appealing to the natural rights philosophy of Jefferson, Luther also hoped to provide a moral justification for what he was asking the workers assembled before him to do—which was essentially break the law by taking part in an extralegal constitutional convention.

Luther's Ideas were coopted the next year by a group of respectable business and professional men from both the Newport and the Providence areas. According to Gettleman, this group muted Luther's radicalism by once again urging the General Assembly to convene a constitutional convention.[69] They called themselves the Constitutional Party, and chose as their intellectual leader a young Whig politician and lawyer from Providence by the name of Thomas Wilson Dorr.

When the Constitutional Party was formed in 1834, it was not necessarily in favor of universal male suffrage. In the General Assembly, Dorr did put forth a proposal to relax the suffrage qualification for the vote on the delegates to the convention, which was to convene later that year; yet, the General Assembly voted the measure down. Similar to the convention held a decade earlier, the delegation assembled at the Constitutional Convention of 1834 was a miniature version of the legislature. At the convention, Dorr opted for a more moderate tack and proposed a taxpaying qualification for the suffrage rather than a property qualification. He did not seek universal white male suffrage. Dorr's moderate proposal received but seven votes.[70] On questions of legislative reapportionment, the convention delegates also did not budge. Moreover, it was clear that most of the convention delegates wanted the convention to fail: on November 10, 1834, the last day before adjournment, a quorum did not appear and no votes were taken. The delegates present moved to adjourn until February 1835. The same thing occurred that February, and a motion of adjournment until June 1835 was passed. In the summer of 1835, the convention finally fell apart when only Dorr and his ally Metcalf Marsh showed up.[71]

After the demise of convention of 1834, the Constitutionalists continued to fight for political change through electoral politics. Initially, they sought a coalition with Whigs in the urban centers opposed to the Jacksonian Democrats in the rural south and west. However, the Constitutionalists found the Whigs reluctant to push their agenda, and they chose to nominate and run their own candidates for political office. At a convention called in 1836, the party nominated Charles Collins to be its gubernatorial candidate. In the election he received only 135 ballots out 7,151 votes cast.[72] The next year, Dorr himself ran for U.S. Congress on the Constitutionalist ticket; he, too, received only scores of votes. By the close of 1837, the brief life of the Constitutionalist Party had come to an end, and Thomas Dorr vowed not to involve himself with electoral politics again unless nonland-holders took the initiative to agitate for the elective franchise.[73]

Although the leaders of the Constitutionalist Party mainly came from the northern industrial towns dominated by the Whig Party, it would be wrong to assume that most Whigs in the state were for even the most mod-erate of the constitutional reforms advocated by Dorr and his followers. Most of the state's Whig leaders did not want an extension of the suffrage to white male laborers for fear of a shift in the political—and economic—balance of the state. According to one opponent of the extension of the suf-frage at the time, the economy of the state had been well managed over the last three decades without the political participation of the nonlandholding masses.[74] Extension of the suffrage would jeopardize that. Thus, the state's Whigs leaders were in the anomalous position of advocating for reappor-tionment to increase representation in the Assembly for Providence and the other northern urban centers while generally objecting to the franchise extension. To make matters worse, the Providence Census in the late 1830s showed a growing influx of "foreigners not naturalized"—mostly Irish Catholics, as I pointed out earlier. The parish pastor in Providence counted a total of nearly seventeen hundred Irish parishioners in 1839; a decade earlier the number was estimated at two hundred.[75] Thus, a new question in the suffrage debate surfaced: what to do with those non-native-born white males? As the 1830s closed, the response to the constitutional ques-tion of reform by the party of Jackson was to do nothing: the Democrats stonewalled on questions of reapportionment and extension of the suf-frage, because reforms in both areas would have diminished the strength of the party in state politics. As for the Whigs, their stance was not much more flexible, and increasingly the party of Anglo merchants in the north-ern industrial towns was becoming consumed by nativist fears. Reformers such as Dorr were faced with the unenviable choice between two parties that colluded to disenfranchise propertyless whites for their separate rea-sons. For the time being, blacks were faced with the same choice.

Discourse, Disenfranchisement, and Reenfranchisement Amid the Chaos of the Dorr War, 1770s–1840

Before moving on to a discussion of the Dorr conflict, I want to return to the circumstances surrounding the disenfranchisement of blacks in 1822 and the underlying competing racial belief systems in Rhode Island throughout the post-Revolutionary period. Earlier, I mentioned that Rhode Island was consumed by Quaker influences over questions of slavery like other colonies during the Revolutionary period. Leaders such as Samuel Hopkins had been preaching against the evils of slavery in Newport since 1770. In 1774 the General Assembly passed a rather weak law that sought to abolish the slave trade that had been so lucrative to the southern port town of Newport. Moral and economic concerns over questions of race and slavery were evidently in conflict in revolutionary Rhode Island. The experience of the state during the war—and more particularly, the performance of black soldiers during the war effort—allowed racial paternalism to take hold and dominate the racial views of the state's leaders for the next several decades.

The performance of black Revolutionary regiments was clear a half-century after that conflict ended. In 1828, Tristam Burges, a Congressman who would become an ally of Dorr, took the floor of the House and described how slaves in Rhode Island had become loyal citizens. "At the commencement of the Revolutionary War," he began, "Rhode Island had a number of slaves. A regiment of them were enlisted into the Continental service, and no braver men met the enemy in battle."[76] Burges further explained that all of them were first granted their freedom before being conscripted. Nearly a decade before, John Eustis of Massachusetts had echoed the same sentiments, explaining that a battalion of four hundred black Rhode Islanders had resisted and repulsed the advance of nearly fifteen hundred troops headed by British Colonel Donop.[77] Reflecting on the same battle in before the Rhode Island Anti-Slavery Society in 1842, Dr. Harris, a Revolutionary War veteran, explained:

> I have another object in view in stating these facts. I would not be trumpeting my own acts; the only reason why I have named myself in connection with this transaction is, to show that I know whereof I affirm. There was a black regiment in the same situation. Yes, a regiment of Negroes, fighting for our liberty and independence—not a white man among them but the officers—stationed in this same dangerous and responsible position. Had they been unfaithful, or given way before the enemy, all would have been lost. ... They fought through the war. They were brave, hardy troops. They helped to gain our independence.[78]

One of the most important figures who kept racial paternalism in the foreground of Rhode Island politics in the late eighteenth and early nineteenth centuries was Moses Brown. Brown was born into one of Rhode Island's leading mercantilist families in the mid-eighteenth century. After the death of his wife in 1773 before he turned thirty, Brown rejected the Baptist faith of his family and instead turned to Quakerism. Brown's family had owned slaves, but on the eve of the Revolutionary War he and other

Quakers such as Samuel Hopkins led the move to abolish the slave trade in 1774. After the war, Brown worked tirelessly for the abolition bill that passed the General Assembly in 1784. Breaking with Quaker practice, Brown involved himself both publicly and privately in politics on the state and federal level. When the Constitution was completed in 1787, Brown opposed its adoption on the grounds that it condoned the slave trade. In October of that year, Brown and the Friends of Rhode Island spoke openly about the slave trade clause (Article I, section 9) as well as the fugitive slave clause (Article IV, section 2). On behalf of the Friends, he wrote that "there is no sensible friend I have conversed on this subject but has not been disagreeably affected." He continued by saying that he was "afflicted to have an article in the constitution of these states so repugnant to the principles of liberty, truth and righteousness."[79]

For the rest of his life until he died at the age of ninety-seven in 1836, Brown adhered to a form of racial paternalism formed from his experiences in the early abolitionist movement of the Revolutionary era. One such example was his involvement in the creation of the African Union Meeting House, the first black church in Providence established in 1820. One of the main purposes of the African Union Meeting House was to provide education for black children to supplant the educational instruction that had previously been provided in white households. Brown provided much of the funding for the construction of the Meeting House and helped to raise the rest. Brown's racial paternalism was spelled out most clearly in a short essay written to commemorate the history of the Meeting House.[80] He contended that "the slavish and gross state of ignorance of the people of colour, has of late years excited the commiseration of those who profess and exhibit themselves the active friends of humanity, and general extension of useful knowledge." With the end of slavery in the state, Brown went on to commend abolitionist societies for creating churches and schools "for the mental and moral improvement of this injured people." Yet, Brown went further, and asserted his belief that the transformation of the "African" was possible through religious and educational instruction:

> The neglected objects of their consultation are the descendents of those miserable Africans, which were insidiously seduced, or violently from their native shores; the consideration of which, apart from the feelings of humanity, or the dictates, of policy, gives them a valid claim to public justice. If (as experience has evinced) there is, more or less, an inseparable connexion [sic] between knowledge and virtue, and ignorance and vice; it would seem to be a patriotic duty to impart to them all the advantages that can be derived from moral and intellectual culture. ... That they are endowed by

an impartial Creator with capacities for such improvement, is now generally admitted; and that the stale imputation of inferiority in mental faculties is rejected; or rather, but few will avow the contrary opinion; although, as Montesquieu shrewdly remarks, "we must suppose them not to be men, or a suspicion would follow that we are not Christians."[81]

Brown combined his own Quaker teaching grounded in compassion for one's fellow man with the Revolutionary rhetoric of natural rights and universal equality, and concluded that servile characteristics of persons of African descent were mutable and able to be transcended:

> An elegant writer has observed with equal brevity and energy: "The authority of Jesus Christ himself must have more weight with Christians, than all the pomp and parade of the most absolute despots on earth. He taught us when we pray to say, 'Our Father.' This alone is sufficient to establish, on an immovable basis, the equality of human beings." … The Africans and their descendents are not only capable of acquiring the common rudiments of education, but the higher branches of science, the most plenary evidence could be adduced.[82]

Moses Brown's *The History of the African Union Meeting House* appeared at a critical juncture in the history of the struggle for citizenship for blacks. It came amid the transition from the dominant racial paternalism of the Revolutionary Era to racial ascriptivism and the accompanying rising hostility and essentialist rhetoric that occurred in the wake of the race riots of the 1820s and early 1830s that I discussed above. When the Rhode Island General Assembly had passed the law manumitting slaves over thirty years before, Moses Brown and his Quaker friends were instrumental in its drafting. The preamble to the bill began with ringing references to Declaration of Independence and its natural rights philosophy. "Whereas, all men are entitled to life, liberty, and the pursuit of happiness," it began, "and the holding mankind in a state of slavery, as private property, which has gradually obtained by unrestrained custom and the permission of laws, is repugnant to its principle, and subversive of the happiness of mankind, the great end of all civil government," the bill went on to suggest that colored persons would be included in the body politic of the state and stand together with whites as "one people."[83] Furthermore, "humanity" required that slaveholders instruct the children of slaves in morality, religion, reading, and writing.

Moses Brown signified the last in a generation of leaders in Rhode Island who approached the racial divide with the paternalistic racial rhetoric found in the Revolutionary era. But as blacks became more independent economically and socially, they were faced with an increasing hostility in the white population of the state. The changes in social conditions that I outlined above played a major role in the ideological transformation that occurred. As Robert Cottrol has argued, this hostility had its origins primarily in the laws of the market: a burgeoning free black population coexisted alongside poor whites in Rhode Island. Yet, whereas previously black slaves worked in the fields and in the households of the white elite, free blacks now competed in an industrialized marketplace for the same jobs as poor whites.[84] With the influx of white ethnics from the late 1820s, an ascriptivist ideology moved to the foreground in the racial discourse.

Joanne Pope Melish concurs on this point. She contends that the legal arrangements around gradual emancipation were the main causal factors in rising hostilities because gradual abolition forced Rhode Island's (and much of New England's) white population to rethink questions concerning citizenship and race.[85] According to Melish, the discourse of "slavery" had, by the 1820s, been supplanted by the discourse of "race."[86] The former was founded on the Revolutionary rhetoric of republicanism and abolitionism, and held at its core Moses Brown's contention that the degraded condition of blacks was due to the historical reality of slavery itself. If the servile characteristics of slaves were a result of the conditions that slavery created, then these characteristics could be transformed by simply changing the conditions. "Freedom" for blacks would effect an amelioration of condition. By 1820, however, the discourse of slavery had given way to a completely different set of assumptions about the differences between the races: now, the emphasis was placed, not on environmental explanations of difference and paternalistic solutions, but on essentialist arguments that characterized blacks as innately and immutably inferior. The solution: remove blacks from what was becoming a "white" polity. Melish analyzes New England society and concludes that, just several years removed from abolishing slavery, whites looked at the continued degraded condition of blacks and argued that "freedom" had not led to any substantial improvements.

For Melish, then, white New Englanders engaged in an "erasure" of their own historical experience.[87] Consequently, the very concept of freedom was reconceptualized, and whites constructed a discourse that placed blacks at a specific point along the continuum of freedom. Freedom now had several "degrees": on the one hand, blacks were free of slavery and were allowed to enjoy the economic fruits of their own labor. On the other hand, because of their inherent inferiority blacks were not capable or responsible enough to enjoy the political fruits of freedom by receiving the full rights of citizenship. This helps explains why the lawyers involved in the Hard Scrabble Riot of 1824 could conclude that destroying black neighborhoods promotes the "morals of the community."

Amid this transformation, blacks were disenfranchised in Rhode Island. It occurred in rather unceremonious fashion. Indeed, very little was written at the time about the changes in the voting laws referred to the racial exclusion, except for a few newspaper articles that reported without commentary on the legislative session of the General Assembly. On January 18, 1822, just four days after the vote was cast to disenfranchise blacks, the *Providence American* ran a story that mentioned the racial restriction on voting almost as an afterthought:

> The Election Law has been so amended, that no one, who is not possessed in his own right, of real estate of the value of 134 dollars, free of encumbrance, shall be entitled to the privileges of a freeman. This amendment, it is obvious, will operate as a sufficient check upon the manufacture of fraudulent votes. The right of eldest sons to vote by virtue of estates belonging to their fathers is abrogated, as being a relick [*sic*] of feudal times, incompatible with the genius of free institutions. An attempt was made to dispense with the existing property qualification of voters; but the House had the good sense to reject the plan by a decided majority. The law was further amended, so as to deny the privilege of voting to all persons except free *white* males.[88]

The very next day, the *Newport Mercury* ran a condensed version of the exact same column; no mention was made of the racial voting restriction in the *Rhode Island Republican* in its summary of the General Assembly's proceedings shortly thereafter.[89] There was little or no outcry from the black community of the state, and very little explanation has been given for the change by either political actors of the time or later commentators.[90] Before 1822, although blacks could legally vote, it has been estimated that few in Rhode Island actually met the $134 freehold qualification and voted.[91]

So why the move to disenfranchise? Let me suggest one hypothesis before returning to a discussion of the reenfranchisement of blacks in the wake of the Dorr War. Because there was no real threat from the electoral strength of the black community, the move to disenfranchise may have been a symbolic act that has its justification in the racial dynamic of the time in states bordering on Rhode Island. Immediately following the War of 1812, state after state revised its constitution. Furthermore, states bordering Rhode Island had enacted constitutional reform with similar racial restrictions in the previous years. Connecticut's state constitution was altered in 1818 and extended the franchise only to white males, whereas in 1821 New York's placed a $250 freehold qualification on black males. Rhode Islanders were certainly aware of the changes occurring outside the state: as early as 1820, the *Manufacturers' and Farmers' Journal* called attention to the Connecticut constitution adopted in 1818 and the constitutional convention recently convened in the state of Massachusetts.[92] Throughout the winter of 1820 and the spring of 1821, the *Journal* ran a series of articles denouncing the Charter and calling for a constitutional convention formed by the people. Echoing George Burrill's Revolutionary rhetoric of the previous generation, the editorials argued that the right of revision of the Charter rested with the king; but since drafting of the Declaration of Independence there was nothing to prevent the General Assembly from granting this power to the people. The *Journal* declared: "This provision of the charter could not be repealed by the general assembly, so long as the controlling power of the crown existed—but, when that power was annihilated by the Revolution, the assembly was enabled to repeal either this, or any other security of the people's rights which the charter contained."[93]

It may well be the case that the General Assembly of Rhode Island saw the changes enacted in neighboring states and followed suit. Whatever the justifications, the disenfranchisement of blacks in Rhode Island in 1822 came as a result of the convergence of economics, politics, and racial ideology. Blacks were forging their own communities and seeking employment in an increasingly industrialized environment, thus pitting them against whites in the labor force. On the other hand, whites were migrating to urban centers, also seeking employment. At the same time, calls for constitutional reform reached a heightened pitch as more Rhode Islanders found themselves disenfranchised. Through the 1820s and 1830s, blacks receded within their own communities and practiced their own uplift ideology. Meanwhile, the rest of Rhode Island, far from a "white man's republic," had become an oligarchy run by the landholding Democratic farmers and the urban Whig merchants.

Reenfranchisement Amid Chaos: The Dorr War, 1841–1843

The election of 1840 brought a landslide victory to the Whig party both at the state and national level. In state elections, Whigs captured the governor's office and took control of the General Assembly. That same year the General Assembly sent James Simmons, a Whig, to the U.S. Senate. And William Henry Harrison trounced Martin Van Buren in presidential balloting. As head of the Democratic State Committee, Thomas Dorr was thoroughly embarrassed by the election results. Yet the election also caused a backlash of sorts, and actually had the unintended consequence of rejuvenating the suffrage movement. Turnout in the state was higher in 1840 than at any other time since 1818; the increasing number of non-landholders saw the excitement created by the election for president and became aroused. Furthermore, the campaign tactics used by the Whigs were copied by the suffragists to jar the nonlandholders of the state from their political slumber.[94] A rejuvenated suffrage movement also became more organized as it geared up in its efforts to mobilize the disenfranchised of the state.

By 1840, Thomas Dorr had moved to forge an alliance with the New York Equal Rights Democrats, also known as the Locofocos, to fight for political change in Rhode Island. Despite his frustration with the partisan deadlock on constitutional reform, Dorr nevertheless switched allegiances and became a "Democrat"—but a member of a small emerging faction of the Democratic Party that was assuming a regional identity. It must be remembered that the local Jacksonian Democrats were vigorously opposed to all reform measures. Nonetheless, by 1840 Dorr's faction and the agrarian, Jacksonian Democrats had entered into an uneasy alliance. In the wake of the election, agitation once again increased around the extension of the suffrage. The Rhode Island Suffrage Association was born on the heels of the 1840 election. It began to publish its own newspaper, the *New Age and Constitutional Advocate,* in November 1840. The *New Age* railed furiously against the landholders and printed acerbic editorials arguing for changes in the constitutional system of government in Rhode Island. It did so by once again invoking the natural rights philosophy found in Revolutionary rhetoric and making an appeal to the inalienable rights granted to all men. In its December 4 issue, it stated:

> The right of suffrage is one of the natural rights of man. Deprived of this, he is incapable of self-protection, unless indeed, superior strength should give him what nature or society had deprived him of. In this case, *might* alone would constitute the quantum of right and justice which he held. ... Deprived of the right of suffrage, we have no protection for either life, liberty, or happiness, other than the will of accidental circumstances which governs others; they may provide for our happiness, and throw the strong arm of law around us to protect our life substance. But even here we are dependent on others, a dependence degrading to a great mind, calculated to degenerate and destroy the natural independence of our soul. For the line of natural and political justice is straight and direct—none can be elevated above it.[95]

In early 1841, the Suffrage Party was created on the strength of the Suffrage Association and immediately held a series of mass meetings calling for an extralegal convention to write a constitution for the state. Originally, Dorr had played no part in the creation of either the suffrage association or the party and declined to be drawn into it as late as May 1841. Yet, when a "People's Constitutional Convention" was called on July 24, Dorr became part of the movement. In August, he was elected as a delegate to the convention, which was to convene on October 4 to draft a new constitution for the state.

With the urging of Dorr and other leaders of the Suffrage movement, elections for delegates to the convention were declared open to all male citizens regardless of nativity or race. By that summer and early fall, however, the issue of race was brought to a head. In September, a Suffrage Association assembly in Providence excluded blacks from participating. The incident stirred a debate in the city's newspapers. A suffrage sympathizer, writing in the *Providence Journal* under the pseudonym of "Town Born," drew on Revolutionary rhetoric to argue for black suffrage:

> Much fault has been found with the Association by some cavaliers, because upon their own principles they do not seem inclined to admit our colored brethren to an equal participation in suffrage. It is said, if "all men are born free and equal," if "the right to vote be a natural and inalienable right," … why does the mere accident of color make a difference?[96]

Yet, Town Born also expressed a keen understanding of the venomous racial animosity among the poor whites in the Association. He argued that, "… we know that, as a general rule, the Association thought it might be too great a shock to public sentiment to allow colored men this privilege, although as a matter of consistency, and to avoid giving offense to our abolitionist friends, the call was so worded as to include them." At the end of his editorial, Town Born cautioned blacks to be patient, for as soon as white universal suffrage was achieved, the Association would turn its attention to the suffrage of blacks. Two days later, a black man responded to Town Born's editorial with a forceful rejoinder on why blacks should not wait:

> From some of the views expressed by "Town Born," in his last number, I am compelled to dissent. If I do not misunderstand him, he is disposed in accommodation to the unreasonable prejudices of the country, to exclude, even under the new dispensation, the approach of which he hails with so much delight, our colored fellow citizens from the right to vote and to be elected to office. To be sure, he encourages them with the prospect of redress, at a different day, when the full blessings of universal suffrage shall come to be felt throughout our borders. In this matter, however, I would submit to no delay, consent to no compromise.[97]

On September 24, the black suffrage leader Alfred Niger was nominated by the executive committee to be treasurer of the Constitutional Convention that was to meet two weeks later. The majority in the committee favored Niger; a minority favored Thomas Green, who was white. As the *Providence Journal* reported on September 27, 1841, the person responsible for nominating Niger was an ardent opponent of Negro suffrage and only nominated him in order to "smoke out" pro-Negro suffrage and pro-abolitionist members of the party. Many other members of the convention objected to a black man in a position of leadership. A vote was taken, and Green was elected by an undisclosed margin.[98]

As the People's Convention convened on October 4, 1841, racial tensions began to flare up within the Suffrage Association. Dorr and fellow suffrage leader Benjamin Arnold continued to plead for universal male suffrage regardless of race. Within the first days of the convention a motion was introduced inserting the word "white" into the suffrage qualification. In response, Dorr introduced a petition by black leader Alexander Crummell, which was read on the floor of the convention. It stated:

> The article to which we refer, disenfranchises that portion of the community generally entitled "colored." The reason for this proscription is seen in the terms employed—it is the existence of the fact *color*. We regard the proscription as unwarrantable, anti-republican, and in tendency destructive; and as such we protest against it. ... We are mostly native born citizens. We have lent our best strength in the cultivation of the soil, have aided in the development of resources, and have contributed our part to its wealth and importance. We have long, but with little aid, been working our way up to respectability and competence. It is evident to open eyes, that, repulsed and disenfranchised as we have been, we have, nevertheless, been enabled to possess ourselves the means and advantages of religion, intelligence, and property. Debarred as we have been of the advantages of learning, and denied participation in civil prerogatives, we unhesitatingly assert that we will not suffer by a comparison with our more privileged fellow-citizens of the same rank, in either religion, virtue, or industry.[99]

Crummell's plea not only drew on natural rights-based, republican principles, but also—and perhaps more important—the very experiences of the black community of Rhode Island over the previous two decades. In attempting to overcome the essentialist rhetoric of those arguing against black suffrage, Crummell and his colleagues argued that blacks had lifted themselves up from slavery to become good and productive citizens, and had proven themselves responsible for all the rights and privileges of citizenship:

Is a justification of our disenfranchisement sought in our want of christian character? We point to our churches as our reputation. In our want of intelligence? We refer not merely to the schools supported by the State, for our advantage, but to the private schools, well filled and sustained, and taught by competent teachers of our own people. Is our industry questioned? This day, were there no complexional hindrance, we could present a more than proportionate number of our people, who might immediately, according to the freeholder's qualification, become voters.[100]

Crummell's petition closed by once again tying the struggle of blacks to both the Revolutionary struggle seventy years earlier and the struggle of the suffragists of the times:

Whether this may be so or not, political experience, the annals of nations clearly teach that there is always danger in departing from clearly defined universal truths, and resorting to unjustifiable and invidious partialities. We trust that your respected body, in the influence you can exert, will not do this. By all humane feeling, by all regard for principle, we entreat, do not this great wrong to us.[101]

After the petition was read, Benjamin Arnold then took the floor and moved to have the word "white" stricken from the suffrage clause. As the *Providence Journal* reported on October 11, Arnold "considered himself bound to make it as a friend of the convention. It was according to all the principles upon which the suffrage association had been founded, and upon which they had hitherto acted. They were now to carry out these principles in action. And it was their duty to be true to them."[102] As proof, Arnold read from the resolutions passed earlier that year at the state meeting in Newport, which allowed for every American citizen to vote regardless of race. As he spoke, Arnold was interrupted by Nathaniel Mowry from Smithfield who complained that Arnold was mistaken: a different body from the Rhode Island Suffrage Association had approved of blacks to vote.[103] He further reasoned that if blacks could vote, they also could be "elected office; and a nigger that might occupy the chair where your honor sits. A pretty look that would be."[104] After the chairman restored order, Arnold responded that he was appealing to "human rights." He stated that he was "for rights and justice and freedom, and [I] joined the Suffrage because [I] thought these were the great causes of that movement." Arnold then concluded by urging his fellow suffragists to act on principle rather than expediency. "[You were] sent to act on fundamentals, not expedients, to form a Constitution in the spirit of truth, justice, and freedom, on the basis of the immutable and eternal principle."[105]

After Arnold spoke, several other delegates rose to speak against the racial exclusion. Colonel Wales stated:

> [I do not] know what right [we] had to form a constitution enfranchising one part of [our] fellow citizens and disfranchising another. ... Did they choose their complexion when they came into the world? They were brought into existence arbitrarily, and ought not to be classed among criminals and malefactors as unworthy of the rights of suffrage. It [is] enough for [me] that they were men and American citizens.[106]

Opposition to the removal of the racial restriction was just as passionate. William Spencer countered that his constituents' ascriptive views would never allow them to vote for a constitution that granted the franchise to blacks. Welcome Sayles also argued from the utilitarian perspective of the "greatest good for the greatest number." "Blacks [have] no right to vote in neighboring states, and under the present conditions of society, there was no sympathy between the whites and the blacks. It [is] endangering the whole project to strike out this word [white], and might prevent the adoption of a republican constitution in this state. It [is] endangering the rights of 15,000 white men."[107]

Thomas Dorr was the last to speak before a vote was taken on the suffrage clause with the word "white" in it. Dorr began by stating that he was:

> Bound to believe the assertions of the members relative to the feelings of [your] constituents, because [I can] not contradict them by any other proof. ... [I do] not think that the people of Rhode Island [are] so illiberal as they [are] represented. [I] had heard before that the people of Rhode Island were narrow and harsh in their prejudice, but [I have] inevitably found them in reverse. This Constitution [is] not democratic in the broadest sense of the word. ... This Convention would be inconsistent with their former declarations, with their bill of rights just adopted and would diverge from the great principles acted out by Roger Williams.[108]

He ended by reminding the delegates that blacks had fought valiantly during the Revolution and that other states had granted the rights of citizenship to blacks on equal footing with whites. Although he closed in passionate defense of the rights of blacks, Dorr's entreaties were to no avail. The delegates quickly voted 46–18 to retain the word white in the suffrage clause. However, Dorr's influence in the convention led to two minor if not altogether inconsequential compromises on the issue. Although blacks were to be disenfranchised, in the People's Constitution, they were also exempted from military service and taxation. Second, Dorr was successful in getting the delegates to agree to a clause in the People's Constitution mandating a popular referendum on the issue of black suffrage at the first annual election after the initial session of the People's Legislature.

Abolitionists both in and outside of Rhode Island vehemently decried the deliberations at the People' Convention. The suffrage association responded immediately with attacks of its own on the abolitionists, accusing them of sabotaging the convention. Amid the proceedings of the Convention, the *New Age and Constitutional Advocate* ran an editorial stating that:

> There are some half-dozen lecturers in this State at present from other States, who are determined to prevent the adoption, as they say of the People's Constitution; although any person on hearing them will see at once that their main object is to break down all organization of both Church and State and convert the people to *transcendentalism.* They openly declare that it is not right to vote for this Constitution with the word "white" out, and still they make that word a reason for going against it. Their force is set against all government regulated by law, and all friends of a regulated government of any sort should be against them, but strange as it may appear many of our opponents who have been so from the commencement have jumped on with this class of disorganizers in hopes to ride down our Constitution.[109]

However, Garrison's *The Liberator* would not relent in its condemnation of the People's Convention. On October 29, it ran a piece written by members of the Rhode Island Anti-Slavery Society announcing the massive attempt underway to defeat the People's Constitution:

> It is time for [the people of Rhode Island] to wake out of sleep and wrestle mightily with a corrupt public sentiment which is crushing humanity to the dust; and making merchandize of the image of God. Especially should they act in a spirited and united manner, at this time, when an attempt is making in Rhode Island, by the pseudo friends of political reform, to make the rights of a man dependent on the hue of his skin![110]

Nearly one month later, the Rhode Island Anti-Slavery Society reported on the mobilization that was gearing up in expectation of the December vote on the constitution. "The free suffrage question was debated with great spirit and at much length; and nearly one thousand dollars were obtained in money and pledges to blot out the proscriptive word 'white' from the new State Constitution which the free suffrage party are soon to present to the people."[111] Included in this effort was Frederick Douglass, who traveled to Rhode Island to assist in efforts to defeat the People's Constitution. But his and the rest of the abolitionists' efforts failed. In December 1841, the People's Constitution was approved overwhelmingly by state voters by a margin of 13,944 to 52. And with it the ties between the radical democratic Suffragists and the state's three thousand black citizens were completely severed.

In late October, after the People's Constitution was completed, black leaders immediately moved to petition the conservative landholders faction to test their support for black suffrage. The landholders were gearing up for their own constitutional convention, which was to take place in November 1841. Earlier that year, and much as they had done since the late 1820s, blacks had petitioned the reactionary General Assembly for the basic right of citizenship. The same Alfred Niger who was nearly elected as an officer to the People's Convention had made the case for black suffrage in an eloquent petition. Once again he drew on the republican principles that had fueled the suffrage debate throughout the previous decade:

> The memorial of the colored citizens of Rhode Island would respectfully represent: that the laws and statutes of the state, now to be amended, the colored population are denied the right of suffrage—debarred from the immunities of citizenship. To your honorable body ... we beg with deference to present our claim and to ask an equal participation in the rights and privileges of citizenship. We are native born citizens descended from an ancestry stretching back to period almost coeval with the first settlers of the country. On American soil, beneath American skies, surrounded by American institutions, we first beheld the light of the impartial sun. Born in no foreign clime, not accustomed to a political creed repugnant to democratic principles and republican usage, we are members of the state of Rhode Island under the government of the United States, familiarized from youth with the nature, features, and operations of our government of our government, whose excellencies and peculiarities are accordant with the flow of our feelings ad the current of our thoughts. ... And we have done service to the country. By the dint of our labour—by hard work and earnest activity, have we for years lent our best strength in the cultivation of the soil, in the development of its resources, and in contributing to its wealth and importance. If at any time danger threatened; the aid and defence we have contributed, has been more than proportionate. There is hardly a Battle field in the country but what is enriched with the blood and bones of colored men. Throughout the entire revolution they contributed their aid. They were seen at Bunker Hill, they were present at YorkTown. The most splendid naval achievements were owing to no small extent to the valor of colored Americans. ... As citizens we have at all taken our part in common burden and expenses; we have

at ways been ready and prompt tax payers. If there is any considerations that may be offered on the part of any of the people, why they
should participate in the privileges of citizenship; we know of no one
who can present more or weightier ones than we. We have been and
are a wronged people—yet have done the country no injury. In the
construction of a State Constitution for which your honorable body
was appointed, and which you now purpose—we beg that our claims
may not be forgotten:—we respectfully ask a participation in the pre-
rogatives of Citizenship.[112]

Blacks had no choice but to turn to the conservative forces—known by
the early 1840s as the Law and Order Party—in control of the government
for help. Although the Law and Order Party opposed the People's Constitution, the product of its own constitutional convention held in November
1841 was no more beneficial to Rhode Island blacks. It, too, barred blacks
from voting. But remaining true to the nativist sentiments upon which
party ideology rested, the new constitution also set a property for naturalized white males at $134. By contrast, the People's Constitution made no
distinction between native born and naturalized white males. The landholders began to release broadsides designed to prey on nativist fears:

By the People's Constitution, should it go into operation, a large body
of foreigners already in the State, would be brought immediately to
the polls. ... Thereby our native mechanics and workingmen would
suffer by the competition, for labor; and the balance of political and
civil power would inevitably be placed in the hands of emigrants
from foreign countries, who would, either directly or indirectly control the State. Let native American citizens pause and reflect, and
honestly decide, if they are or are not willing to become subject to
such control; and then act accordingly.[113]

Although the conservative forces created a media blitz in support of
the "Legal" Constitution, it failed by the small margin of 676 votes out of
16,702 cast. Buoyed by the "ratification" of the People's Constitution and
the defeat of the Legal Constitution, the Suffragists immediately called
for an election to vote for state officers. In April 1842, Thomas Dorr was
elected to the governorship in an election where only 6,539 votes were
cast. In May, he moved to seize the Providence arsenal and the reigns of
government. By this time, the conservative forces had been promised federal assistance from President Tyler in the event of civil unrest. Within a
few days, the conflict fizzled as Dorrites scattered and Dorr himself fled the
state. However, while in exile, Dorr promised to return to Providence and
capture what in his eyes was his constitutional and hence legitimate right

to power. In the meantime, he traveled to other states garnering support for his cause, finding it in many places. For example, Dorr was received warmly by New York's Democratic machine Tammany Hall in mid-May 1842 and was promised armed assistance from several units of the New York militia should they be needed. William Cullen Bryant's *Evening Post* supported Dorr's cause, and on his departure the Democratic Party hosted a colorful parade to honor Dorr attended by prominent politicians such as Samuel Tilden and Ely Moore.[114] This outside support gave Dorr the confidence to believe that he could actually win in an armed insurgency.

In June he returned to Rhode Island with a rebellious army upwards of eleven hundred men ready to march on Providence. The "legal" government officials were ready. On June 25, Governor Samuel King declared martial law and assembled nearly three thousand troops in Providence. At the request of the Law and Order Party, Providence's black community raised two companies and nearly two hundred men, which eventually became part of the Providence Home Guard and helped patrol the streets of the city. The army of the chartered government was quick in putting the Dorr rebellion down: by July 2, all government forces had returned to their home stations to resume civilian activities, and on July 4—the day the People's Legislature was to reconvene with a Governor Dorr in the executive branch—the Providence militia held a massive parade to celebrate its victory.

Some commentators have asserted that the victory of the government's forces was in large part a result of the help of the black community in and around Providence.[115] Whether this is the case or not is less important than the political calculation made by both Rhode Island's blacks and the Law and Order Party amid the Dorr turmoil. Faced with exclusion from the Suffrage Party's push for the extension of the franchise, the black community had no choice but to seek a political alliance with the Law and Order Party. In turn, the Law and Order Party was for all intents and purposes indebted to blacks, and in return for their support, many leaders of the constitutional convention called in September 1842 advocated striking the word "white" from the suffrage clause. When the constitution was completed and ratified, blacks were granted the franchise, but foreign-born males in Rhode Island would have to meet the $134 freehold qualification. In the last days of the convention, the delegates voted to drop the word "white" from the suffrage clause by a vote of 45–15.[116] In November 1842, the constitution was approved 7,024–51—although Dorr and the Suffragists urged their supporters to boycott it, which they did. By January 1843, as a result of the extraordinary events that flowed from the Dorr War, blacks were granted the right to vote in Rhode Island.

Conclusion

Reflecting on the extraordinary events of the Dorr War, Frederick Douglass commented that, "we cared nothing for the Dorr Party on the one hand, or the 'law and order' party on the other. What we wanted, and what we labored to obtain, was a constitution free from the word *white*."[117] Indeed, blacks had made a political calculation in the midst of the conflict that worked to their advantage. Chased out of a coalition with Thomas Dorr and the Suffrage Association, they had little choice but to throw their weight behind the Law and Order Party during the conflict. Blacks emerged on the winning side of the conflict and achieved their objective of the elective franchise—they found themselves in the right place at the right time. However, to begin and end with such political exigencies would be to overlook the changing dynamic of race formation that preceded the Dorr War and the factors that essentially made it possible for blacks to be "in the right place at the right time" and exploit the situation for advantage.

From the 1820s on, blacks in Rhode Island had lifted themselves up and out of slavery. Yet, by 1840 blacks could well make the case that they had been "industrious," and they pointed to their black churches and black schools, and the members of the community who had become well-to-do and respectable in the eyes of whites. By that time, they had become fairly organized. During the Dorr conflict, for example, petition after petition was submitted by black leaders Alfred Niger and Alexander Crummell containing extraordinary rhetorical devices: they drew upon fundamental aspects of the American belief in industry, fairness, and equality. But they were more than mere rhetoric. Once the Dorr conflict ensued, their justifications for equal citizenship were backed up with some solid evidence of their "worthiness" because of their economic independence and industriousness.

Yet, that same black "industriousness" amid the isolation nonetheless created racial and economic tensions with what would become the core base of the Suffrage movement: poorer and foreign-born whites. By the early 1840s these social, demographic, and economic realities structured the partisan nature of the conflict. The nativist sentiments in the Law and Order Party had reached such proportions that, to the minds of the leaders of the Party, blacks posed less of a threat than white, largely Catholic immigrants. As Elisha Potter, Whig politician who had served as president of the constitutional convention of 1824, noted in the wake of the Dorr conflict: "[The Law and Order Party] would rather have the negroes vote than the d——d Irish."[118] Nativism cut to the center of the Dorr conflict. Furthermore, nativism became connected in a significant way to the abolitionist movement that had by the 1830s become highly organized. We shall also see the impact of nativist fears on Massachusetts politics during this time period in the next chapter. Here it should be pointed out that Rhode Island abolitionists fought against slavery in the South but became intensely involved in promoting free suffrage for blacks at home throughout the Dorr War. Let us return for a brief moment to Dorr sympathizer William Goodell, who underscored this point after the conflict:

> If abolitionists may stand aloof from the oppressed *white* men of Rhode Island, because they, and their friends in other states, stand aloof from the oppressed *colored* men of the country, then may the oppressed whites of R. Island, and their friends, on the same principle, stand aloof from the efforts of abolitionists, on the ground that they do not care, equally, for the rights of the poor and the wronged *whites*. Such a prejudice against abolitionists has extensively existed, from the beginning, because, it has been said, there are aristocrats in their ranks. ... If abolitionists can see white liberty crushed in Rhode Island, without alarm and sympathy, the objection will acquire vast force.[119]

Nativism and abolitionism combined to give blacks a space for political opportunities amid the conflict. But that space was created *only after* the suffrage movement had succumbed to ascriptivism, against the wishes of some of its most important leaders.

Ultimately, my contention is that these contingent forces allowed for the (re)emergence of racial paternalism in Rhode Island during the Dorr conflict. Racial ascriptivism may have infected the Suffrage movement, but in the final instance it was not Rhode Island's Whigs who maintained political power. In the case of Rhode Island, racial paternalism had its direct roots in the experience of the tiny rebelling colony during the Revolutionary era. As a New York newspaper at the conclusion of the Dorr War put it:

> The colored people of the Rhode Island deserve the good opinion and kind feeling of every citizen of the State, for their conduct during the recent troublous times in Providence. They promptly volunteered their services for any duty to which they might be useful in maintaining law and order. Upwards of a hundred of them organized themselves for the purpose of acting as a city guard for the protection of the city, and to extinguish fires, in case of their occurrence, while the citizens were absent on military duty. The fathers of these people were distinguished for their patriotism and bravery in the war of the Revolution, and the Rhode Island colored regiment fought, on one occasion, until half their numbers were slain. There was not a regiment in the service which did more soldierly duty, or showed itself more devotedly patriotic.[120]

The actions on the part of blacks during the Revolutionary War, which both fed and justified the racial paternalism of the Revolutionary era, were played out again during the Dorr War. Blacks had proven themselves—once again—worthy of the rights of citizenship among the white elite of the Law and Order Party. Their reward was the elective franchise. Once again, Goodell understood the paternalistic sentiment undergirding the choice of the Law and Order political leaders to grant the franchise to blacks:

> Up to [May 1841], as we know, the suffrage party were hooted at, for wishing to admit the "low Irish and the niggers to the polls." ... But the tune has turned now. When the contest came lately, to the sword, the city aristocracy were [sic] willing to have the help of the colored people, the most of whom were their dependents, their laborers, their coachmen and their domestics. They enrolled them as firemen, and admitted some of them into the military ... the admission of the dependent colored people to vote, as well as to fight, and the boast of their support, *answers their selfish purposes and is impudently trumpeted to their praise.*[121]

These are the factors that allowed blacks to be "in the right place at the right time" when the Dorr War ensued. Black enfranchisement was the outcome.

I would be remiss if I closed this chapter without making one last—and perhaps tangential—point on race formation in Rhode Island. The evidence presented above supports the claim that a realignment of Rhode Island's political parties took place as a consequence of the Dorr conflict. My sense is that race formation played a significant role in that realignment *before* the Dorr War. The partisanship displayed by the Whigs and the Democrats in Rhode Island was structured more by statewide demographic and sectional conflicts than by national ideological divisions. Thomas Dorr himself began his political career as a Whig, became a founding member of the Constitutional Party in the mid-1830s, switched his allegiance to the Democrats in the late 1830s, and then aligned himself with the Suffrage Association and its offshoot, the Suffrage Party. Indeed, the suffragists transcended conventional partisan lines, as Richman makes clear: "As for the Dorr Rebellion and national party politics, there is a sense in which at first there no connection between them. The suffragists were composed of Whigs and Democrats alike."[122] After the Dorr War, two political parties of Rhode Island aligned more closely with the national parties on the issue of race. The Democrats indeed became the Jacksonian "white man's party" after the conflict, while the Whigs formed an alliance with blacks until their demise in the mid-1850s. Cottrol estimates that somewhere between seven hundred and one thousand blacks voted consistently—comprising anywhere from nearly 5 percent to 22 percent of the vote—after their enfranchisement in 1843.[123]

At times, it was the difference between winning and losing. For instance, the Whigs lost the gubernatorial race of 1845 by a few hundred votes but managed to win it the following year by less than one hundred votes. During the election of 1848 in which the slaveholding Whig Zachary Taylor was matched against Democrat Lewis Cass and Free Soiler Martin Van Buren, the Whig newspaper *Providence Journal* drew on the paternalism that had led to the enfranchisement of blacks and reminded them of the alliance they had formed. The day before the election that November, it stated:

> The party which gave you the right to vote asks for your votes tomorrow. The men who have always stood by you ask you to stand by them. They ask you to do no new thing, to support no new principles, but only to stick by your old friends and your old principles. They ask you to stand by the Whig Party, which is our party and your party;—the party of freedom and liberality and of all enlightened progress. ... After having enjoyed the right of suffrage for six years and during all that time maintained the character of orderly citizens, will you now make Dorrites of yourselves by voting for Martin Van Buren. ... It is almost an insult to ask such questions. We know that you will not; we know that you will vote tomorrow just as you have always voted and will give another evidence of your attachment to correct principles and sound government.[124]

One cannot help but note the irony in the choice black Rhode Islanders had between a slaveholder in Taylor and the person largely responsible for effectively disenfranchising thousands of New York's blacks in Van Buren, as we saw in Chapter 2. Nonetheless, despite misgivings about voting for a slaveholder, blacks in Rhode Island voted the Whig ticket faithfully that year and continued to do so until antislavery and nativism completely consumed the party in the mid-1850s.

CHAPTER 5

"The Vaunted Superiority of the White Race Imposes Corresponding Duties"

Massachusetts—The "Exception" to the Rule

The Persistence of Racial Paternalism in Antebellum Massachusetts

Charles Sumner stood before the Supreme Court of Massachusetts on December 4, 1849, to argue the case of Sarah Roberts, a five-year-old black girl who was denied entrance into one of Boston's all-white Common Schools.[1] Segregated schools had existed in Boston for over a half-century and were largely the by-product of black agitation in the years following the Revolution. In 1787, a group of black Bostonians first petitioned the state legislature to furnish education of some sort because they received no benefit from the free schools of Boston.[2] Suspicion and prejudice created a hostile environment for their children that stamped them with a badge of inferiority. The Massachusetts legislature refused the plea, but a well-organized black community and its white benefactors persisted. A decade later, with financial backing from prominent Bostonians, the Revolutionary War hero and black activist Prince Hall founded a school for black children in his home. The project was short-lived because of a yellow fever epidemic. But continued pressure was placed on city officials, and by 1806 the first permanent school for blacks settled into the basement of the African Baptist Church. Now, nearly fifty years after the successful struggle to create all-black schools in Boston, Sumner was before the highest court in the state at the behest of black and white abolitionists to argue that the same system of segregation did irreparable harm to both black *and* white children.

Sumner's challenge in *Roberts v. City of Boston* was to find a constitutional basis on which to rest his claim of equal protection of the law for Sarah Roberts. The contentious struggle over the passage of the Fourteenth Amendment—a roiling debate in the 39th Congress in which Sumner himself would be at the epicenter—was still twenty years down the road. With no federal recourse thus available, Sumner instead turned to the Massachusetts Declaration of Rights found at beginning of the State Constitution of 1780. The Declaration was drafted by one of the patriarchs of Massachusetts politics in the Revolutionary Era, John Adams, and reflected the natural rights philosophy circulating in the newly created states. It contained this simple statement in the First Article: "All men are born free and equal; and have certain natural essential, and unalienable rights, among which may be reckoned the right of enjoying and defending their lives and liberties."[3] Sumner used these principles to argue that *all* citizens of Massachusetts enjoyed what he called "equality before the law," and that the object of the State Constitution of Massachusetts "was to efface all political or civil distinctions, and to abolish all institutions founded upon *birth*."[4] To Sumner, Boston's segregated schools created a caste system much like that found in India. That system was not only inherently unequal, it was also patently "evil." He maintained that "the school is the little world where the child is trained for the larger world of life. It is the microcosm preparatory to the macrocosm. ... And since, according to our institutions, all classes, without distinction of color, meet in the school, beginning there those relations of Equality which the Constitution and Laws promote to all."[5] In other words, Sumner argued that the laws of the city should be applied in a colorblind fashion, but doing so would lead to a diverse student body that would better prepare Boston's children—*both white and black*—for the racialized world surrounding them.[6]

Although Justice Lemuel Shaw found much to agree with in Sumner's argument, he ultimately ruled against Sarah Roberts. His opinion for the unanimous court laid the theoretical groundwork for the "separate but equal" doctrine put forth by the Supreme Court fifty years later in *Plessy v. Ferguson* (1896). To be sure, Shaw never used the phrase "separate but equal." But the decision nonetheless hinted at its premise strongly, as he contended that any governmental entity had the power to classify citizens according to race as long as it was done "reasonably." Shaw explained that:

> In the absence of special legislation on this subject, the law has vested the power in the [school] committee to regulate the system

of distribution and classification; and when this power is *reasonably exercised*, without being abused or perverted by colorable pretences, the decision of the committee [to segregate students] must be deemed conclusive.[7]

The crux of Shaw's argument rested on the idea that equality and racial classification were not inherently incompatible—which, of course, was the opposite conclusion Chief Justice Earl Warren would come to a century later in the *Brown* case. In words that Justice Henry Billings Brown would quote nearly verbatim in the majority opinion of the *Plessy* case some fifty years later, Shaw concluded: "It is urged, that this maintenance of separate schools tends to deepen and perpetuate the odious distinction of caste, founded in a deep-rooted prejudice in public opinion. This prejudice, if it exists, is not created by law, and probably cannot be changed by law."[8] As long as the decision to segregate children along racial line was arrived at reasonably—or rather, as long as the decision was ostensibly grounded in the "reasonable prejudice" of public opinion—the school committee was justified in doing what it did. Sarah Roberts would have to continue to attend the all-black Boston school.

The decision outraged black and white abolitionists in Boston who had been agitating for school desegregation for over a decade. The list of activists involved in the struggle included the most fervent proponents of abolitionism throughout the antebellum North: William Lloyd Garrison, Wendell Phillips, Theodore Parker, Charles Lenox Remond, William C. Nell, and Francis and Edmund Jackson, to name but a few.[9] Unbowed in the wake of Shaw's ruling, they continued the struggle. By then, the national conflict over slavery had transformed electoral politics in Massachusetts. The 1840s saw the rise of the antislavery Liberty Party, which drew a significant amount of votes from both Whigs and Democrats. In 1851 a remarkable coalition consisting of Democrats and Free Soilers ousted the dominant Whig Party statewide. Three years later, the Know-Nothing Party, running on an antislavery and anti-immigrant platform, swept into power by capturing the mayor's office in Boston, the governor's mansion, every seat in the state Senate, and 351 of 359 seats in the lower House.[10] In 1855, the Massachusetts legislature passed a law stating that any child entering public schools in the Commonwealth shall not be denied entry "on account of race, color, or religious opinions of the applicant or scholar."[11] Thus, some six years after the *Roberts* case and six years before the onset of the Civil War, Massachusetts had completely desegregated its public school system.

In doing so, the state had removed yet another vestige of legal discrimination against blacks. No doubt wanton acts of prejudice, racism, and violence persisted. But the legal rights of citizenship had been extended further to blacks in Massachusetts than in any other part of the country outside New England. On the eve of the Civil War, blacks in Massachusetts could legally intermarry with whites. They were allowed to ride in the same train cars, worship at the same churches, go to the same theatres, and sleep in the same hotels as whites. Black children were allowed to attend the same schools as white children. After several setbacks, Massachusetts had also passed a personal liberty law for runaway slaves. And black males in the state had been legally entitled to the franchise since the abolition of slavery in the state in the 1780s.[12] The only rights of citizenship denied to blacks in antebellum Massachusetts were the right to sit on a jury, the right to testify against whites in court, the right to own a passport, and the right to serve in the militia.[13] These formidable restrictions notwithstanding, the evidence is undeniable that Massachusetts remained one of the most racially liberal states in the period between the Founding and the Civil War.

The *Roberts* case has cast its shadow over significant portions of the ongoing conflict surrounding race and the law for the last 150 years. It was the first desegregation case in the United States and served as a precursor to all subsequent cases leading up to *Brown v. Board of Education* (1954). Sumner's eloquent argument and Shaw's lucid opinion both lie at the foundation of the debate that has raged in civil rights jurisprudence over colorblindness and equal protection from *Plessy* right up to the present.[14] *Roberts* also provided the major conceptual framework for the drafting of the Fourteenth Amendment in the 39th Congress during Reconstruction.[15]

Yet I want to suggest that *Roberts* also casts a shadow back in time, and serves as a lens through which to view race formation in Massachusetts in the period before the Civil War. A snapshot of the dominant racial attitudes of Massachusetts is contained in the ostensibly innocuous way Sumner chose to close his argument before the Massachusetts Supreme Court that December day in 1849. After his long discourses on the concept of equality before the law in Western thought, on the concept of caste in India, and on the concept of "the Christian spirit" from which is derived the "solemn assurance of the Equality of Men, as an Ordinance of God," Sumner concluded by saying:

> That is not all. The vaunted superiority of the white race imposes corresponding duties. The faculties with which they are endowed, and the advantages they possess, must be exercised for the good of all. If the colored people are ignorant, degraded, and unhappy, then should they be especial objects of care. From the abundance of our possessions must we seek to remedy their lot. And this Court, *which is parent to all the unfortunate children of this Commonwealth,*

will show itself truly parental, when it reaches it down, and, with the strong arm of Law, elevates, encourages, and protects our fellow colored citizens.[16]

Sumner ended his argument in *Roberts* not only by contending that whites were superior to blacks in social condition but by intimating that whites also were superior in natural faculties. But with that superiority came "corresponding duties" to care for blacks the way parents care for their children. And the Court, "the parent to all unfortunate children of this Commonwealth," had a special responsibility in the uplift of the black race. Where Sumner had earlier contended that all institutions should be "effaced" of all distinctions based on race, by the end of his argument he had suggested that the true promise of equality—if it existed at all—could only be manifested through racial paternalism. Concomitantly, the government of Massachusetts had to be imbued with an institutional sense of paternalism toward blacks and granted the power to act on these sentiments.

The views expressed in Sumner's closing comment fit seamlessly within the larger paternalistic attitudes manifested throughout the North in the antebellum period we have seen in the previous chapters. Yet, the state of Massachusetts is somewhat "exceptional" in this regard: racial paternalism remained particularly strong in the Bay State throughout the antebellum era. It took hold in the decade before the Revolutionary War when the discourse of natural rights first appeared in the arguments of white elites of the Bay Colony as they began to buck the British Crown. It dominated the thinking on race in the state in the last quarter of the eighteenth century when slavery was abolished and blacks were granted the right to vote. Racial paternalism held sway in the thinking of most political leaders and shaped the dynamic of racial politics in the state through the first and second party periods. This was the case when Federalists and Republicans competed vigorously for power right up to the election of John Quincy Adams to the presidency in 1824. As we shall see, however, it continued even in the thinking of many Massachusetts Democrats in the second-party era who had been aligned with their Jacksonian counterparts in the South on most national issues but who broke ranks with them beginning in the 1830s with the "gag rule" and more generally on questions of citizenship and slavery in the decades that followed. Whereas Democrats in other states north of the Mason Dixon Line held fast to ascriptive views and acted upon them by attempting to disenfranchise blacks from the electorate, many antislavery Democrats in Massachusetts rarely exhibited the same sentiments publicly or sought the same course of action. In short, racial ascriptivism did not take root in Massachusetts to the extent that it did in other northern states. It was nowhere near a potent force in state party politics as we have seen in either Pennsylvania and New York, or even neighboring Rhode Island, where it derailed the working class, biracial coalition that formed during the Dorr Rebellion.

Most important, paternalism also lay at the heart of the dominant racial ideology of the abolitionist movement when it emerged in Boston in the early 1830s. Though abolitionism did not become influential in national politics until the 1840s, it was a formidable agent in mitigating and blunting the effects of racial ascriptivism in state politics from the 1830s on. When many abolitionists broke with William Lloyd Garrison and turned from moral suasion to political action in the late 1830s and early 1840s, racial paternalism ran through the development of electoral politics via the state's Whig Party and the split between the "Conscience Whigs" and the "Cotton Whigs," into the creation of the Liberty Party, the Free Soil Party, the Know-Nothing Party, and finally the Republican Party.

The question, of course, is why racial ascriptivism never took root in Massachusetts the way it did in other states I have analyzed here. Put differently, why was Massachusetts the "exception" to the rule? In one sense, I agree with Bruce Laurie's lucid assessment of the racial politics of Massachusetts when he writes in his excellent work *Beyond Garrison: Antislavery and Social Reform:* "Race relations in Massachusetts, and perhaps the region at large, generally leaned toward the paternalistic end of the spectrum ... paternalism set the tone in law as well as social relations, without erasing other forms, and that for a want of a realistic alternative blacks tended to comply even as they struggled for equal rights."[17] Laurie states that the racial paternalism of Massachusetts was part of a larger "Yankee culture." In the closing pages of an incredibly detailed and comprehensive description of antebellum Massachusetts politics, Laurie concludes, "Racial paternalism was very much part of that [Yankee] legacy. It was not equality [between blacks and whites], to be sure, but it was as far as Yankees were prepared to go."[18]

Laurie is reacting, partly, to an early review of his work that questions whether or not his assessment of Massachusetts politics in the antebellum era can be described simply as "Massachusetts Exceptionalism." Laurie's response can be characterized as a qualified yes: "Massachusetts was undeniably different in degree and in kind on the question of antiforeignism and race."[19] This was indeed the case, and Laurie's trenchant analysis bears out these conclusions. When it comes to voting rights for blacks, Massachusetts was certainly the exception to the rule—just as we have seen with other civil rights that the state afforded to its black population. Yet, although Laurie's response to the question of the inherent exceptions in Bay State politics is accurate, the reasons that he concludes Massachusetts was so different do not fully satisfy my search for an explanation. Political culture sets the boundary conditions for the larger political dynamic at work; but it must be viewed within the context of that larger dynamic. As I have emphasized in previous chapters, racial paternalism is but one part of race formation as it developed in each state as well as across state lines. So, too, with Massachusetts. There were other underlying factors at work in conjunction with the racial narratives put forward by leaders in the state. Massachusetts underwent its own "exceptional" development with respect to both demographic and partisan shifts, which, considered in conjunction with the persistence of racial paternalism, help us to explain why blacks were granted the right to vote early in the state's history and why that right was never denied to blacks.

It is to these underlying factors that I first turn before analyzing the discursive developments in the state. In the next section, I address the demographic changes Massachusetts underwent in the antebellum period. There I argue that the state's small black population, combined with what I call the "arrested development" of white (mainly Irish) immigration, both served to reinforce the dominant racial paternalism. Blacks made up a tiny minority of the state's population throughout the antebellum period. Moreover, in contrast to other Northern states such as Pennsylvania and New York and, to a lesser extent, Rhode Island, the black density in the population consistently decreased. Blacks did not migrate to Massachusetts in the late eighteenth and early nineteenth centuries to the extent that they did to other Northern states. Accordingly, the "race threat" hypothesis failed to fully materialize in the political discourse the way we saw, for instance, with Pennsylvania. Curiously, Massachusetts was on the front lines of the rhetorical wars over slavery from the 1830s on, but was never on the front lines geographically the way Pennsylvania was. Coupled with that is the fact that white immigration—and particularly Irish immigration—was relatively small until the 1830s and 1840s. The antiforeign exclusionist politics that lay at the heart of Know-Nothingism really did not take shape until the 1850s, after the Irish fled the famines in Ireland. Whereas in other states the arrival of the Irish allowed political actors seeking partisan advantage to play on racial fears and espouse ascriptive views concerning blacks early in the state's history, the same set of factors did not take place in Massachusetts. The arrested development of white immigration thus served to arrest the development of racial ascriptivism until the second-party period.

But, as I contend later in the chapter, by that time it was too late: during the second-party period, racial paternalism had become entrenched as the dominant view throughout the political party structure in the state. Despite heightened partisan competition in both the first-party period, race was a secondary issue in state politics. During the first two decades of the nineteenth century, Federalists and Republicans oftentimes competed vigorously for office. Yet, unlike in New York and Pennsylvania, race remained in the background. Partisan competition, in other words, did not bring race to the center of the political debate as elsewhere. By the 1830s and 1840s, political actors in Massachusetts began to take prominent stances on the issue of slavery. In doing so, they heightened attention to the rights of blacks back in their home state. Each time they focused on slavery in the South, they were forced to address the issue of rights for blacks in their own backyard. As Laurie points out, this had a damaging effect on the Democratic Party in the state.[20] Because many Democrats and Whigs (as well as the members of the Liberty and Free Soil Parties) were largely antislavery, the parties were consequently forced toward a consensus of sorts on the rights for blacks in Massachusetts, further imposing paternalistic tendencies among the state's leaders. I argue that the arrival of Garrison and abolitionism in the 1830s furthered these dominant attitudes in the state and kept the pressure on political leaders to protect and expand blacks' rights.

Later, I come back to the racial discourse of the state and argue that, beginning as early as the 1760s, racial paternalism became the dominant racial belief system in the state. Like Laurie, who terms the racial views peculiar to Massachusetts part of the "Yankee culture," I contend that leading partisans and abolitionists mostly adhered to these sets of racial attitudes. Yet, placed in the context of the other states we have looked at here, the racial paternalism of Massachusetts looks similar to that in other states even if it is more entrenched and dominant. The discussion in Section IV focuses on the views of party leaders from Federalists and Republicans in the first-party era to Whigs, Democrats, Libertyites, and Free Soilers in the second-party era. Finally, I analyze the thinking of William Lloyd Garrison in closing. Garrison's views were certainly radical or "egalitarian" in nature. Yet, my intent on highlighting them is to make the case for his relevance in keeping state party leaders in their more racially paternalistic stances in the state from the 1830s to the Civil War.

My argument here is that blacks maintained the right to vote in Massachusetts because of the "exceptional" way that the three components of race formation developed in the state in the antebellum period. One more point should be made before proceeding. In many ways, what follows is the story of the "nonevent" of the racial disenfranchisement of blacks in Massachusetts. Unlike the other states I have analyzed, there was no climactic debate waged on the issue. The franchise was granted to blacks in the early 1780s and was never legally denied to them throughout the antebellum period. It was not debated in the state Constitutional Conventions of 1779, 1821, and 1853. Part of the reason, of course, is because of the relatively tiny black population—blacks neither provided a decisive electoral advantage nor posed a real political threat to any political actors. In proceeding, I am fully aware of the argument that one may not find a "there there" in my analysis.

Yet, although small in population, the black communities of Massachusetts were well organized and fought valiantly for their civil rights, as Lois and James Horton have shown.[21] I accept and agree to an extent that expediency guided many political leaders in these decisions—quite plainly, denying the right to vote for blacks would get them nowhere, especially when leaders from Massachusetts played such a prominent role in the debates around slavery and would look hypocritical if they rolled rights back at home. But, as I hope to show, principle plays a role in explaining why blacks were not denied the right to vote at a time when blacks in other states were being disenfranchised. The racial attitudes of the abolitionists and their moral crusade against slavery in the South protected the rights of blacks in the Bay State. This lies at the crux of Laurie's Massachusetts Exceptionalism—and I agree with it. But the narratives they constructed about race and citizenship must be placed within the larger concept of race formation that I have attempted to sketch out in detail in other states.

From Slavery to Freedom: Demographic Development in Massachusetts

Slavery was introduced into the colony of Massachusetts in 1638. It came on the heels of the arrival of Pilgrims escaping religious persecution from England. In 1641, the first statute justifying slavery in the New World was passed in Massachusetts. Known as the Body of Liberties, it provided that slaves would not be found in the Bay Colony "unless it be lawful captives in just wars, as willingly sell themselves or are sold to us, and such shall have the liberties and Christian usage which the law of God established in Israel concerning such persons doth morally require; provided this exempts none from servitude, who shall be judged thereto by authority."[22] Rather than outlawing slavery outright, the Body of Liberties actually legalized the enslavement of Indians and Africans in Massachusetts.[23] And its roots were religious in nature. In a report issued by the Massachusetts House of Representatives in 1822 on the migration of "Negroes and Mulattoes" into the state, Federalist politician Theodore Lyman commented that the statute proved "that our ancestors were much governed in their notions concerning bondage by the doctrines of the Levitical Code ... and it is probably owing to the provisions made by Moses in favor of slavery, that they themselves were afterwards made to regard it with some degree of complacency."[24] In contrast to Pennsylvania, where German Quakers reasoned as early as the 1680s that *any* form of slavery violated the laws of Christianity, slavery in Massachusetts was introduced, justified, and perpetuated on biblical grounds.

By 1676, there were nearly two hundred slaves of African descent in the colony. The number of slaves remained fairly constant until the end of the seventeenth century, when a precipitous rise in their importation occurred. From 1698 to 1707, two hundred slaves were imported to Massachusetts—approximately the same number as the previous sixty years.[25] The sharp rise in the number of slaves startled the white colonists, and in 1704 the Selectmen of the town of Boston responded by issuing a decree to the British Crown. In it, they stated that they "are desired to promote the encouraging of white servants, and to put a period to Negroes being slaves."[26] The next year, a law was passed imposing a duty of 4 pounds on every Negro imported into the colony. The duty was refunded if the slave was exported within a year or died within six weeks.[27] In 1708, Governor Dudley issued a report that suggested that slaves were not as desirable as white servants because the latter could be used in the militia as well as in the fields.[28] The colony also sought to limit the number of Indians slaves— particularly those from the Tuscaroras Tribes of South Carolina—by passing a law prohibiting their importation.[29] Despite these attempts, however, slavery continued to proliferate in the colony. By 1720, the number of slaves expanded to two thousand. Fifteen years later, there were twenty-six hundred slaves in Massachusetts.

If resistance to slavery existed in the Bay Colony in the first half of the eighteenth century, it was leveled predominantly on economic and material rather than on moral and religious grounds. The small Quaker minority in Massachusetts provided the only moral opposition to slavery during this period. In 1700, the Quaker judge Samuel Sewall spoke out against the buying and selling of human beings as un-Christian. His published remarks drew spirited responses from his Calvinist counterparts.[30] Williams contends that the Quaker minority in Massachusetts remained fervently but "secretly" opposed to slavery for fear of reprisal by the "Puritans."[31] The Puritanical code was thus used as a justification for separating persons of African descent from Europeans and denying them the rites of Christianity. African slaves were routinely denied baptism during this period. Baptism implied humanity, and any person who was human could not be held in bondage. Similarly, a law passed in 1705 specifically prohibited any "Christian" from marrying a Negro.

The predominant thinking on slavery in Massachusetts changed precipitously in the wake of the First Great Awakening. By the middle of the eighteenth century, slavery became a moral problem to Quakers and Calvinists alike. In 1755, the town of Salem instructed its representative

Thomas Pickering to petition the General Court against the further importation of slaves. The petition is noteworthy because it was the first of its kind to be made on moral grounds.[32] A decade later the town of Worcester requested that its representative do everything he could "to obtain a law to put an end to that unchristian and impolitic practice of making slaves of the human species ..." Boston followed with a similar request a year later.[33] The colony's legislature was soon inundated with petitions. In 1767, the first bill seeking to "prevent the unwarrantable and unlawful Practice or Custom of inslaving [sic] Mankind" was introduced into the House of Representatives. The bill died because of resistance from the larger towns, but a growing sentiment against slavery grounded in the natural rights philosophy of the period had taken root in Massachusetts. For the next ten years, bills abolishing slavery were introduced into the legislature. As was the case in other colonies, the arguments against slavery were joined with arguments against the oppression of the British Crown, which rested on the "inalienable rights of man." However, the experience of Massachusetts was different in one significant respect: blacks themselves took a more activist role in the abolition of slavery in the Bay Colony than perhaps anywhere else in the rebelling colonies.

As early as 1766, black slaves began to sue in the Massachusetts courts for their freedom, a right granted to them indirectly through the colonial charter. Court cases involving slaves continued through the Revolutionary years and culminated in the Quock Walker cases of 1783, which by most accounts abolished slavery in the Bay State. The first petition by blacks objecting to their enslavement was sent to the King's Governor and the House of Representatives in 1773. A year later, the General Court submitted a bill abolishing slavery, but Governor Hutchinson refused it, claiming that the Crown had not granted him authority to act on it.[34] In 1777 the Assembly introduced another bill abolishing slavery that also went nowhere. That same year, slaves in the state submitted a second petition claiming their "natural and inalienable right to ... freedom."[35] In 1778, lawmakers of the state drafted a restrictive constitution that protected the practice of slavery on the one hand and denied the right of suffrage to free blacks on the other. When the new constitution was put to a vote that same year, it was defeated decisively. Some scholars have concluded that an absence of a bill of rights as well as its antiblack provisions were significant causes for its failure.[36]

Two years later, the citizens of Massachusetts ratified a more liberal constitution that formed the foundation for both the abolition of slavery and the right to vote for black males. As mentioned at the outset of this chapter, its first article was drafted by John Adams and declared that "All men are born free and equal and have certain natural essential, and unalienable rights, among which may be reckoned the right of enjoying and defending their lives and liberties ..." Furthermore, the document set qualifications for voting on the basis of sex, age, and property. Race was not mentioned. Black activists quickly took advantage of the ambiguous nature of the state constitution. In 1781, Revolutionary War hero and renowned black seamen Paul Cuffe and his brother petitioned the town fathers of Dartmouth and inquired "whether all free Negroes and mulattoes ... have the same privileges ... as white people ... respecting places of profit, [and] choosing officers."[37] Richard Collens, the town Constable of Dartmouth, accepted their tax payment and provided them with a receipt. Reflecting on the Cuffes' petition in his *Colored Patriots of the American Revolution*, black abolitionist William C. Nell concluded: "It was ascertained by these proceedings, that taxes must be paid, the receipts being forwarded; and this case, although no action followed in Court, settled the right of the colored man to the elective franchise in the state of Massachusetts."[38]

Thus, within a crucial four-year period between the late 1770s and early 1780s, slavery was abolished and blacks were granted the right to vote in Massachusetts. The Constitution of 1780 provided the legal justification for each. Despite the controversy surrounding the Quock Walker cases of 1783, scholars have come to the agreement that they did in fact put an end to slavery.[39] The first national census taken in 1790 listed 5,463 blacks in the state, none of whom were identified as slaves.[40] Blacks would continue to enjoy the right to vote without interruption throughout the antebellum period.[41]

The high levels of activism on the part of the small black community in Massachusetts during the Revolutionary years is a significant factor in explaining why slavery ended when it did on the one hand, and why blacks were granted the right to vote so early in the state's history on the other. Blacks and sympathetic whites utilized the natural rights discourse of the Revolutionary era to their fullest advantage in arguing for the equal rights of citizenship. Movement politics, coupled with arguments for black citizenship grounded in the environmentalist, natural rights philosophy of the Revolutionary era, continued to play a causal role in the successful struggle for black rights in Massachusetts throughout the antebellum period. Both, however, must be understood within the context of the development of party politics. I will come back to a discussion of each of these factors a bit later. For now, it is important to fasten onto the underlying socioeconomic and demographic shifts in Massachusetts during this period to assess their impact on the politics of race. Despite some similarities, the demographic development of Massachusetts in the period between the Revolution and the Civil War was quite different than states to the south such as New York and Pennsylvania. Development in Massachusetts also differed to a large extent from its New England counterpart, Rhode Island.

TABLE 5.1 Black Population, Density, and Rates of Increase in Massachusetts, 1790–1860[42]

Year	Black Population	Black Density (%)	Black Rate of Increase from Previous Census (%)	White Rate of Increase from Previous Census (%)
1790	5,463	1.44	—	—
1800	6,452	1.52	18.01	11.66
1810	6,737	1.43	4.41	11.63
1820	6,740	1.29	0.04	10.98
1830	7,048	1.15	4.56	16.83
1840	7,993	1.10	13.00	20.87
1850	9,064	0.91	15.39	35.17
1860	9,602	0.85	5.93	23.94

Similar to national trends in the years between 1790 and 1860, Massachusetts experienced an absolute numerical increase in the number of free blacks. Much as we have seen in Pennsylvania, New York, and Rhode Island, the Commonwealth's black population showed an increasingly urban orientation during these years. Blacks in Massachusetts moved from rural areas to urban centers—particularly from the western part of the state to the eastern part to settle in and around Boston. However, unlike Pennsylvania and, to a lesser extent, New York and Rhode Island, Massachusetts did not experience a sudden or sustained influx of blacks moving into the state from elsewhere. The density of blacks in the overall population began declining in the middle decades of the eighteenth century and continued to decline in every decade except one before the Civil War. In addition, the rate of growth in the black population paled in comparison to that of the larger white population, as Table 5.1 makes clear.

The overall density of the black population in the antebellum years peaked in 1800 at just over 1.5 percent. The largest increase in the black population occurred in the decade between the First and Second Census, taken respectively in 1790 and 1800. The 1790s was the only decade where the black rate of increase surpassed the white rate of increase. Even during the height of the abolitionist movement and the Underground Railroad network operating in Boston from the 1830s to the 1850s, the rate of white increase in the population surpassed the rate of black increase. On the eve of the Civil War, blacks made up less than 1 percent of the overall population of the state.

As manufacturing rivaled maritime and agricultural commerce as the linchpin to the state's economy in the opening decades of the nineteenth

Table 5.2 Population and Density in Boston, 1742–1845[43]

Year	Total Population	White Population	Black Population	% White	% Black
1742	16,382	15,008	1,374	91.61	8.39
1765	15,520	14,672	848	94.54	5.46
1790	18,320	17,534	766	95.82	4.18
1800	24,937	23,763	1,174	95.30	4.70
1810	33,787	32,319	1,468	95.66	4.34
1820	43,298	41,558	1,740	95.98	4.02
1825	58,281	56,364	1,917	96.71	3.29
1830	61,392	59,517	1,875	96.95	3.05
1835	78,603	76,846	1,757	97.76	2.24
1840	85,000	83,012	1,988[44]	97.66	2.34
1845	114,366	112,524	1,842	98.34	1.61

century, Boston and its satellite towns became more populated vis-à-vis the rest of the state.[45] In 1790, the population of Boston made up just 4.83 percent of the state's population. In 1840, the number had nearly tripled to 12.65 percent.[46] In the same period, blacks continued to migrate eastward toward Boston.[47] Yet, the influx of blacks into the urban centers in and around Boston did nothing to dramatically change the racial makeup of the city. Black density increased only twice in a hundred-year period between the 1740s and the 1840s, each time only slightly, as Table 5.2 indicates.

Tables 5.1 and 5.2 reveal that blacks constituted a tiny portion of the overall population of Massachusetts throughout the antebellum period. This, coupled with the downward trends in black densities over the same period, helps explain why there was very little concern by whites that blacks migrating to the state from elsewhere would overrun the state. The "race threat" argument did not materialize in Massachusetts to the extent that it did elsewhere. In fact, only once during the antebellum period was the issue of black immigration seriously debated, and it came in response to restrictive laws passed elsewhere in the North.

The debate occurred in the early 1820s amid a wave of state constitutional conventions and the uproar over the Missouri Compromise of 1820. In 1821, the state House of Representatives asked a select committee to determine whether a bill should be passed limiting the influx of free blacks and mulattoes into the state. The Committee was charged with determining the necessity of "checking the increase of a species of population, which threatens to be both injurious and burdensome ..."[48] It cited the state's prison population as cause for concern: as of January 1821, black inmates comprised "146th part" of the overall black population of the state, while white convicts formed but "2140th part" of the white population of the state. Referring to anti-black immigration laws passed in other states, the committee then considered a similar bill meant to "protect the population of this Commonwealth from all dangers and injuries, whether affecting morals or health."[49]

Although the committee referred to the racial makeup of the state prisons, it did not rely on statistics depicting the overall racial makeup of the state's population. It is not clear if accurate data were available to them. Yet, data gathered in subsequent censuses reveal that black migration into Massachusetts was virtually nonexistent in the opening decades of the nineteenth century. Black density in the state had decreased from 1.52 percent in 1800 to 1.29 percent in 1820. The overall black population rate of increase was about 4.5 percent in the same period, but just .04 percent from 1810 to 1820. Thus, although the passage of restrictive laws in other states served to sound the race threat alarm bells in Massachusetts, the evidence does not indicate that a real race threat existed.

The interesting thing about the committee's decision, however, is that it rejected the race threat hypothesis altogether in its conclusion: the committee based its findings neither on the *perception nor the reality* of black migration into the state. The Federalist politician Theodore Lyman was charged with drafting the committee's report. In it, he referred to the racially liberal tradition of the state dating back over the previous century and recommended that no restrictive law be passed. He reasoned that:

> a law, which should produce that effect [of barring free blacks and mulattoes from the state], would entirely depart from that love of humanity, that respect for hospitality and for the just rights of all classes of men, in the constant and successful exercise and maintenance of which, the inhabitants of Massachusetts have been singularly conspicuous.[50]

Political leaders in Massachusetts resisted the race threat argument that was being used elsewhere to justify the restrictions of rights of blacks. Lyman and the House committee instead fell back upon the dominant paternalistic racial ideology of the state that had predominated since the Revolution. In reality, there was indeed no cause to fear a sudden and precipitous increase in black migration: unlike Pennsylvania, Massachusetts was not physically on the frontlines of slavery. And, unlike New York City, Boston was not attracting significant numbers of blacks just up from slavery from either the South or other parts of the North. Yet Lyman and his committee chose to rest their arguments on racial paternalism.

We need to add here, however, that racial politics also developed differently in Massachusetts as a result of patterns of white immigration to

Massachusetts in the early part of the nineteenth century. Massachusetts did not experience massive immigration by non-English aliens in the late eighteenth and early nineteenth centuries as in other states in the North. Handlin asserts that the number of immigrants landing in Boston before 1830 never exceeded a total of 2,000.[51] Irish immigration was virtually non-existent throughout this period: from 1821 to 1836, a total of only 4,180 Irish entered Boston by sea.[52] After 1840, Irish immigration to Boston increased rapidly, such that by 1850 thirty-five thousand Irish resided in the city—or about 25 percent of the population.[53] The precipitous increase particularly in the Irish population of the city exacerbated the ethnic and racial cleavages of party politics during the 1840s and into the 1850s, when the nativist movement in Massachusetts culminated in the landslide victory of the Know-Nothings in the election of 1854. We will come back to this point later. For now, I only want to note that the trickle of Irish immigration into Massachusetts in the late eighteenth and early nineteenth century pales in comparison to the experiences of Pennsylvania and New York. Recall that in both of these states the Irish became a loyal constituency of the Jeffersonian Republicans as early as the 1790s. Democratic Party leaders were quick to utilize the Irish as a political wedge against their Federalist rivals in their attempt to paint the latter as decidedly pro-black.

The crucial point is that ethnic, racial, and party politics all converged in the first party era in these other states. This was not the case in Massachusetts. We might say that Massachusetts underwent a form of arrested development in terms of white migration. I contend that the absence of these ethnic and racial conflicts in the first party period in Massachusetts helps in our search to explain why the Democratic Party never successfully played the race card in the state once it developed and competed for power in Massachusetts in the second party system. The racial ascriptivism never took hold there in the early decades of the nineteenth century. This was at least partly a result of the economic and social development of the state. The white elites in both the Federalist and Republican parties of Massachusetts remained decidedly paternalistic in their racial attitudes. Furthermore, the small number of black voters neither posed a threat to party leaders nor provided a decisive advantage in electoral politics. This is not to suggest that the Jeffersonian Republicans did not compete for power with the Federalists during this period. On the contrary, party competition was at times quite vigorous in the state, as we shall see. But unlike Pennsylvania and New York, racial conflict was not a major factor in the dynamic of party competition in the opening decades of the nineteenth century. By the time the Democrats emerged in Massachusetts in the early 1830s, the abolitionist movement had taken root in the state and had begun to exert its influence on racial matters, particularly in state politics.

Abolitionism blunted the development of an ascriptive racial ideology of the Massachusetts Democratic Party at a time when Jacksonian Democracy became identified with it elsewhere.

Race, Partisanship, and Abolitionism, 1780s–1850s

Party Competition in the First-Party Period

Established political parties with consistent voting patterns were present in Massachusetts well before the Revolutionary era.[54] Patterson makes the case that the Court and Country "factions" functioned with a high degree of cohesion in the late provincial period. They aligned more clearly along sectional lines (eastern and western) amid revolutionary fervor in early 1774. While the Revolutionary War was being waged against the British Crown, western farmers found themselves pitted against eastern mercantile interests in a battle for rule at home. In 1777–1778, as Massachusetts debated a new constitution, the legislature passed a set of economic programs favored by coastal interests that further exacerbated the sectional conflict.[55] Nearly a decade later, the ongoing struggle would erupt full force in Shays' Rebellion in Western Massachusetts, an event that shook the foundations of the banking and merchant elite, prompting calls for a Constitutional Convention in the summer of 1787.

The Federalist/Anti-Federalist rivalry in Massachusetts thus had its origins in the economic conflict that had existed along sectional lines since pre-Revolutionary times. These old fissures persisted as delegates met in Boston in late 1787 to debate the ratification of the Constitution. Not surprisingly, eastern merchants supported the Constitution, while western farmers opposed it. With the delegation evenly divided, Governor John Hancock and his backers signaled that he would throw his support behind ratification if amendments protecting individual liberties from the federal government favored by the western faction were agreed to. Anti-Federalists such as Samuel Adams signed on, and, one week later, Massachusetts became the seventh state to ratify the Constitution.[56]

John Adams drafted Massachusetts' first Constitution in 1780. A decade later, he was part of the new federal government serving as vice president, aligning himself with Secretary of Treasury Alexander Hamilton and the incipient Federalist Party at the national level. In Massachusetts, Adams's Federalist allies held political power throughout the 1790s. Both Federalists and the minority Republicans supported Adams in his bids for president in 1796 and 1800. Although partisan competition intensified after Jefferson's election in 1800, Federalists continued to dominate Massachusetts politics for most of the next two decades. High levels of partisanship occurred particularly in the years before and during the War of 1812. Massachusetts Federalists were at the center of resistance to the national government's war effort. Partisanship declined during the "Era of Good Feelings." With Republican James Monroe in the White House, the Federalists nonetheless continued their political dominance in Massachusetts. Partisanship intensified briefly in 1823–1824 as the Republicans captured the governor's office in two highly contested elections. The first-party era abruptly ended in the state when John Quincy Adams was elected to the presidency in 1824. The Federalist Party ran its last candidate for governor in 1826 and then dissolved into the shifting Republican factions.

Scholars tend to agree that one measure of heightened partisan competition is an increase in voter turnout. The first party period in Massachusetts bears this out. Goodman contends that high voter turnout in Massachusetts at this relatively early stage is attributed to well-developed state party organizations that responded to an expanded electorate.[57] Formisano concurs that voter turnout increased precipitously after 1805 but reaches a different conclusion on the question of party organization. He asserts that the early party battles in the state were not at all organized.[58] Regardless of the differences in opinion on the levels of party organization during the first-party period in Massachusetts, two things are certain: first, although the Federalists held control for most of the last decade of the eighteenth century and first two decades of the nineteenth century, the Republicans competed vigorously for office. Second, levels of voting increased with party competition, particularly between the years 1805–1815, as Table 5.3 makes clear.

Only twice in the period between 1800 and 1825 did the Federalists receive over 60 percent of the vote for governor. The Republicans attained this feat once—in the uncontested election of 1825. Furthermore, Table 5.3 suggests a high correlation between party competition and higher voter turnout. In the years between 1805 and 1815, the Federalists and Republicans competed vigorously for the governor's office as victory margins remained slim throughout most of the decade. Those same years witnessed a dramatic increase in turnout. According to Formisano, turnout went from a low of just above 30 percent in 1804 to 70 percent in 1812. It dipped to under 50 percent in the years following the War of 1812 but spiked again to near 60 percent in the highly contested elections of 1823–1824 before falling off once again after the demise of the Federalists.[59]

Thus, party competition between Federalists and Republicans was stiff at times during the first party period. Jefferson's embargo and the onset of the War of 1812 stoked the flames of partisanship. In New England, where Federalism was particularly strong, objections to the war effort and the policies of the Virginia Dynasty in general led to the Hartford Convention

Table 5.3 Party Vote, Percentage, and Total Vote in Governor's Elections, 1800–1825[60]

Year	Federalist Vote	Republican Vote	Vote Total
1800	19,630 (50.3%)	17,019 (43.6%)	39,059
1801	25,452 (55.6%)	20,184 (44.1%)	45,816
1802	29,983 (60.5%)	19,443 (39.2%)	49,583
1803	29,199 (67.3%)	13,910 (32%)	43.409
1804	29,993 (55.1%)	24,006 (44%)	54,499
1805	35,204 (51.0%)	33,518 (48.6%)	68,986
1806	37,740 (50.2%)	37,109 (49.3%)	75,216
1807	39,234 (48.1%)	41,954 (51.5%)	81,516
1808	39,643 (48.9%)	41,193 (50.8%	81,147
1809	47,916 (51.3%)	45,118 (48.3%)	93,322
1810	44,079 (48.5%)	46,541 (51.2%)	90,813
1811	40,142 (47.8%)	43,328 (51.6%)	83,917
1812	52, 696 (50.6%)	51,326 (49.3%)	104,156
1813	56,754 (56.6%)	42,789 (42.7%)	100,223
1814	56,510 (54.8%)	46,502 (45.1%)	103,163
1815	51,099 (53.2%)	44,505 (46.4%)	95,963
1816	49,527 (51.1%)	47,321 (48.8%)	96,970
1817	46,610 (54.6%)	38,129 (45.1%)	84,496
1818	39,538 (55.7%)	30,041 (42.4%)	70,927
1819	42,875 (53.7%)	35,271 (44.2%)	79,885
1820[61]	31,072 (58.3%)	21,927 (41.7%)	53,297
1821	28,608 (58.3%)	20,268 (41.1%)	49,086
1822	28,487 (57.1%)	21,177 (42.5%)	49,849
1823	30,171 (46.2%)	34,402 (52.7%)	65,330
1824	34,210 (46.8%)	38,650 (52.9%)	73,051
1825	—	35,221 (94.1%)	37,426

in 1814. Federalists who gathered there seriously pondered secession. But moderates at the meeting were successful in deflecting the discussion toward reform measures, which included the proposal of seven constitutional amendments directed at Republican policies on the national level. Although it had little impact on the war effort, the Hartford Convention nonetheless provided a significant outlet for antiwar sentiment against "Mr. Madison" and the Republicans.[62] Even in the wake of the war effort, Federalists still dominated Massachusetts politics for the next decade.

Yet, for all the partisanship during this period, there was a certain consensus around which Federalists and Republicans in Massachusetts united. Party leaders on both sides of the political divide were guided by what Formisano describes as "antipartisan assumptions about the nature of politics and society."[63] Although passionate in their political convictions, Federalists and Republicans nonetheless expressed an antipartyism premised on a higher allegiance to the principles of the Revolution. The period between the 1780s and 1820s—or roughly the first-party era—possessed a split personality: partisan, on the one hand, but antiparty, on the other. Formisano calls this unlikely combination of centrism and antipartyism the "Politics of the Revolutionary Center."[64]

The Politics of the Revolutionary Center thrived because the leaders of both parties were all men of the Revolutionary generation. As such, they claimed to be true heirs to the Revolutionary Spirit of '76. What they disagreed about was who was more "patriotic" and loyal to that spirit. Republicans looked to the war effort and the Declaration of Independence drafted by their leader, Thomas Jefferson, and professed to be guardians of liberty. Federalists couched the war effort in the context of the larger process by which the American government was created, and emphasized the importance of heroes such as Hamilton who were Revolutionary Consolidators. Party identification thus took a back seat to this higher political identity. For Formisano, the Revolutionary Center is most clearly seen through the selection of state party leaders. For instance, every Massachusetts governor between the 1780s and the mid-1820s was a Revolutionary hero in some fashion: from John Hancock to John Brooks, all took part in the Revolutionary War effort, no matter what side of the political aisle they found themselves on in its aftermath.

But if it is true that this consensus formed out of a common experience and guided political actors throughout the first-party period, I want to make the claim that a consensus also formed in matters pertaining to race. Part of the common experience of the generation of political leaders in Massachusetts in the early national period included the discourse of "natural rights" of the Revolutionary era. The natural rights discourse ultimately provided the moral and normative justifications for their rebellious actions against the British. Nowhere was the "natural rights" of the colonialist and the "inalienable rights" of the slave tied together more closely than in the early abolitionist movement found in parts of New England. A narrative about race and citizenship that had been molded in the 1760s and 1770s remained in place in Massachusetts throughout the first party period. Whether Republican or Federalist, a defender of the Spirit of '76 or the Constitution, the political leaders of the state throughout this period had been acculturated to racial paternalism during the Revolutionary era. And the static nature of Massachusetts society during this period served to reinforce this consensus, unlike New York or Pennsylvania where the shifting underlying socioeconomic dynamic allowed politicians seeking partisan advantage to successfully utilize an alternative, ascriptive narrative about race and citizenship.

The Rise and Demise of the Whig Party

The election of John Quincy Adams in 1824 brought an end to both the Federalist Party and the first party period in Massachusetts. Quincy had broken ranks with the Federalists as early as 1808. He served in James Monroe's administration and helped to formulate the Monroe Doctrine. A majority of voters in Massachusetts supported its native son in the presidential elections of 1824 and 1828. By the time he lost to Jackson in 1828, party politics in the Bay State was at the end of a gradual transition to the second-party period.

During Quincy's term in office, former Federalist Daniel Webster emerged as a leading voice in state politics on the pressing issues of the day. By 1828, Webster had become one of the leading advocates for protectionist trade policies. Webster staked out a position that had grown popular with the new manufacturing elite of Massachusetts. By the second decade of the nineteenth century, large-scale cotton manufacturing had come to rival maritime trade as the principal economic activity. Cotton manufacturing drove the industrialization and urbanization of the state from the 1820s on. As we saw earlier, Boston and its surrounding towns became the center of economic activity as the population grew in Suffolk and neighboring counties. Much of the economic change can be traced back to the founding of the Boston Manufacturing Company by Frances Cabot Lowell in 1813.[65] By 1820, Lowell, Massachusetts, had become the cotton manufacturing center of New England. Webster's protectionist policies also favored the growing investment in the cotton industry by smaller local merchants. By the time that Jackson won the presidency in 1828 on a platform of free trade, the merchant class of Massachusetts had aligned behind Webster's protectionism. Jackson's opposition to internal improvements and his attack on the Bank of the United States further alienated business and political leaders of the state. By 1832, when Jackson successfully opposed Clay's American System, most of the political leadership of Massachusetts was solidly protectionist and largely anti-Jackson.[66] Two years later, the Massachusetts Whig Party was born.

The Whig Party of Massachusetts consisted of a coalition of cotton manufacturers, merchants, and native laborers who viewed high tariffs as needed job protection from detested immigrant labor. It pulled support from nearly every section of the state. In Laurie's view, the party's strength rested on an evangelical Protestantism mixed with secular corporatism.[67] Its economic ideology derived mainly from the old Federalist developmental focus on a strong national government and a stable manufacturing base. But Whiggery also contained an underlying ambivalence toward the shifting socioeconomic landscape of American society. The Whigs took an immediate interest in promoting sectional harmony with their southern counterparts, as the big manufacturers of the state worked closely with King Cotton in the South. Despite defections of prominent "Conscience" Whigs such as Charles Sumner and Charles Francis Adams with the onset of the Mexican-American War in 1846 and the nomination of Zachary Taylor as the party's presidential standard bearer in 1848, Massachusetts Whigs remained unified from 1834 to 1854 in opposing all attempts to implement any national policies that would alienate the Southern Whigs.[68]

The Whigs dominated state politics for the first two decades of the second party period. Whigs elected their candidate to the governor's office in every year except two between 1834 and 1848. In the same period, they controlled both houses of the legislature each year but one. Every United States Senator and twenty-seven of the thirty-one Representatives that served in the House were Whigs during this period. On the presidential level, Whig candidates captured the state's electoral vote four straight times—Webster in 1836, Harrison in 1840, Clay in 1844, and Taylor in 1848.[69]

Yet the seeds of the Whig demise in Massachusetts were sown in the nature of its coalition. On the one side, the manufacturing elite of the party opposed all denunciations of slavery and slaveholders. The big manufacturers of the state were business partners and close friends with southern slaveholding cotton producers. In principle, they argued that abolitionism in the North was unnecessary because the peculiar institution of slavery was protected by the Constitution. Abbott Lawrence summed up this position when he wrote to his friend Cassius Clay: "I am in favor of maintaining the compact established by our fathers. I am for the Union as it is. ... The abolition of slavery in the States is exclusively a State question and one with which I do not feel that I should meddle or interfere in any shape or form."[70]

Lawrence best exemplified the "Cotton Whig" position. Against the Cotton Whigs stood a group of antislavery men considered the old "Brahmins" of Massachusetts society—men such as John Quincy Adams, Charles Allen, and later Adams's son Charles Francis and Charles Sumner.[71] These Conscience Whigs were not tied to the cotton manufacturing elite of Massachusetts. They had in fact been displaced socially by the rise of the nouveau riche cotton manufacturers. Loyal Whigs nonetheless, they were left with the choice of either convincing Whig party leaders aligned with the cotton manufacturers that an antislavery stand would strengthen rather than weaken the party, or making an attempt to take control of the party altogether. At first, they opted for overtaking the party.[72] By the mid-1840s, the schism in the Whig Party had become irreparable. Since the late 1830s, John Quincy Adams had waged his lonely but fierce battle in Congress against the southern-supported Gag Rule on antislavery petitions. His efforts energized Conscience Whigs back in Massachusetts. Conscience Whigs became more adamant in their calls for abolition and began to justify their antislavery stances by referring back to the natural rights doctrines of the Revolutionary era. In a speech to fellow Whigs in Boston in 1846, Charles Sumner stated that "The Whigs should be the conservators of the ancestral spirit ... they should profess that truest and highest conservatism which watches, guards, and preserves, the greatest principles of Truth. Right, Freedom, and Humanity. Such a conservatism is the conservatism of '76."[73]

Conscience Whigs bolted from the Whig Party at the urging of John Quincy Adams and others in the aftermath of the Mexican-American War—precisely when the expansion of slavery resurfaced as the major national issue. It came amid the presidential election of 1848 as Cotton Whigs were determined to stand behind Whig nominee and slaveholder Zachary Taylor. Conscience Whigs placed their support behind Henry Clay. When Taylor was nominated at the national convention, Massachusetts Conscience Whig delegate Charles Allen denounced the nomination and addressed the convention by stating: "I declare to this convention my belief that the Whig Party is here and this day dissolved."[74] Allen's prediction was not far from the truth: that year many Whigs in Massachusetts supported former Democrat and Free Soil candidate Martin Van Buren. Two years later the Massachusetts Conscience Whigs became part of a remarkable coalition between the Free Soilers and Democrats. Their sole goal was to defeat what remained of the Whig Party. The "Coalition" captured state power briefly in 1851 and 1852. The Whigs returned to power in 1853, in time to narrowly defeat a new state constitution drafted by a delegation consisting largely of Coalition members. The vote across the state followed party lines with one exception: the burgeoning Irish Catholic community in Suffolk County, normally loyal to the Democratic Party, aligned itself with the Whigs and voted against the new constitution. The Irish vehemently opposed any form of antislavery measure and thus distanced themselves from the Democratic-Free Soil Coalition. One year later, with both antislavery and anti-immigrant sentiment percolating in Massachusetts, the Know-Nothings swept into power, essentially undoing what remained of the Whig Party in Massachusetts.[75]

The Democratic Party of Massachusetts

Throughout the second party period, the Democratic Party remained in the minority in Massachusetts. This is not to suggest that the Democrats were altogether an inconsequential force in state politics. During the 1830s and early 1840s, the Democrats consistently polled about 35 percent of the vote.[76] Between 1836 and 1848, Democratic gubernatorial candidates averaged roughly 41 percent of the vote and at times surpassed the 44 percent mark.[77] Twice in this period the Democrats won the governor's office—in 1840 and 1843, when perennial gubernatorial candidate and party leader Marcus Morton broke through to capture power. As we have seen, from 1850 to 1852 the Democrats controlled the state government by entering into an anti-Whig alliance with the Free Soil Party. The rise of Know-Nothingism put an end to both the Whigs and the Democrats as the state experienced a major political realignment in the 1850s.[78] With the passage of the Fugitive Slave Act in 1850, the election of Democrat Franklin Pierce to the presidency in 1852, and the Kansas-Nebraska Act in 1854, the Know-Nothings emerged abruptly in the struggle for the anti-Democratic movement in Massachusetts. The Know-Nothing Party, comprised of a coalition of antislavery and anti-immigrant forces, held power briefly from 1854 to 1857 before giving way to the emergent Republicans. Radical Republicans would hold power in Massachusetts until the 1870s. The Democrats, by contrast, became a casualty of the political changes of the 1850s and receded into the minority for the next twenty years.

The coalition that comprised the Massachusetts Democrat Party consisted of farmers, urban immigrant laborers, and small coastal fishermen. All were united in their hatred for the state's business and political elite. To Democrats, Whiggery had two faces: the cotton manufacturer Abbott Lawrence, on the one hand, and perennial Whig Senator Daniel Webster, on the other. Both symbolized the domination of urban wealth and social position that had existed in the state since the Revolutionary era. The Democrats of the 1820s and 1830s were the sons of the anti-Federalists of the late 1700s, and the arrival of Jacksonian Democracy signaled a revitalization of a forgotten antiaristocratic ideology that provided the impetus for the Democratic Party's political and ideological strength in the second-party period. As Irish immigrants streamed into Boston and its environs in the 1840s, they came under attack by rival workers. In response, the Irish naturally became allied with the Democratic Party and, like the Irish immigrants in other states across the North, actively resisted the abolitionist movement. But their alignment with the Democrats helped to create an influential minority party that had support across the different geographical regions of the state and had a significant impact on the development of politics until the Democratic demise in the 1850s.

The Massachusetts Democrat Party aligned itself with the national party on most of the critical issues, including the questions surrounding internal improvements, the rechartering of the United States Bank and the protective tariff.[79] Darling contends that its ideology was on the whole consistent with Jacksonian Democracy: a largely agrarian, democratic response, rooted in Jeffersonian Republicanism, to the aristocratic, urban ideology of Whiggery that traced its origins back to the Federalists.[80] Yet the Massachusetts Democrats differed significantly in one important respect that bears great significance on our purposes here. Although Jacksonian Democracy was becoming synonymous with the "white man's republic" across the country in the 1830s and 1840s, the Democratic Party of Massachusetts first struggled with the issue of race and then ultimately resisted the basic tenets of the white republic ideology.

As early as 1831, a rift appeared over the question of slavery. It emerged between two leaders of Massachusetts Democracy: Marcus Morton, on one side, and David Henshaw, a rich Boston druggist and owner of the Boston Statesmen, on the other.[81] Early on Morton had expressed his differences with John Calhoun over slavery and nullification. These differences have to be viewed within the larger sectional conflict over slavery. As early as 1822 Massachusetts had become embroiled in a bitter dispute with South Carolina in the wake of the Denmark Vesey slave uprising. That year, South Carolina passed a law prohibiting any free black from entering the state. The law affected many Massachusetts blacks who made their living as seamen. If the law was enforced, Massachusetts blacks coming to port in Charleston would be jailed. The conflict persisted for two decades. In 1842, while Morton was governor of the state, the Massachusetts legislature authorized funds to defend imprisoned blacks in southern state courts. The next year, the state sent two agents to the ports of Charleston and New Orleans to prosecute cases for blacks at the expense of the Commonwealth. On their arrival, the agents were met by mobs and quickly run out of town.[82]

The simmering conflict between Massachusetts and South Carolina over slavery produced a schism between Massachusetts Democrats and the Southern wing of the party. Southern Democrats continually argued that Northern blacks did not enjoy the same rights as whites. At the risk of appearing hypocritical, the Democracy in Massachusetts could only point to the rights that blacks already enjoyed in the Bay State.[83] If the Massachusetts Democratic Party did not actively work for the expansion of rights for blacks in the state, then it did not work against them by espousing the same ascriptive views toward blacks that Democratic Party leaders in both the South and elsewhere in the North did. As the leader of the Democratic Party for most of the 1830s and 1840s, Morton was thus caught between the dominant racial ideology of paternalism in his state and the national ascriptive policies of his own political party.

Through it all, Morton remained resolutely opposed to the Southern Slave Power—if for no other reason than by virtue of the fact that he opposed any form of aristocracy, which is how he viewed the slave system in the South.[84] On the other side, Henshaw continued to reassure southern Democrats that the Democratic Party of Massachusetts did not approve of abolition. The issue of slavery thus divided the Massachusetts Democrats much the same way it divided the Whigs. Morton became the leader of the antislavery wing of the party, whereas Henshaw, with the Irish of Boston aligned behind him, took the more traditional Democratic approach.[85] Eventually, Morton and the antislavery wing of the party would win out. But that "victory" also would prove to be the Democratic Party's undoing.

The critical point for the Democrats came at the moment the Whigs were being ripped apart by the slavery issue. As mentioned earlier, Conscience Whigs began to leave the party during the presidential election of 1848 when the Whigs nominated Zachary Taylor. That year Van Buren finished in second place in the balloting in Massachusetts, largely on the strength of Conscience Whigs and antislavery Democrats who crossed party lines.[86] With the Whig majority crumbling in the state, the Democrats, under the leadership of Morton and fellow antislavery Democrat George Boutwell, entered into coalition two years later with the Free Soil Party. They controlled the state government from 1851 to 1852, but the coalition began to crumble during the presidential election that fall.[87] The Whigs swept back into power before ultimately being devoured by the antislavery and anti-immigrant forces that were unleashed in the state. Those same forces eventually devoured Massachusetts Democrats as well, for in 1857 the Republicans emerged as the dominant party in the state and remained so through the Civil War and Reconstruction. The Democrats were relegated further to minority status.

From Abolitionism to the Rise of the Radical Republicans

Partisanship during the second-party period cannot be understood without a consideration of the extent to which abolitionism impacted on the state.[88] On New Year's Day 1831, William Lloyd Garrison published the first edition of his abolitionist paper *The Liberator* from the city of Boston. For the next thirty-five years, Garrison would produce more than eighteen hundred weekly editions of his newspaper singularly dedicated to the cause of uplifting the black race. To be sure, abolitionism had existed in New England since the middle decades of the eighteenth century, when Quakers and Calvinists had objected to the subjection of the black race in both the North and South. In this sense, that Garrison chose Boston as the place to launch what would become the origins of the contemporary abolitionist movement was not surprising. In 1829, he spent over a month in a Baltimore jail on a libel charge resulting from a piece that appeared in Benjamin Lundy's *The Genius of Universal Emancipation* on November 20.[89] There, Garrison saw firsthand fugitive slaves awaiting return to their masters further South. The experience galvanized his thinking on slavery and, on his emergence from prison, Garrison went on a lecture tour arguing for immediate abolition. Free blacks in the North immediately warmed to his ideas, but his immediatism put him at odds with his mentor Lundy and the rest of the Quaker abolitionist community. When Garrison arrived in Boston in 1830, religious leaders such as Lyman Beecher refused to take up the mantle of his cause. So Garrison came to the realization that he and he alone had to begin the struggle for immediate emancipation.

What was indeed different and shocking about *The Liberator* was the tone Garrison adopted in its pages from the first issue. Garrison denounced gradual abolition as a possible solution to the nation's moral dilemma of slavery and instead preached an immediatism that resembled the radical message of black abolitionists such as David Walker, who in 1829 had stunned both the North and the South with the violent message of his *Appeal*. In the very first issue, Garrison stated bluntly: "I will be as harsh as truth, and uncompromising as justice. On this subject I do not wish to think, or speak, or write with moderation."[90] He promised the nation's 320,000 free blacks—half of whom lived above the Mason-Dixon Line— that he would not only fight for the immediate emancipation of slaves in the South but also for the rights of free blacks everywhere, including right there in Massachusetts. He then proceeded to denounce the forty-five-year-old state law banning inter-racial marriages.[91]

Garrison and his followers held firmly to two tenets. The first was that abolitionists should push their cause through "moral suasion" rather than political action. Aileen Kraditor asserts that "moral" in Garrisonian terms meant that an abolitionist could petition a legislature, testify before a committee, or question a candidate on his views on slavery for publication.[92] These activities could be carried out by individuals or by antislavery societies. In addition, an abolitionist exerted "moral" influence by voting for an antislavery candidate over a proslavery candidate. But the latter was to be conducted solely on individualistic terms—no abolitionist organization could advocate for one candidate over the other. Most important, any activity had to be conducted nonviolently.

The second tenet on which Garrisonians fastened was deeply connected to the first. Garrison disavowed what he thought to be direct political action of any type for the simple reason that to engage in politics in the American system of government was to assume that the Constitution on which it rested was a legitimate document. For Garrison and his early followers, the Constitution was a pro-slavery document through and through; to entangle oneself in the political system was to essentially join into a union with slaveholders. "The Constitution is a covenant with death and an agreement with hell."[93] To vote for any political candidate for office was thus an act that legitimated a system so morally corrupted it was beyond reform. For Garrison, joining a political party or, worse, advocating for the creation of a party based on the "one ideaism" of abolitionism was simply out the question.

By the late 1830s, Garrison's positions on both issues were being questioned by abolitionists who thought that the movement should begin a campaign of direct political action that included engaging in electoral politics. The schism in the abolitionist movement is well documented and does not need to be rehashed here.[94] Suffice it to say that the rift led to the creation of new organizations that challenged Garrison's abolitionist worldview by advocating for direct political action. The Massachusetts Abolition Society was created in 1839 to rival the Massachusetts Anti-Slavery Society. And the American Anti-Slavery Society developed into the American and Foreign Anti-Slavery Society.[95] The schism in the abolitionist movement also led to the creation of the first political party dedicated solely to the abolition of slavery. Founded on April 1, 1840, in Albany, New York, the Liberty Party sought the overthrow of slavery "within the limits of national jurisdiction"[96] and based its moral justification, not only on the Declaration of Independence but also, more important, on the Constitution of the United States. The Liberty Party thus owed its origins in many ways to the hard work of Garrison and his followers for the last decade—but the very principles on which it rested violated Garrison's core belief in the strategy and tactics of the abolitionist movement.

With James Birney and Thomas Earle at the top of the ticket, the Liberty Party garnered just under seven thousand votes nationally in 1840. Four years later, the Liberty Party would expand its vote total to about sixty-two thousand. In Massachusetts, it did not fare much better. The Liberty Party got about 1 percent of the presidential vote in 1840. At its height, it received about 9 percent of the votes cast in state elections in 1846. Brauer asserts that the Liberty Party did hold the balance of power in the gubernatorial elections of 1843 and 1844.[97] By 1848, most of the members of the party had aligned themselves with the newly organized Free Soil Party. Short-lived as it was, however, the Liberty Party was significant because it signaled a radical change in the strategy in one wing of the abolitionist movement. And as Laurie points out, the racial paternalism of the Liberty Party became infused in the political system in a way that the abolitionist movement could not achieve.[98] The upshot is that, during the 1840s, abolitionists became deeply engaged in electoral politics—a phenomenon that would not subside even with the dissolution of the Liberty Party.

In 1848 the antislavery movement took another dramatic turn with the creation of the Free Soil Party—a coalition comprised of New York Barnburner Democrats, radical antislavery Whigs, and the bulk of the Liberty Party.[99] Although the Liberty Party was unable to make an impact nationally, the Free Soil Party posed a real threat to the Northern wings of both the Democrats and Whigs. It did so by making a calculated decision not to take a stand on black rights in its national platform. Party leader and presidential candidate Martin Van Buren reasoned that many Northern whites would support a party that specifically advocated for the prohibition of slavery in the territories. They would *not* support a party that advocated for the equal rights of blacks.[100] Free Soil Party ideology was thus an amalgam of the ideology of antislavery and the ideology of the white republic. Frederick Douglass understood this clearly when he wrote in his newspaper *The North Star* in 1849: "The cry of Free Men was raised, not for the extension of liberty to the black man, but for the protection of the liberty of the white."[101]

For the abolitionists from Massachusetts who had left the Liberty Party to join the Free Soilers in the late 1840s, there was essentially nowhere else to go politically. They remained strong advocates for abolition and the equal rights of blacks even though the national party remained silent on both issues. By 1852, many of the Democrats and antislavery Whigs who formed the basis of the Free Soil Party had drifted back to their former parties, leaving what George Julian described as a "residuum of permanent adherents of the cause."[102] The national Liberty Party platform reflected the more radical stance of what remained of the Free Soil Party. It went further than the document of 1848 and stated that slavery was "a sin against God and a crime against man." However, it did not demand equal rights for blacks. In 1852, the Democrats recaptured the White House. In Massachusetts, Democrat Franklin Pierce outpolled the Free Soil candidate John Hale, though both were defeated by Whig Winfield Scott.[103] On the state level, the Whigs wrested power from the Coalition comprised of Free Soilers and Democrats. One year later, Free Soilers in Massachusetts would enter into another coalition—this time joined with the nativist wing of the Whig Party—which swept into power throughout the state on a platform of antislavery and anti-immigration. Know-Nothingism would remain in power from 1854 to 1857, although the anti-immigrant policies advocated by the Know-Nothings were vigorously opposed by the antislavery wing of the party.[104] Differences proved to be the undoing of the Know-Nothings as the radical antislavery elements of the party drifted toward the newly formed Republican Party. Republicans captured the governor's office in 1857. The radical wing of the Republican Party would continue to hold power in the state throughout the Civil War and Reconstruction.[105]

We should take several things away from this discussion of party politics in the first- and second-party period in Massachusetts. First, although partisan competition was stiff at various times between the Federalists and Republicans in the opening decades of the nineteenth century, the rights of blacks—and particularly voting rights of blacks—remained a peripheral issue. Partisanship did not lead to calls for the disenfranchisement of blacks the way it did in New York and Pennsylvania or to an extent in Rhode Island. I argue that the reason is threefold. First, political leaders throughout this period all adhered to the racial paternalism that was dominant since the Revolution. Second, the overall population of blacks remained inconsequential throughout the first-party period. The small numbers of blacks in the state and the lack of migration from elsewhere help explain why the race threat argument failed to materialize. Third, white immigration to Massachusetts played a comparatively small role in party dynamics in the first-party period. In this sense, the state underwent "arrested development": Irish immigration in particular was small in the opening decades of the nineteenth century and hence had virtually no impact on the ideological development of Jeffersonian Republicans as it had elsewhere. Racial ascriptivism thus remained subordinated to paternalism.

The second thing we should take away from the discussion is that, during the second-party period, the Democratic Party of Massachusetts failed to propound the "white republic" ideology to the extent that it was promulgated elsewhere in the North. The Democratic Party remained in the minority for most of the period between the 1830s and 1850s. When it captured power briefly in the early 1840s and again the early 1850s, it adopted an antislavery stance. In the early 1840s, Massachusetts was front and center in the bitter dispute over slavery with southern states. In the early 1850s, the Democrats captured power with the help of antislavery Free Soilers. In both instances, an ascriptive ideology on which one wing of the party rested was effectively silenced. Many Democratic Party leaders themselves either sidestepped the issue of race altogether or advocated for the rights of blacks—including Marcus Morton, who led the party for two decades.

Finally, the rise of the abolitionist movement centered in Boston kept the political pressure on state leaders to promote and protect the rights of blacks from the 1830s on. Even as abolitionists entered electoral politics and found themselves making deal after deal with "the devil" by entering into coalitions with political groups not completely committed to abolition, they managed to steer the state's political parties toward expanding black rights. Although the right to vote had never been denied to blacks, the evidence of the abolitionists' success are evident: before the 1830s, blacks in Massachusetts attended separate schools. They could not intermarry with whites. And they were forced to sit in segregated areas in places of worship, amusement, and transportation facilities. By the 1860s, these legal barriers had been removed. The impact that the abolitionist movement had on Massachusetts politics is difficult to refute. At its core, abolitionism ascribed to racial paternalism and utilized successfully the discourse of paternalism that had been in place in Massachusetts since pre-Revolutionary times.

The Discourse of Racial Paternalism in Antebellum Massachusetts

In Chapter 1, I laid out the logic of "environmentalist" arguments about race that are found most prominently in Winthrop Jordan's *White Over Black*. Jordan makes the case that "no line of reasoning … could have better typified the changed pattern of thought in the Revolutionary era" than "the flowering of environmentalism."[106] In Massachusetts, environmentalist arguments against slavery began to appear in the middle decades of the eighteenth century. The racial paternalism that emerged coevally with environmentalism remained dominant in the state throughout the antebellum period. As early as 1755, petitions began to appear before the General Court of Massachusetts Bay requesting that the slave trade be stopped on moral grounds. Calvinist and Quaker conscience was further awakened during and after the French and Indian War.[107] In 1764, Bostonian James Otis was the first to combine the natural rights and antislavery doctrines into a coherent theoretical argument. Otis wrote in his *Rights of the British Colonies* that:

> The Colonists are by the law of nature free born, as indeed all men are, white or black. No better reasons can be given, for enslaving those of any color than such as baron Montesquieu has humorously given, as the foundation of that cruel slavery exercised over the poor Ethiopians, which threatens one day to reduce both Europe and America to the ignorance and barbarity of the darkest ages. Does it follow that tis right to enslave a man because he is black? Will short curl'd hair like wool, instead of Christian hair, as tis called by those, whose hearts are as hard as the nether milestone, help the argument? Can any logical inference in favor of slavery, be drawn from a flat nose, a long or a short face. … There is nothing more evident says Mr. Locke, than "that creatures of the same species rank promiscuously born to all the same advantages of nature and the use of the same faculties, should also be equal one among another, without subordination and subjection, unless the master of them all should by any manifest declaration of his will set one above another, and confer on him by an evident and clear appointment, an undoubted right to dominion and sovereignty." "The natural liberty of man is to be free from any superior power on earth, and not to be under the will or legislative authority of man, but only to have the law of nature for his rule." This is the liberty of independent states; this is the liberty of every man out of

society, and who has a mind to live so, which liberty is only abridged in certain instances, not lost to those who are born in or voluntarily enter into society; this gift of God cannot be annihilated.[108]

Otis's pamphlet was circulated widely throughout the colonies.[109] It began a flood of antislavery literature in Massachusetts that increased particularly after the passage of the Stamp Act.[110] As mentioned earlier, the first abolition bill was introduced in the Massachusetts General Court in 1767. It sought to "prevent the unwarrantable & unusual Practice … of inslaving [sic] Mankind in the Province."[111] Two years later, Samuel Webster of Salisbury urged his fellow colonialists to enact immediate emancipation: "What then is to be done? Done! For God's sake break every yoke and let these oppressed ones go free without delay—let them taste the sweets of liberty, which we so highly prize, and are so earnestly supplicating God and man to grant us: nay, which we claim as the natural right of every man."[112] In 1770, Samuel Cooke devoted his election sermon to "the cause of our African slaves."[113] Three years later, the issue of abolition was the subject of the Harvard College commencement debate. Abolition remained a major issue in Massachusetts politics until it was finally achieved in the wake of the Quock Walker cases of 1783.

The discourse of natural rights and antislavery was pervasive enough in the state such that it shaped the thinking of slaves, who in turn used it to argue on behalf of their own cause. On April 20, 1773, four Boston slaves petitioned the Massachusetts legislature for their freedom. They wrote that:

> The efforts made by the legislative of this province in their last sessions to free themselves from slavery, gave us, who are in that deplorable state. A high degree of satisfaction. We expect great things fro men who have made such a noble stand against the designed of their *fellow-men* to enslave them. We cannot but wish and hope Sir, that you will have the same grand object, we mean civil and religious liberty, in view of your next session. The divine spirit of freedom, seems to fire every humane breast on this continent, except such as are bribed to assist in executing the execrable plan.[114]

Slaves would continue to petition the state legislature as well as sue in the state courts for their freedom on the grounds that slavery violated their natural rights. Paul Cuffe drew on the same principles in arguing for the right to vote in the town of Dartmouth in 1781. White abolitionists also proceeded to make their case. During the Constitutional Convention of 1780, the town of Pittsfield adopted the following declaration and instructed its delegation to present it to the convention: "No man can be deprived of liberty, and subjected to perpetual bondage and servitude, unless he has forfeited his liberty as a malefactor."[115] In the wake of the ratification of the state constitution that year, it was left to the courts to decide the constitutionality of slavery. Ultimately, the natural rights doctrine was used as justification for abolition. Relying on the Declaration of Rights found at the beginning of the new constitution, Chief Justice Cushing, who presided over the Quock Walker case in 1783, wrote that:

> [Slavery] has been heretofore countenanced by the Province Laws formerly, but nowhere is it expressly enacted or established. It has been a usage ... our Constitution of Government, by which the people of this Commonwealth have solemnly bound themselves, sets out with declaring that all men are born free and equal—and that every subject is entitled to liberty and to have it guarded by the laws, as well as life and property—and in short is totally repugnant to the idea of being born slaves. This being the case, I think the idea of slavery is inconsistent with our own conduct and Constitution; and there can be no such thing as perpetual servitude of a rational creature, unless his liberty is forfeited by some criminal conduct or given up by personal consent or contract.[116]

Consensus in the First-Party Period

I suggested earlier that racial paternalism transcended partisan lines throughout the first-party era in Massachusetts. Federalists and Republicans alike opposed slavery on natural rights grounds and continued to construct narratives of citizenship based on racial paternalism once slavery was abolished. Federalist leaders such as John Adams and Caleb Strong, on one side, and Republicans such as Elbridge Gerry and Samuel Adams, on the other, all reached a consensus in their opposition to slavery during the Revolutionary period. Reflecting on this toward the end of his life, John Adams would write that "the turpitude, the inhumanity, the cruelty, and the infamy of the African commerce in slaves have been so impressively represented to the public by the highest powers of eloquence that nothing that I can say would increase the just odium in which it is and ought to be held. Every measure of prudence, therefore, ought to be assumed for the eventual total extirpation of slavery from the United States."[117] The Federalist George Thatcher had argued vehemently—albeit in vain—against compromises on slavery in the Constitutional Convention of 1787. Undaunted, he continued his attacks on the practice once in Congress, where he argued in 1799: "This government originated from, and was founded on, the rights of man, upon which ground we mean to protect it, and could there be any propriety in emanating a government from ours, in which slavery is not only tolerated, but sanctioned by law? Certainly not."[118]

Massachusetts Republicans also were active participants in the trans-formation of the discourse from natural rights and antislavery to argu-ments for the rights of citizenship for blacks. Revolutionary hero William Eustis was the last Republican governor of the state in the first-party era, winning election in 1823–1824. Eustis had been the only Jeffersonian from Boston to serve in Congress in the first decade of the nineteenth century. In 1809, he was appointed by James Madison to be Secretary of War. He returned to Congress in 1819. One year later, he found himself front and center in the national debate over the Missouri Compromise. On Decem-ber 12, 1820, Eustis took to the floor of the House to argue against a clause in the Missouri Constitution, which forbade free blacks from entering the state. Eustis argued against racial ascriptivism by asserting that blacks in Massachusetts had enjoyed the basic rights of citizenship because the state had abolished slavery. Drawing on his own personal experiences, he began by discussing black military service during the Revolution. "At the com-mencement of the revolutionary war," he recollected, "there were found in the Middle and Northern States, many blacks, and other people of color capable of bearing arms; a part of them free, and a greater part of them slaves. The freemen entered our ranks with the whites." Eustis continued:

> The war over, and the peace restored, these men returned to their respective States; and who could have said to them, on their return to civil life, after having shed their blood in common with the whites in the defence [sic], of the liberties of the country—You are not to participate with us in the rights secured by the struggle, or in the liberty for which you have been fighting? Certainly no white man in Massachusetts. The gentleman from Virginia says, that the term "We the people" ... does not mean or include Indians, free Negroes, and mulattoes. If it shall be made to appear that persons of this descrip-tion, citizens at the time, were parties to and formed an integral part of that compact, it follows, that they are and must be included in it. To justify the inferences of the gentleman, the preamble should read "We, the *white* people." But this was impossible; the members of the convention who formed the constitution, from the Middle and Northern States, could never have consented, knowing that there were in those States many thousands of people of color, who had rights under it. They were free—free from their masters. Yes, in the first instance, they also became freemen of the State, and were admitted to all the rights and privileges of citizens, and have con-tinued to exercise them from the peace of 1783 to this day. In Mas-sachusetts, they constituted, and were, in fact, an elementary part of the federal compact. They were directly represented as the whites, in

the initiatory process; and from their votes, in common with those of the whites, emanated the Convention of Massachusetts, by whom the federal constitution was received and ratified. Is not this proof? Is it not demonstration that they are entitled to, that they hold and exercise federal rights in common with our other citizens? ... Not only the rights, but the character of these men, do not appear to have been understood; nor is it to me, at all extraordinary, that gentleman from other States, in which the condition, character, the moral faculties, and the rights of men of color, differ so widely, should entertain opinions so varient [sic] from ours. In Massachusetts, sir, there are among them those who possess all the virtues which are deemed estimable in civil and social life. ... Now we ask only that in a disposition to accommodate others, their avowed rights and privileges be not taken from them.[119]

Just three days before Eustis delivered his speech, Federalist Harrison Gray Otis—who would actually lose the Massachusetts gubernatorial election to Eustis in 1823—had taken the floor of the Senate to make his own case against the proposed Missouri Constitution. His speech exemplified the extraordinary extent to which a consensus had been attained between Massachusetts Federalists and Republicans on the issue of race. Otis took Eustis's argument one step further to highlight the fact that the "privileges and immunities" clause of the Constitution guaranteed citizenship to blacks no matter where they resided or traveled. Otis claimed that "in any state ... if a man of color should be a citizen there, he would carry his privilege elsewhere ... if he possesses these rights, and stands in this relation to the State, he is a citizen. In Massachusetts many persons of color [stand] in this relation to the State and ... until the contrary was shown, that the same was true in every State in the Union."[120] He continued:

But with these convictions, I shall strenuously and forever oppose the extension of slavery, and all measures which will subject a freeman, of whatever color, to the degradations of a slave. Believing, therefore, that every free citizen of color in the Union is joint tenant with myself in the public lands of Missouri ... and that he is entitled to his protection equally with those born to a happier destiny, I cannot consent to an act which would divest him of his property and rights, and interdict him from even passing into a country of which is a legitimate coproprietor [sic] with myself.[121]

Despite the partisan differences that existed, both Eustis and Otis were in agreement on the dominant racial ideology in Massachusetts.

Rising Conflict and the Nationalization of Race in the Second-Party Era

Although slavery was far removed geographically from the boundaries of the state, the speeches delivered by Eustis and Otis in Congress during the debate over the Missouri Compromise demonstrate that, by 1820, Massachusetts was already at the center of the political dispute simmering over slavery. Once on the national stage, political leaders of Massachusetts of all parties were further impelled toward a consensus on matters pertaining to race. That consensus would hold more or less throughout the antebellum period. The reason is fairly straightforward: few Massachusetts politicians openly supported slavery. Furthermore, many found it impossible to argue against the degrading practices of the South if back home the state had been guilty of denying the rights of citizenship to its own black population. The political leaders of the state had to inoculate themselves from the "glass house" argument. Yet, expediency and political calculation were not the only motives—in Bruce Laurie's term, it was part of their "Yankee culture," but that I argue was actually dominant throughout the North during the Revolutionary era. At each turn, political leaders of Massachusetts sought to portray the condition of blacks in the best light by extolling their virtues, on the one hand, and the rights of citizenship they enjoyed, on the other. They did it by offering a narrative of race and citizenship grounded in the dominant paternalistic ideology. On the other side, southern politicians charged Massachusetts with hypocrisy, claiming that the state had not provided equal citizenship to blacks.

This war of words between Massachusetts politicians and southern politicians escalated in the wake of the Denmark Vesey slave uprising of 1822. As I mentioned earlier, South Carolina had passed a law that essentially banned all free blacks from entering the state. These actions drew ire from Massachusetts' politicians who rushed to protect the state's black seamen from imprisonment when traveling to ports such as Charleston. The state's political leaders consistently petitioned the federal government for support. Meanwhile, the state took its own action. In 1836, a Massachusetts joint legislative committee investigated the practices of South Carolina and concluded that:

> It is a matter of surprise ... that so gross a violation of the rights of our citizens, and one which has so long and invariably been put in operation against them, should have been permitted to have passed without the attention of the government, whose duty it is to protect their citizens. ... This right is claimed by the meanest citizen, and his voice ought to be heard. ... If it be said, the laws complained of bear most hardly upon. ... Negroes, be it so, does this alter the case?

Are they not citizens? The rights and liberties of citizens will not be taken from them, without the aggressors being made fully sensible that Massachusetts will protect them, whether they be rich or poor, bond or free, white or black.[122]

A full exposition of South Carolina's defense did not come until 1843, when the federal House of Representatives supported a grievance on behalf of 150 Boston memorialists who argued successfully before the federal government that imprisoning free blacks was a violation of the Privileges and Immunities clause of the Constitution. In response, South Carolina reverted to what would become the standard nineteenth-century states' rights reading of Article 4, section 2 of the Constitution. The state contended that "citizenship" as outlined in the privileges and immunities clause of the federal Constitution did not reach so far as to include state citizenship. Thus, South Carolina was justified in imprisoning any free black who entered the state. But ultimately the political leaders of South Carolina sought to place their northern counterparts on the defensive by turning the spotlight back on the practices of Massachusetts. "Are free Negroes, even in Massachusetts entitled to *all* the rights and privileges conferred by her institutions upon the highest class of society?" asked Kenneth Raynor of South Carolina. "Certainly not," he concluded, and presented as evidence the fact that blacks and whites could not intermarry.[123]

From the 1820s on, political leaders in Massachusetts thus found themselves in a peculiar position: on the one hand, many moved—whether willingly or reluctantly—to the forefront of the growing national debate over slavery. On the other hand, each time they stepped out on the front lines they were forced to address in some way the issue of rights for blacks back home. Put another way, the more slavery became a national issue the more attention race relations back in Massachusetts received. Not surprisingly, political actors responded to the growing national crisis in one of several ways: they either took strong public stances on the issue of slavery or sought to play it down altogether. But the record indicates that very few political leaders of the state argued openly in support of slavery. The most notable exception was the future Whig Edward Everett, who stated on the floor of Congress in 1826: "Domestic slavery is not, in my judgment, to be set down as an immoral and irreligious institution."[124] But Everett was the rare exception. More important, even fewer Massachusetts politicians would argue in front of a national audience that the rights for blacks back in Massachusetts should be restricted. The voting rights for blacks were therefore rarely questioned and never in jeopardy of being repealed.

The Democratic Party

Although it spent most of the second-party period in the minority, the Massachusetts Democratic Party on the whole consistently expressed an unwillingness to side with their southern counterparts on slavery. The views of the dominant wing of the party are best exemplified in the career of Marcus Morton. Morton served in the House of Representatives from 1817 to 1821, was associate justice of the State Supreme Court from 1825 to 1840, and Governor from 1840 to 1841 and 1843 to 1844. Morton was a radical democrat in many ways. He considered the southern slave power to be an aristocracy. In 1842, he was one of the only politicians outside Rhode Island to support Thomas Dorr in his rebellion against the Landholder's Party. During the Constitutional Convention of 1853, Morton argued passionately for the expansion of voting rights to naturalized citizens. Although he was an early supporter of the pro-slavery southern Democrat and his close friend John C. Calhoun, Morton had openly broken ranks with Calhoun and the Southern wing of the party on the issue of race and slavery by the 1830s.[125] He opposed slavery on moral grounds, and yet was reluctant to call himself an "abolitionist." Morton's thinking on slavery was more in line with the Jacksonian philosophy of states' rights than the racial ascriptivism we have seen in other northern Democrats. In 1835, he responded to an abolitionist minister by stating:

> I have a deep and strong conviction of the unrighteousness of hold-ing our fellow men in servitude, and of the magnitude of the curse of slavery to our country. … [Nonetheless] Can we interfere with the conduct of the slave holder towards their slaves? The power of holding slaves is guaranteed to a portion of the union by the sacred instru-ment which we are all bound to support. And we have great reason to fear that any interference with what the slave holders deem to be there domestic rights and their legal property will in any degree, tend to ameliorate the condition of the slaves of to facilitate their eventual emancipation.[126]

At other times Morton expressed his disdain for slavery through the natural rights lens of the Revolutionary era, which the abolitionist move-ment had promulgated. "For one human being to hold others, whom the Almighty has created his fellows, in bondage, is entirely repugnant to that principle of equality which is founded in religion as well as in natu-ral right," he wrote in a letter to George Bancroft in 1837. "That princi-ple of equality knows no distinction of race or condition, includes in its benevolent embrace the whole human family."[127] Although Morton con-sistently refused to side with political abolitionism, he nonetheless made very similar arguments about the evils of slavery. The difference, of course, was that Morton believed abolition could only come about through either southern state action or individual acts of emancipation on the part of slaveholders. If there was a link between Morton and the southern wing of the party, it was in states' rights—not slavery rights.

During his first term of governor, Morton steered clear of the issue of slavery. Yet with the rise in influence of the Liberty Party by the time of his second term in 1843, Morton became more open about his views on slavery. In a way, those views would lead to his downfall in the Massachusetts Democratic Party. In 1845, Morton's pro-slavery Democratic rival David Henshaw and the members of his faction launched an all-out attack on Morton, claiming he was both anti-Catholic and an abolitionist. In order to salvage his political career, Morton had to refute the charges—most important, the charge of being an abolitionist. In fact, Morton's allies came to his defense by publishing a thirty-two-page pamphlet titled *A Refutation of the Charge of Abolitionism … Against the Hon. Marcus Morton.* In it, they addressed each of the charges against him. When Henshaw and his cronies accused Morton of being for interracial marriages, Morton's defenders shot back: "Mr. Henshaw seems to forget that he lives under a Republican Government where nature alone authorizes marriages, leaving matters of color entirely to the taste of the parties concerned. … There was in our statute books an old law, interfering with this law of nature, [which] was repealed with the approval of Governor Morton."[128] Such an unapologetic stance on issues of race and civil rights from a Northern Democrat and his supporters was rare if completely unheard of.

The Whig Party

The Whig response to slavery was varied in the second-party period because of the split I discussed earlier between Cotton Whigs and Conscience Whigs. Many Whig politicians in Massachusetts detested slavery and publicly argued for its restriction. They differed, however, on strategy toward the peculiar institution in existing Southern states. Many such as Abbott Lawrence and Daniel Webster detested abolitionism as much as they did slavery. Yet, at the state level, few openly sought to restrict the rights of blacks. Nonetheless, responses to the national debate over slavery did have repercussions back home. Daniel Webster and John Quincy Adams are two very different cases in point.

From the time that he was elected to Congress in 1812, Webster had been opposed to the extension of slavery. Webster had argued against provisions of Henry Clay's Missouri Compromise in Congress and spoke out in his typical eloquent manner at a meeting of the fledgling antislavery movement at the Boston State House on December 3, 1819.[129] Over the next thirty years, Webster's ongoing presidential ambitions would lead to a rocky and ultimately disastrous relationship with the abolition movement. By the 1820s, he had become a firm supporter of the textile manufacturers of Massachusetts, having come down decisively in their favor on the issue of tariff protection. In return, they continued to be his staunchest supporters for the rest of his life. For many years, manufacturers and merchants had given to the "Webster annuity," a fund that supplemented Webster's governmental income while he did their bidding in the Senate.[130] In 1846, when Webster was looking for a way back into the Senate after serving in the Harrison and Tyler administrations, forty businessmen were successful in raising $37,000 so that he could afford to remain in Washington.

Webster understood the dynamics of the Whig Party he led. As early as 1838, he had courted its Southern wing in the hopes of capturing the presidential nomination. At the same time, Webster remained steadfast in his opposition to the expansion of slavery. He was keen to the fissures in the party over slavery that had appeared by the late 1830s, and how continuing developments were leading not only his party, but the entire country down a dangerous path. With the outbreak of the Mexican-American War, Webster's ambivalence became apparent. He expressed to a friend:

> My own opinion is, that the Anti Slavery feeling is growing stronger and stronger every day; and while we must be careful to countenance nothing, which violates the Constitution, or invades the rights of others, it is our policy, in my opinion most clearly not to yield the substantial truth, for the sake of conciliating those whom we never can conciliate, at the expense of the loss of the friendship and support of those great masses of good men, who are interested in the anti-slavery cause.[131]

In the wake of the war, Webster called the Wilmot Proviso his "thunder" in the Senate and spoke out passionately against the annexation of Texas, claiming it was nothing more than "a scheme for the extension of slavery of the African race."[132] But his tough antislavery stance cost him the support of Southern Whigs. In 1848, Webster lost the presidential nomination to Zachary Taylor. The experience caused him to rethink his position in the hope of receiving the presidential nomination in 1852. At the same time, developments continued to drive the nation toward the final showdown on the issue of slavery. In 1850, the head of the Southern wing of the Whig Party Henry Clay proposed his "compromise" legislation, which sought to combine the regulation of the newly acquired territories, the issue of slavery in Washington, D.C., and the problem of fugitive slaves escaping the South under one omnibus bill. Included of course was the Fugitive Slave Bill, which abolitionists all across the North had labeled the Bill of

Abominations. At Clay's urging, Webster backed the Fugitive Slave Bill, hoping that its passage would help "save the Union." He expressed his support on the floor of the Senate in his famous "Seventh of March" speech. After relating in brief the history of the problem of slavery in his usual fluent manner, Webster gave his reasons for supporting the bill:

> I desire to call the attention to all sober-minded men at the North, of all conscientious men, of all men who are not carried away by some fanatical ideas or some false impression, to their constitutional obligations. ... What right have they, in their legislative capacity, or any other capacity, to endeavor to get round this Constitution, or to embarrass the free exercise of the rights secured by the Constitution to the persons whose slaves escape from them? None at all; none at all. Neither in the forum of conscience, nor before the face of the Constitution, are they, in my opinion, justified in such an attempt. ... I say that the South has been injured in this respect, and has a right to complain; and the North has been too careless of what I think the Constitution peremptorily and emphatically enjoins upon her as a duty.[133]

Webster's support for the Fugitive Slave Bill brought immediate wrath from the all quarters in Massachusetts. Sumner accused him of "elaborate treason." Ralph Waldo Emerson called it a "filthy enactment" and announced that he would refuse to obey it.[134] John Murray Forbes cited Webster's speech as the reason for bolting the Whig Party. "The scales fell from my eyes, and I gave up the Whig Party and acted in my quiet way with the Republicans." Within a year, the Whig Party would be defeated resoundingly by the Democrat and Free Soil Coalition in Massachusetts. By 1854, the Party would virtually cease to exist. In 1852, Webster, revered across the country as the quintessential American statesman for the first half of the nineteenth century, made one last bid for the presidency. He received but six delegate votes from New England and none from the southern planters. "After having done my duty to my Southern brethren, they had neither the courage nor the kindness to place me on the record of that convention."[135] Despite four decades as the face of Federalism and Whiggery in Massachusetts, Webster died a discredited man only a few months after the Convention adjourned.

Unlike Webster, John Quincy Adams's stance on slavery in this period brought him to the height of his political powers in Massachusetts after he departed the White House. Like both his father and mother before him, Adams had despised slavery throughout his political career, dating all the way back to his break with the Federalists in 1808. In 1820, as Madison's Secretary of State, he openly decried the Missouri Compromise. But, as president, Adams had carefully dodged the slavery question. When he was elected to the Congress at the age of sixty-three in 1831, Adams was still far from an abolitionist. But his thinking was transformed as he was inadvertently thrust into the center of the slavery debate. Adams would remain there from the mid-1830s to his death—literally on the floor of the House of Representatives in 1848.

It began with his first speech in Congress in which he presented fifteen petitions from citizens of Pennsylvania praying for the abolition of the slave trade in Washington, D.C. Southern congressman fumed in protest. For the next eight years, Quincy would wage a lonely war against the Gag Rule that prohibited any petition pertaining to slavery. His efforts endeared him to abolitionists all across the North. On the Fourth of July 1843, Adams reaffirmed his connection with the values of the Declaration of Independence in an incessant attack on slavery before an abolitionist audience:

> The extinction of slavery from the face of the earth is a problem, moral, political, religious, which at this moment rocks the foundations of human society throughout the regions of civilized man. It is indeed nothing more nor less than the consummation of the Christian religion. It is only as *immortal* beings that all mankind can in any sense be said to be born equal, and when the Declaration of Independence affirms as a self-evident truth that all men are born equal, it is precisely the same as if the affirmation had been that all men were born with immortal souls. ... Hence it is, too, that, by the law of nature and of God, man can never be made the property of man.[136]

As Adams enjoyed prestige across the North in the aftermath of his battle against the Gag Rule, the experience also led him to support the protection and expansion of black rights back in Massachusetts. Throughout the Gag Rule battle, the aging Adams was a firsthand witness to the state conflict between the Cotton Whig and Conscience Whig factions of the party, of which I have already spoken. By the middle of the 1840s, Adams was clashing with other state Whigs such as Abbott Lawrence and Daniel Webster. He stood shoulder to shoulder with leaders who opposed the North-South Cotton Whig alliance and, in the wake of the annexation of Texas, openly advised his younger "Conscience Whig" colleagues to bolt from the party. Though he died before the presidential election of 1848, Adams' advice was heeded as those younger colleagues left the Whigs to form the Free Soil Party in Massachusetts. Among them included some of the staunchest abolitionists in Massachusetts: Adams' son Charles Francis Adams, who was the Free Soil Party vice presidential candidate in 1848; Stephen Phillips, the Free Soil candidate for Governor; former Whig Congressman John Palfrey who also left the party in 1848;[137] and Charles

Sumner, the future Republican Senator who would argue the *Roberts* case before the Massachusetts Supreme Court one year later.[138]

The Liberty Party

Liberty Party politicians also took a tough abolitionists stance, but they went further than any other political actors to argue for the equal rights of blacks in Massachusetts. And they did it sooner. As we've seen, the Liberty Party was founded in New York in the spring of 1840 and dedicated itself to the cause of ending slavery in the South and promoting equal rights for blacks in the North. For the next eight years, the Liberty Party continued to press its extraordinary calls for racial equality up until its dissolution when it merged with the Free Soil Party. In Massachusetts, the party issued broadsides depicting both major parties as violators of the principles found in the Declaration of Independence and the Constitution, meanwhile depicting itself as the "Good Samaritan" for the entire black race. For the members of the Liberty Party, "The Right Sort of Politics" was founded upon the racial paternalism, as it announced in 1843:

> There is a LIBERTY PARTY organized on the principles of '76, founded on the truth that "Honesty is the best policy," that "Righteousness exalteth a nation"—a sort of Good Samaritan Party, which "don't pass by on the other side." The members of this party find that there is one question in the politics of this country, which must be settled right before any other can be settled at all; and till that great question is settled right, our glorious revolution is incomplete, and out national history unfit to be written. They find that under the form of republicanism, the country is really governed by a combination of about 250,000 slaveholders, who hold, on an average, ten or eleven slaves each, and contrive to wield the power and patronage of the federal government, directing it this way and that way, as they think it necessary to make their property in those slaves secure and profitable. Now, this property in human beings is immeasurably more tyrannous and oppressive, than that usurpation against which our fathers took arms in '76. ... The Liberty Party [seeks to] reconcile the "hostile elements" by establishing justice for the slaves, treat them as our fathers wished to be treated when they said, "We hold these truths to be self-evident," Etc. No matter if the slaves were as bad as they are black, and no sane man doubts that their hearts are at least as white as those of their oppressors, it would be honester [*sic*], safer, and cheaper to have them friends, than to have them enemies. We may take the side of their oppressors, do their unrighteous bidding, be their humble volunteer slaves, and as our reward, obtain

their contempt, drain our purses to support them in idle luxury, and our veins to protect them against the just retributions of Heaven. But when we go down with them, we and our children, into the gulf of national perdition, will it be a very great consolation to us, that their skins were white and their ancestors Anglo Saxon?[139]

Later that year, the Liberty Party held its annual convention, where it rededicated itself to social and political equality between the races:

> *Resolved,* that the fundamental truths of the Declaration of Independence, that all men are endowed by their Creator with certain inalienable rights, among which are life, liberty, and pursuit of happiness, was made fundamental law of our National Government, by that amendment of the constitution which declares that no person shall be deprived of life, liberty, or property, without due process of law. *Resolved,* That this Convention recommends … to the friends of Liberty in all those free [states] where any inequality of rights and privileges exists on the account of color, to employ their energies to remove all such remnants … of the slave system. Resolved, that we cordially welcome our colored fellow citizens to fraternity with us into the *Liberty Party,* in its great contest to secure the rights of mankind and the religion of our christian country.[140]

Although at times it held the balance of power in the state during the 1840s, the Liberty Party never managed to garner more than 9 percent of the total vote at the polls. Its impact on the politics of Massachusetts is nonetheless significant, for it provided discursive continuity on the question of race during a transition period when issues of strategy and tactics were dividing the abolition movement from moral suasion to political action. The Liberty Party acted as an important bridge through which the discourse of racial paternalism passed from Garrison and the abolitionists, to the Massachusetts Free Soilers and Know-Nothings, and finally to the Republican Party that was created and captured power in the mid-1850s.

Garrison and Abolitionism

From the 1830s on, William Lloyd Garrison and the abolition movement had a major impact in maintaining the dominant discourse of racial paternalism in Massachusetts. In the very first issue of *The Liberator,* he laid down his reasons for coming to Boston, stating plainly to blacks living above the Mason-Dixon Line that "your moral and intellectual elevation, the advancement of your rights, and the defence [*sic*] of your character, will be the leading object of our paper."[141] Echoing David Walker's words from his *Appeal,* Garrison then attacked the forty-five-year-old law banning interracial marriages. For the next thirty-five years until the end of the Civil War, Garrison would use the pages of *The Liberator* to continue that attack by espousing and promoting racial paternalism.

To analyze in detail the pages of more than eighteen hundred issues of *The Liberator* or Garrison's other main work *Thoughts on African Colonization* is well beyond the scope of my inquiry here. What follows is the core of Garrison's overall argument against racial inequality. The upshot is that Garrison's writing betrays an extraordinarily consistent set of attitudes about the basis of American political culture, about the moral and intellectual competency of blacks, and about the duty of whites to assist in the uplift of the black race in America. That is to say, it is the embodiment of racial paternalism.

Garrison took his bearings from the environmentalist thinking that formed the backdrop to the American Revolution. Garrison ardently believed in the Enlightenment principles that all men were endowed with the gift of reason and universal equality. In his *Thoughts on African Colonization*, Garrison argued that:

> Man is created a rational being; and therefore he is a subject of moral government, and accountable. Being rational and accountable, he is bound to improve his mind and intellect. With this design, his Creator has outstretched the heavens, and set the sun in his course, and hung out the burning jewels of the sky, and spread abroad the green earth, and poured out the seas, that he might steadily progress in knowledge. The slaves are men; they were born, then, as free as their masters; they cannot be property; and he who denies them as opportunity to improve their faculties, comes into collision with Jehovah, and incurs a fearful responsibility. But we know that they are not treated like rational beings, and that oppression almost entirely obliterates their sense of moral obligation.[142]

Because human beings were rational and accountable, they were capable of self-improvement. Self-improvement transcended racial bounds, thus making the question of the rights for blacks a universal human right. In *The Liberator*, the Garrison explained:

> I am prepared to show, that those who have entered into this CON-SPIRACY AGAINST HUMAN RIGHTS are unanimous in their mode of attack; unanimous in proclaiming the absurdity, that our free blacks are natives of Africa; unanimous in propagating the libel that they cannot be elevated and improved in this country; unanimous in opposing their instruction; unanimous in exciting the prejudices of the people against them; unanimous in apologising [*sic*]

for the crime of slavery; unanimous in conceding the right of the planters to hold their slaves in a limited bondage; unanimous in their hollow pretence for colonizing, namely, to evangelize Africa, unanimous in their *true motive* for the measure—a terror lest the blacks should rise to avenge their accumulated wrongs.[143]

By the time that Garrison had begun his publication and brought the abolition movement to life, ascriptivism had become the dominant racial paradigm throughout the country. The American Colonization Society had been in existence for some fifteen years and had published justification after justification on why free blacks had to be removed to Africa. As Richard Newman points out, antislavery in Massachusetts before Garrison meant colonization; up to the early 1830s, only free black communities across the North had doggedly opposed it.[144] Garrison now lent his powerful voice to their cause. Yet, in order to combat racial ascriptivism propounded by the ACS, Garrison had to revive the principles of the Declaration of Independence and reconstruct the narrative of race that had become dominant. To do so, he argued, much as Otis had done some seventy years before, that "natural" equality was far different from an essentialist emphasis on skin color:

> Nature, we are positively assured, has raised up impassable barriers between the races. I understand by this expression, that the blacks are of a different species from ourselves, so that all attempts to generate offspring between us and them must prove as abortive, as between a man and a beast ... in truth it is often so difficult in the slave States to distinguish between the fruits of this intercourse and the children of white parents, that witnesses are summoned at court to solve the problem! Talk of the barriers of Nature, when the land swarms with living refutations of the statement! ... As long as there remains among us a single copy of the Declaration of Independence, or of the New Testament, I will not despair of the social and political elevation of my sable countrymen.[145]

If Garrison argued stridently that blacks were not "naturally" equipped to be slaves, he defended just as feverishly the free populations of blacks across the North and South. Although not denying some of the charges against the degraded social condition of free blacks in the North, Garrison nonetheless took umbrage at the American Colonization Society's characterizations by comparing them to white immigrants who were pouring into the country in the opening decades of the nineteenth century:

> I repel these charges against the free people of color, as unmerited, wanton and untrue. It would be absurd to pretend, that, as a

class, they maintain a high character: it would be equally foolish to deny, that intemperance, indolence and crime prevail among them to a mournful extent. But I do not hesitate to assert, from an intimate acquaintance with their condition, that they are more temperate and industrious than that class of whites who are in as indigent circumstances, but who have certainly far greater incentives to labor and excel; that they are superior in their habits to the hosts of foreign emigrants who are crowding to our shores, and poisoning our moral atmosphere; and that their advancement in intelligence, in wealth, and in morality, considering the numberless and almost insurmountable difficulties under which they have labored, has been remarkable. … The truth is, the traducers of the free blacks have no adequate conception of the amount of good sense, sterling piety, moral honesty, virtuous pride of character, and domestic enjoyment, which exists amongst this class.[146]

Garrison understood that blacks as a class were lowly and degraded. But there was nothing racially essentialist about indolence, immorality, and crime. Anticipating the potency of nativist arguments that lay dormant but would emerge in Massachusetts once Irish immigration increased in the 1840s, Garrison argued that whites emigrating from elsewhere were just as "immoral." Furthermore, free blacks proved themselves to be industrious by improving their social condition across the North against relentless discrimination. "In Baltimore, Philadelphia, New York, and other places," Garrison contended, "there are several colored persons whose individual property is worth from ten thousand to one hundred thousand dollars,"[147] thus demonstrating that blacks were capable of mental, moral, and physical improvement.

Garrison's racial paternalism mirrored the paradigm of the Revolutionary era in another way: although he continued to make his own arguments about race and point out the inconsistencies of racial ascriptivism, Garrison insisted that the world hear blacks express their own ideas in their own words. His publications were the platform on which those ideas could be aired. Blacks obliged by offering their own version of the natural rights argument that echoed the themes raised in petitions by slaves during the Revolutionary period. The second part of his *Thoughts on African Colonization* is entitled "Sentiments of the People of Color" and contains letters and writings of blacks from all across the country—many of them reprinted from *The Liberator*. On September 1, 1831, a group of blacks in Pittsburgh convened to denounce the American Colonization Society. The wealthy black businessman John Vashon chaired the meeting and submitted to Garrison the resolutions of the meeting, which included the following:

Resolved, That "we hold these truths to be self-evident: that all men are created equal, and endowed by their Creator with certain inalienable rights; that among these are life, liberty, and the pursuit of happiness"—Liberty and Equality Now, Liberty and Equality Forever! … Resolved, that we are freemen, that we are brethren, that we are countrymen and fellow-citizens, and as fully entitled to the free exercise of the elective franchise as any men who breathe; and that we demand an equal share of protection from our federal government with any class of citizens in the community.[148]

Throughout the rest of the antebellum period, Garrison would remain singularly focused on the discourse of racial equality. Despite the crosscurrents of electoral and movement politics that surrounded him, he would return time and again to a few simple principles upon which his brand of abolitionism was based: complete racial equality, universal and inalienable rights, the duty of whites in the cause of uplifting the black race. Garrison espoused a racial narrative that had come into existence in the decade before the Revolutionary War. He drew on the ideas first expressed by Benjamin Otis and others in the 1760s, which combined a natural rights philosophy with elements of Christian doctrine. To that he added the ideas embodied in the Declaration of Independence. And he unrelentingly took the message everywhere in his attempt to combat the discourse of ascriptivism that had dominated the thinking on race during the height of the colonization movement. As he addressed an all-black audience in June of 1831:

Colonizationists generally agree in asserting that the people of color cannot be elevated in this country, nor be admitted to equal privileges with the whites. Is this not a libel upon humanity and justice—a libel upon republicanism—a libel upon the Declaration of Independence—a libel upon Christianity? "All men are born equal, and endowed by their Creator with certain inalienable rights—among which are life, liberty, and the pursuit of happiness." What is the meaning of that declaration? That *all* men possess these rights—whether they are six feet five inches high, or three feet two and a half—whether they weigh three hundred or one hundred pounds—whether they parade in broadcloth or flutter in rags—whether their skins are jet black or lily white—whether their hair is straight or woolly, auburn or red, black or gray—does it not. … Colonizationists too generally agree in discouraging your instruction and elevation at home. They pretend that ignorance is bliss; and therefore 'tis folly to be wise. They pretend that knowledge is a dangerous thing in the head of a colored man; they pretend that you have no ambition; they pretend that you have no brains; in fine, they pretend a thousand other absurd things—they are a combination of pretences. What tyranny is this! Shutting up the human intellect—binding with chains the inward man—and perpetuating ignorance.[149]

Although the racial narrative Garrison espoused was not new, he advanced it further and more successfully than the earlier generation of abolitionists had.

Conclusion

Although despised by Northerners and Southerners alike, the abolitionists nonetheless persisted in the middle decades of the nineteenth century in their crusade to end slavery. John L. Thomas remarks that, more than any other American, William Lloyd Garrison "was responsible for the atmosphere of moral absolutism which caused the Civil War and freed the slaves."[150] Just days before his assassination, Abraham Lincoln had come to a similar conclusion, telling Daniel Chamberlain that "I have only been an instrument. The logic and moral power of Garrison, and the anti-slavery people of the country and the army, have done all."[151] When the Civil War ended, Garrison was carried through the streets and raised in the air on the shoulders of black Bostonians. Although he never saw action in a Civil War battle, Garrison ended the war effort every bit the war hero. With the war over and the slaves freed, he ceased publication of *The Liberator*. His reason for coming to Boston in 1831 was completed.

Thomas goes on to suggest that Garrison, in convincing his followers to boycott elections during the 1830s, also challenged "the democratic process" because he "refused to take the step which he believed an abandonment of principle."[152] The implication is that abolition worked outside the "democratic" system that surrounded it in the antebellum period and would only become engaged if a radical reconstruction of the system occurred. In one sense, Thomas is right: Garrison consistently refused to participate in electoral politics, calling it a personal "sin" to vote. Laurie suggests that Garrison's relationship to politics was more complex than that—Garrison was in effect more political than Thomas gives him credit for.[153] Certainly, Garrison realized the importance of the ballot in the ultimate goal of abolition. "We have never opposed the formation of a third party as a measure inherently wrong," Garrison wrote in *The Liberator*. "Abolitionists have as clear and indisputable [a] right to band themselves together politically … as their fellow-citizens who call themselves whigs or democrats."[154] It is true that Garrison thought the "one-issueism" of the Liberty Party was wrong, but only because he believed withdrawing into one party would isolate abolition, thus allowing the two major parties to ignore the cause.

But, in another sense, Thomas is certainly mistaken about where Garrison and abolitionism stood in respect to the democratic process. Social movements are an integral part of the "democratic process" precisely because they are a challenge to it. My point, however, is a different one. Garrison's brand of abolitionism drew upon one of the fundamental aspects of the "democratic process" brought into existence in the United States in the Revolutionary era. For the abolitionist movement he sparked in Boston in the early 1830s relied on a narrative about the democratic process that was already deeply ingrained in the political culture of the United States by the middle decades of the nineteenth century. It was certainly ingrained in the "Yankee" culture of Massachusetts, which gave the state and the rest of New England its rather exceptional disposition. I would argue that this is one of the major reasons that Garrison's arguments resonated to the extent that they did. This narrative consisted of the language of natural rights, of universal equality, and of the moral and physical uplift of the black race by whites—in short, the discourse of racial paternalism that had been formed during the first wave of abolitionism in the middle decades of the eighteenth century, which Garrison and his abolitionist supporters inherited and used successfully through the middle decades of the nineteenth century.

This is not to suggest that the power of that discourse alone was the decisive factor in any successes that the abolitionist movement enjoyed throughout the antebellum period. But what it does suggest is in Massachusetts the racial paternalism remained a powerful set of ideas to be tapped from the time of the Revolutionary period right through to the Civil War. Garrison and the abolitionist movement exploited this dominant racial ideology and used it successfully to press the cause for blacks both at the national and state level. My concern in this chapter has been with the latter, that is, in explaining why blacks were granted the right to vote early in the state's history and were never denied that right. As I said at the outset, in a peculiar way I was engaged in explaining a "nonevent"—in other words, why the right to vote for blacks was granted when it was and why it was *not* denied to blacks when other states across the North were becoming more racially restrictive. As this chapter further suggests, paternalism remained strong in the state for the half-century after the Revolution as a result of the consensus reached by political elites in both parties during this time. Socioeconomic forces did not disturb that consensus or force political leaders to reassess it to the extent that we have seen in other northern states. By the 1830s, abolitionism and the racial paternalism it espoused played a large role in not only protecting the rights of blacks in Massachusetts, but also in expanding those rights in the antebellum period. The arrested development of immigration patterns, the nature of partisan conflict, and the national attention placed on Massachusetts as a result of the high profile of many of the state's leaders in the simmering national debate over slavery also had a significant impact. But the abolitionist movement kept racial paternalism alive in Massachusetts in the 1840s and 1850s, right up to the onset of the Civil War.

In his study of Garrison and of Boston's blacks, Donald Jacobs asks the question, "What if *The Liberator* had never been published in Boston, and Garrison had gone to Washington as he had originally planned? He concludes that the "direction taken by Boston's black community" would have been quite different.[155] Counterfactuals in political science are taboo simply because it is impossible to predict the outcome of an event that never took place. But what we can say is that, from the time abolition settled in the state to the Civil War, the rights of blacks in Massachusetts were *expanded*: the Jim Crow laws were dropped and the miscegenation laws were done away with. Because of abolition's influence, black and white children attended the same schools; blacks and whites rode on the same trains, slept in the same hotels and worshipped in the same churches; blacks and whites could legally intermarry if they desired. And the right to vote for black men, instituted during the height of the Revolutionary War, remained a fundamental right.

CHAPTER **6**

Epilogue

Reconstructing the Two Reconstructions:
Antebellum Race Formation and the
Nationalization of Party Politics

President Lyndon Johnson sat on the bed in his quarters at the White House on the evening of July 2, 1964, with several newspapers spread about him. The headlines were similar: in one way or another they all referred to the Civil Rights Act that Johnson had just signed that day. Johnson's press secretary Bill Moyers walked in and, sensing the president's glum mood, asked why his signature on the most important piece of legislation since Reconstruction was not cause for celebration. Johnson replied, "Because Bill, I think we just delivered the South to the Republican Party for a long time to come."[1]

In the short term, of course, Johnson's fears were unfounded. He coasted to victory that fall, garnering over 61 percent of the popular vote and racking up 90 percent of the Electoral College total. But with his uncanny nose for politics, Johnson saw the writing on the wall: signing the Civil Rights Act would most certainly demolish the southern base of his Democratic Party. The crowning achievement of the Second Reconstruction up to that point also announced the beginning of the end of the Solid South. In the fall of 1964, Johnson lost just six states—Louisiana, Mississippi, Alabama, Georgia, South Carolina, and Barry Goldwater's home state of Arizona. But the speed with which parts of the South turned on Johnson and the Democrats is telling and foreshadowed things to come in the decades since. In South Carolina, Goldwater received about 59 percent of the popular vote. In Alabama, the figure was just under 70 percent. And in Mississippi, where three civil rights workers had been murdered just two weeks before Johnson signed the Civil Rights Act, Barry Goldwater received an incredible 87 percent of the popular vote. The walls were beginning to crumble—and Johnson knew it.[2]

It does not take much analytical acumen to appreciate Johnson's prescience that July evening in 1964. Indeed, the story of how race realigned the political parties in the South in the wake of the Second Reconstruction is a familiar one. But a couple of examples are worth noting here. In 1968, after Johnson was chased out of the presidential race by his failures in Vietnam, the segregationist George Wallace won the electoral votes of eight of the eleven former confederate states. Nixon won Florida and Virginia, while Humphrey captured only Johnson's home state of Texas. In 1972, with his "Southern Strategy" firmly in place, Nixon swept the entire South. Carter's electoral victory in the South in 1976 is somewhat anomalous, given his Southern roots, his fervent religious convictions, and the explosive fallout over Watergate. In the three presidential elections between 1980 and 1988, Democratic candidates won the electoral votes of exactly *one* state in the Deep South—that was Jimmy Carter who won his own state of Georgia in 1980. Even Clinton's electoral successes in the South in 1992 and 1996 come with an asterisk: the only states where he won a majority of the vote were in Arkansas in 1992 and 1996 (roughly 53 percent each time) and in Louisiana in 1996 (52 percent). Al Gore was shut out of the South in 2000, including in his home state of Tennessee. So, too, was John Kerry in 2004.

When the 89th Congress convened in January 1965, the Democratic Party held veto-proof majorities in both houses: 295–140 in the House, 68–32 in the Senate. Going into the elections in the fall of 1964, the Democratic Party held nearly 90 percent of the Southern seats in the House and over 95 percent of the Southern seats in the Senate. Yet, by the time that the 93rd Congress convened in the winter of 1973, the Republican Party had captured 30 percent of the Southern seats in both House and Senate.[3] And by the time the 109th Congress convened—the same Congress that passed the Voting Rights Reauthorization Act of 2006—the partisan transformation of the South had more or less been completed. In the sixteen southern states from Delaware to Texas, Republicans held a 95–59 majority in the House and a 22–10 majority in the Senate. The Republican House majority leader was from Texas. The Republican Senate majority leader claimed Tennessee as his home state. Nine of the sixteen governors of these states were Republicans.[4] And, of course, another Texan was in the White House—but this time representing the GOP.

Despite the shortcomings and unfinished business of the Second Reconstruction, it is beyond doubt that the Civil Rights Movement of the 1950s and 1960s shaped contemporary American politics in fundamental ways. At its core, the Second Reconstruction destroyed the four pillars of the Jim Crow system in the South that V. O. Key outlined in his monumental work *Southern Politics in State and Nation:* disenfranchisement, malapportionment, the institutional and ideological structure of segregation, and the one-party system.[5] This is just a small indication of the extent to which one-party politics in the South has evaporated, as Lyndon Johnson knew it would once the other three aspects of Jim Crow that Key analyzed had been destroyed. And, as Richard Valelly points out, black enfranchisement since the 1960s has been coupled with a sharp increase and healthy sustenance of black officeholding all across the South at the local, state, and congressional levels.[6] Not surprisingly, the overwhelming majority of these black elected officials are in the Democratic Party. Before J. C. Watts retired from Congress in 2003, he was the only Black Republican in the House of Representatives. Since his retirement, every black member of Congress resides in the Democratic Party.

Do a search on the Web for J. C. Watts and one will find this about him: "J.C. Watts is a rare breed, a black Republican, the first elected [to Congress] from a southern state in over 120 years."[7] In and of itself, the statement does not seem out of the ordinary because it is an accurate description of both Watts and the historical reality that his election to Congress in 1994 represented. And yet, the reality is extraordinary in two respects. First, it is a shocking reminder of where we are today in American politics, and the extent to which race has fundamentally transformed our two-party system in the wake of the Second Reconstruction. Second, this description of Watts and his election to Congress in the year of the Republican Revolution also reminds us of a longer historical reality, dating back to the *First Reconstruction.* Yes, Watts was the first elected Black Republican in Congress from a southern state since the 1870s—since that all-too-brief period when blacks who were allowed to vote would cast their lot with the Republican Party, and when *every* black officeholder in the South at the local, state, and national level was a *Republican.*

Would it be overstating it to suggest that race has turned the two political parties inside out in the period since the First Reconstruction? Perhaps not, but my intent here is certainly not to argue this point by retelling the story of the Two Reconstructions. That, too, has been told and retold often. For our purposes here, let us stipulate that race was the most important factor on which the Republican Party was founded in the 1850s, developed during the periods of the Civil War, Reconstruction, and Jim Crow, and transformed into its current sectional, ideological, and institutional shape after the Second Reconstruction. The crucial turning point came in 1964 when Lyndon Johnson and the Democrats opted for civil rights while the Republicans with Barry Goldwater out front opted for states' rights. Conversely, the same can be said about the Democratic Party during this stretch as it transitioned from the party of the Confederacy, the Solid South, and "Segregation Forever" to the party that, as I write this, has its first serious black contender for the presidency in Senator Barak Obama from Illinois. Obama comes from the same state Abraham Lincoln did, but not from the same political party. And yet, today the Democratic Party is closer to the Party of Lincoln than the Republicans will be for some time to come, if history is our prologue.

What do the forgoing pages have to do with this history? What relevance, if any, do the voting rights of black men in four northern states in the antebellum period hold for understanding the Two Reconstructions—or our contemporary racial politics for that matter— in a different light? Can any conclusions be drawn, any connections made between race formation as I have defined and explained it in New York, Pennsylvania, Rhode Island, and Massachusetts and what has happened since, when race and party politics are considered?

It goes without saying that political scientists and historians do not necessarily write histories merely to uncover the past. As important as that is, students of American political development also seek to pinpoint recurring patterns—economic, institutional, ideological, social, and cultural—in the past that shape and limit the choices political actors make in the present, hence bringing the present more fully into focus. Certain political scientists with a historical emphasis call this "path-dependence."[8] And when done properly, political scientists and historians not only succeed in their jobs of predicting the past, they may actually get a few things right if they are so bold as to make an attempt at predicting the future.

I will not lay claim to the belief that the history and development of the two parties between the Two Reconstructions and since was "caused" by race formation in the antebellum North in any fundamental way. There is no argument for path dependence made here. Yet, the outlines of what took place in the wake of the Civil War and since had already formed in the antebellum North in the decades leading up to the Civil War. This point has not been heretofore acknowledged in the way that I shall here in these closing pages. It may be because of the way that historians and political scientists view that extraordinary historical period. For, much like the Revolutionary War, the Civil War era holds a special place in most accounts of American history, not simply because these periods were extraordinary or of great interest—they were—or brought forward great individual deeds on the part of great historical figures—they did. Rather, the Civil War (like the Revolutionary War) is viewed by many as a significant break in the continuity of American political history. This is why, for example, Sean Wilentz's latest work *The Rise of American Democracy: Jefferson to Lincoln* would begin and end where it does.[9] Focusing only on the antebellum period when writing about the crucial expansion of American Democracy is simply a method, an effective and compelling one to be sure, but it is nonetheless a way of organizing and telling the story—and as such, it is both a "natural" and a man-made periodization of American history. Scholars of political party history engage in spirited debates about when party "realignments" actually took place, which elections were "critical" and which were not, how many "party systems" have endured over the course of United States history, and whether we have entered a new period of party decline or "dealignment." Within these frames, the Civil War is always seen as a "critical turning point" in the development of American politics.

Rightfully so. No one would deny that the attempt, however flawed or halfhearted, to lift four million souls into citizenship from slavery was a fundamental shift from our own past. Nonetheless, when the impact of race on American political development is considered, the Civil War and its aftermath are also regularly seen as a "break" with the past rather than the continuation of it in some modified form. The bare bones outline of the Two Reconstructions I alluded to earlier, and how they transformed the two parties, is comprehensible in most accounts of race and American political development because, at base, there is a traceable continuity in the development of our two-party system from the Civil War to the present. No such continuity is easily traceable when one is attempting to connect race in the antebellum period to that later history—that is, to the Two Reconstructions.

This fact bothers the political scientist who scours history to uncover recurring patterns of political development. And so, in closing, I want to briefly suggest ways in which the politics of race *displayed continuity* from the period I have focused on in this work, into the First and Second Reconstructions, and up to the present.

At its core, my argument in *Between Freedom and Bondage* has been that the question of black enfranchisement in these four states has to be approached with an eye toward two views at once: first, we needed to look at them separately—as four independent case studies with different outcomes, different dynamics, and peculiar developments over time. Yet, when searching for an explanation of why some states disenfranchised blacks and others didn't, we also needed to view them through a similar lens: through the changing economic structure of racial conflict, through the changing partisan structure of race affiliation, and through the changing discursive structure of racial coalitions. In other words, we needed to at once view each state independently of one another through the same concept of race formation in order to arrive at an explanation.

The reader will decide if the explanation offered here has any merit. But one thing should be clear from the analysis I have presented. The question of voting rights for blacks in each of these northern states became inextricably tied to the development of the political parties in each state on the one hand, and across states lines on the other—moreover, at a time when political parties were developing into coalitions on a national scale. This is one of the basic features of the second-party system in the nineteenth century. My account traces how each of the state parties in New York, Pennsylvania, Rhode Island, and Massachusetts moved into alignment with the national parties on the issues of race and slavery. In important ways, the question of voting rights for blacks in each state lay at the foundation of that alignment. It was both a cause and a consequence of that larger dynamic.

Scholars are fond of pointing to Martin Van Buren as the architect of the mass political party.[10] As early as 1827, Van Buren is on record as stating that the creation of national party allegiances would mitigate sectional prejudices.[11] He then went about building the Democratic Party through the vehicle of Jacksonian Democracy. Van Buren was right as long as an issue rooted in sectional prejudices did not became of national concern. His theory failed once slavery became the overriding issue during the second party period; party politics thus became *nationalized* and *sectionalized* within a span of several decades. It was in many respects a volatile combination that would reoccur over the next century and more when we consider the issue of race.

Thus, if the Civil War represents a certain break in the continuity of American politics in some respects, it also was a continuation, and an *aggravation,* of the movements we find in the antebellum era—the nationalization of political parties on one hand, and the sectionalism of issues and prejudices on the other. At the heart of that development during and after the First Reconstruction of course are the issues surrounding race that by now have become familiar. It is here that the recurring patterns of race formation I have sought to uncover in the antebellum North—the economic structure of racial conflict, the racial structure of partisan competition, and the discursive structure of racial coalition formation—reemerge in the First and Second Reconstructions.

We see this in the South during the First Reconstruction, when the paternalistic relationship between the Republican Party and black Southerners is reproduced in a similar (albeit modified) way to that which had been formed in the early days of the nineteenth century with Federalists and blacks in New York, or Whigs in Pennsylvania, or the Law and Order Party in Rhode Island, or most of the political establishment in

Massachusetts. As Valelly points out, Southern blacks and Reconstruction Republicans forged a biracial winning coalition in 1867–1868.[12] As long as blacks were allowed to vote and hold office in the South, and white Republican Party leaders who were calling the shots in Washington maintained their political will, this racial coalition would last. As we know, it did not endure for long. On the other side, the Democratic Party fell back on racially ascriptivist arguments about race and citizenship for the newly freed slaves similar to those that had been used to argue for black disenfranchisement across the antebellum North. In the South, Bourbon regimes fought Reconstruction Republicans in order to capture and then hold on to electoral power. They did it by preying on the economic and racial fears of poorer Southern whites, thus driving a wedge between them and black Southerners. Jim Crow was as much a strategy to maintain the political and social bonds between the white elite and the white masses as it was an attempt to disempower black Southerners and their white Republican benefactors. The strategy unfolded in the post-Reconstruction South as it had done in the antebellum North. Even the agrarian revolts of the 1890s, which sought to link the forces of exploited black and white farmers and workers, proved unable to overcome the racial ascriptivism which held the Democratic Party in the South together like an ideological glue.

The net result of course was the "system of 1896," which virtually destroyed party competition throughout much of the country. Once the Republican Party realized that it could maintain its hold on national power without the electoral support of Southern blacks or Southern whites (and with Democratic defections in the Northeast and the continued support of Western states), it could advocate racially paternalistic views by paying lip service to the cause of equal rights for blacks in the South without having to back those words with legislative action or political will. Republican presidents such as William McKinley and Teddy Roosevelt courted black leaders such as Booker T. Washington and encouraged the economic and political "separateness" he outlined in his famous "Atlanta Compromise" speech in 1895. Equal rights usually meant "separate but equal" in the paternalism of the Republican Party—no matter how benign the spirit in which it was uttered. Similarly, once the Democratic Party realized that it could maintain its hold on the South without capturing power in Washington, it would come to accept the existing institutional and sectional arrangements, and could thereby put in place the elaborate structures their brutal brand of racial ascriptivism demanded with virtual impunity. Although the Democratic Party was essentially shut out of national power until Woodrow Wilson's election in 1913, racial acriptivism prevailed throughout the country. Its most succinct statement came in the *Plessy v. Ferguson* case when Justice Brown, in writing for the Court, argued:

It is claimed by the plaintiff in error that, in an mixed community, the reputation of belonging to the dominant race, in this instance the white race, is "property," in the same sense that a right of action or of inheritance is property. Conceding this to be so, for the purposes of this case, we are unable to see how this statute deprives him of, or in any way affects his right to, such property. If he be a white man, and assigned to a colored coach, he may have his action for damages against the company for being deprived of his so-called "property." Upon the other hand, if he be a colored man, and be so assigned, he has been deprived of no property, since he is not lawfully entitled to the reputation of being a white man.[13]

Justice Brown made the important distinction in *Plessy* between "social" and "political" equality, which then allowed him and seven of his colleagues to interpret the Fourteenth Amendment as allowing for "separate but equal" protections. Homer Plessy could easily get from New Orleans to Slidell at the same time as whites if he rode on the same train for the exact same fare—he just had no legal right to sit in the same car because that would be diminishing the worth of the white man next to whom he sat.

During the days of Jim Crow, Whiteness as Property lay at the core of the racial ascriptivism of the Democratic Party. It held together the coalition. Racial paternalists, by contrast, put forward a counter argument that would not take hold until the middle decades of the twentieth century. That line of reasoning is found in Justice John Marshall Harlan's lone dissent in *Plessy*. Harlan, a former slave owner himself, would give organizations such as the NAACP the legal and conceptual basis on which to attack segregation in public schools across the South when he introduced into the American legal lexicon the notion of "colorblindness" for the very first time. Yet, Harlan also argued that perfect equality between the races did not—nor would ever—exist:

The white race deems itself to be the dominant race in this country. And so it is, in prestige, in achievements, in education, in wealth, and in power. So, I doubt not, it will continue to be for all time, if it remains true to its great heritage, and holds fast to the principles of constitutional liberty. But in view of the constitution, in the eye of the law, there is in this country no superior, dominant, ruling class of citizens. There is no caste here. Our constitution is color-blind, and neither knows nor tolerates classes among citizens. In respect of civil rights, all citizens are equal before the law.[14] [emphasis added]

Today, of course, Harlan is widely celebrated as a seer of sorts—as someone who lived before his time and spoke about things to come. The concept of colorblindness has come to dominate the legal arguments over civil rights since *Plessy*. Yet, few seem to remember Harlan's conditional phrase which comes before his great pronouncement of "colorblindness"— namely, that the white race shall be dominant "for all time, if it remains true to its great heritage ..."

Harlan's views cut to the core of paternalism: we can fight for some form of equality between the races without ceding the notion that whites will remain true to their heritage by staying on top.

To be sure, there were arguments for complete equality between the races made during this period by others. But if members of the Republican Party thought it, they also knew the electoral costs of fighting that battle outweighed the benefits. And so the GOP practiced an early form of "benign neglect." Their political dominance nationally held together until the Great Depression and the election of Franklin Roosevelt in 1932. By then blacks had begun to flee the political persecution and economic discrimination of the South and migrate North. Roosevelt's dominant coalition consisted of the improbable fusion of the Solid South, labor, urban ethnic workers, and Northern urban blacks. As blacks continued to flow into cities such as New York, Philadelphia, Chicago, Boston, Providence, Cleveland, Detroit, they became loyal voting members of the Democratic political machines they encountered. They also acquired more resources and sophistication in order to push the cause of civil rights.[15] Yet, it was in the urban centers of the North in the years after World War II that the racially ascriptive views that dominated the Democratic Party began to crumble. As Paul Frymer rightly points out, blacks became electorally "captured" by the Democratic Party during this period.[16] But with electoral capture came a transformation in the racial belief system of Democratic Party leaders—or at least some of them. Although Roosevelt did not sign federal antilynching laws, his wife Eleanor championed the cause of civil rights throughout his years in the White House. As we know, the New Deal coalition could not hold together as long as white Southern ascriptivists were in the same party as Northern paternalists. This was precisely the choice that Lyndon Johnson pondered that evening in July 1964 after he signed the Civil Rights Act. Yet, with blacks effectively disenfranchised in the South and kept at bay from competing economically with Southern whites because of Jim Crow laws, the Democratic Party could continue to operate without fear of reprisals. Once blacks won back the right to vote, partisan alignments would surely shift. Furthermore, once the Civil Rights Act, which prohibited discrimination in employment, was enacted and enforced, blacks would enter into economic competition with whites across the South in ways that had not been realized during the previous eighty years since the end of slavery. In other words, the economic structure of racial conflict would exert pressure on the political system and thereby feed directly into those partisan (re)alignments. And so, the Second Reconstruction represented another fundamental shift in race formation just as it had done before the Civil War and the First Reconstruction.

Out of power during the years of the New Deal, the Republican Party nonetheless held to its paternalistic views. By the 1950s, with many northern Democratic leaders questioning the racial ascriptivism that Southern party leaders propounded, the vast majority of Republicans and Democrats outside of the South reached an uneasy consensus on race—in principle, that is. That consensus was expressed by former Republican governor and Supreme Court Chief Justice Earl Warren in the *Brown* decision of 1954. Chief Justice Warren effectively accepted Justice Harlan's position of "colorblindness" advocated almost sixty years earlier, when in a unanimous decision Warren argued that separate but equal in the field of education was inherently "unequal" and hence unconstitutional. It was a position that the NAACP and the liberal establishment had been advocating for decades. It also represented a fundamental transition in the dominant racial belief of the country from ascriptivism to paternalism in the intervening years from *Plessy* to *Brown*. Service in World War I and II, much like service during the Revolutionary War or the Dorr War, proved to be a major catalyst. The historian Daryl Michael Scott describes this transition as one from "contempt" for African Americans in the white mind to one of "pity."[17] I would argue that, in addition to the notion of "pity" and the "damaged psyche" which Scott describes, the *Brown* decision was built on a racially paternalistic view that in fact came to dominate the logic of integration in education from the 1960s right up to the present. But one must look closely in the *Brown* decision for it. At the crucial moment in his argument, Justice Warren quotes a passage from the decision of the Kansas court that formed part of the set of cases the Supreme Court was reviewing:

> *Segregation of white and colored children in public schools has a detrimental effect upon the colored children.* The impact is greater when it has the sanction of the law; for the policy of separating the races is usually interpreted as denoting the inferiority of the negro group. A sense of inferiority affects the motivation of a child to learn. Segregation with the sanction of law, therefore, has a tendency to [retard] the educational and mental development of negro children and to deprive them of some of the benefits they would receive in a racial[ly] integrated school system.[18] [emphasis added]

No one would certainly argue that segregation did not have a detrimental effect on black children. One need not get into a debate over the Court's reliance on Kenneth Clark's famous "Doll Test" to come to that conclusion. What is extraordinary about this statement is precisely what is *not* said, namely, that segregation of white and colored children in public schools has a detrimental effect on *both white and colored children.* Somehow the Court overlooked the pathological effects of segregation on Southern white kids, not to mention the rest of white America. Maybe it was unintentional. Or maybe they reasoned that segregation really didn't affect whites at all ... either way, the course of action going forward was clear: all one had to do to reverse the effects of Jim Crow was to send the black child with her damaged psyche to a school with a "normal" white child. All would be made right. This is the exact opposite line of reasoning found in the racial ascriptivism of the *Plessy* decision. But in the new racial paternalism, there is a strangely familiar logic that undergirds the *Brown* opinion. It is all right for blacks to be near whites because now their enhanced value depends on it. The transformation from the ascriptivism of *Plessy* to the paternalism of *Brown* lies in a shift in concern from the damage integration would do to the "property" of whites, to a concern for what continued segregation would do to the "damaged psyche" of blacks.

I am not suggesting that integration was the wrong policy, even if the evidence is clear that unintended consequences such as white flight has led to a failure in its implementation across the country. There were no easy choices here. My concern is with the underlying logic that flows from a certain set of assumptions about how race operates in America. But one can see why Southern whites, told all their lives that segregation was necessary and ascriptivism was the norm, would resist such a shift in racial ideology once the Democratic Party chose racial paternalism in the Second Reconstruction. One can further see why all across the South whites bolted the cities for the suburbs rather than allowing their children to go to school with blacks. They had lived in the ignorant bliss of racial ascriptivism their entire lives. One-party rule in the South from the 1880s to the 1960s was merely the means by which race formation was held static in this period, and now that equilibrium was gone. The economic, partisan, and ideological transformations in the South began well before that night in July 1964 when Johnson spoke to Bill Moyers about losing the South for the foreseeable future. But at that point there was no turning back. In the wake of the Voting Rights Act of 1965, blacks in the South registered to vote and immediately pulled the lever for the people which they believed freed them from the ideology of ascriptivism—the Democratic ticket. It was a vote to end the Solid South.

Today, it is the Republican Party that stands for complete "color-blindness" in the interpretation of the Constitution. Meanwhile, Democratic Party leaders have embraced a "color-conscious" interpretation of the Constitution that was premised on a distinction made by Thurgood

Marshall in various Supreme Court decisions. Marshall argued that there is a fundamental difference between "invidious discrimination," on the one hand, and "benign discrimination," on the other. Jim Crow is of the former type; affirmative action the latter. Race-conscious liberals support race-based remedies, whereas the Texas Republican George Bush calls them "the soft bigotry of low expectations." In other words, Bush accuses racial liberals of being paternalistic. Not surprisingly, with Republican presidents winning the White House twenty of the twenty-eight years between 1980 and 2008, the Supreme Court has restricted the use of race in admissions policies and hiring to the point at which race-conscious remedies for past discrimination are hanging by a thread.

I would certainly not attempt to make the case that the "colorblindness" advocated by the Republican Party today is merely racial ascriptivism as it was promulgated in the past in disguise—it is not. Nor would I contend that the racial policies of the Democratic Party consist purely of racial paternalism—they do not. How far racial paternalism and ascriptivism lay beneath the surface of the contemporary debate over race is anyone's guess. My sense is not too far—in other words, there is more continuity with the past than rupture from it in the respective ideologies. That said, one of the true success stories of the Second Reconstruction has been the degree to which the country has moved well beyond overt racial paternalism and ascriptivism as it appeared in earlier periods. The tenets of classical liberalism that we tell ourselves we hold fast to and live by in this country—equal opportunity, individual merit as a means of advancement, political equality under the eyes of the law—have always been a fiction of sorts. But aren't all political narratives? When considering race, it is even more so. The successes of the Second Reconstruction have moved us somewhat closer to a liberalism which holds true to the belief that in our society race no longer matters—that all individuals are treated as such, *qua* individuals. If it is a noble goal, we also know that we are not "there" yet.

We may never get there. We may never know when we arrive. But knowing where "there" is begins with the genealogical record of these ideas and developments that lead to the Two Reconstructions.

Endnotes

Chapter 1

1. Alexis de Tocqueville, *Democracy in America*, vol. 1 (New York: Alfred A. Knopf, 1948), p. 356.
2. "President Bush Signs Voting Rights Act Reauthorization and Amendments Act of 2006," July 27, 2006. http://www.whitehouse.gov/news/releases/2006/07/20060727.html.
3. Charles Wesley, "Negro Suffrage in the Period of Constitution-Making, 1787–1865," *Journal of Negro History*, vol. 32, no. 2 (1947), p. 166. See also Alexander Keyssar, *The Right to Vote: The Contested History of Democracy in the United States* (New York: Basic Books, (2000), Table A.5, p. 354).
4. Black males were reenfranchised in 1842 in the wake of the Dorr War.
5. New York did not restrict the franchise to white males outright, but placed a higher property qualification for voting on blacks ($250).
6. Rogers Smith, *Civic Ideals: Conflicting Visions of U.S. Citizenship* (New Haven: Yale University Press, 1997); Alexander Keyssar, *The Right to Vote: The Contested History of Democracy in the United States* (New York: Basic Books, 2000); Ron Hayduk, *Democracy for All: Restoring Immigrant Voting Rights in the United States* (New York: Routledge Press, 2006).
7. Keyssar, xvii.
8. Richard Valelly, *The Two Reconstructions: The Struggle for Black Enfranchisement* (Chicago: University of Chicago Press, 2004).
9. Vermont, Maine, New Hampshire, and Massachusetts made no attempt to restrict the franchise to white males in the antebellum period. See Charles Wesley, "Negro Suffrage in the Period of Constitution-Making, 1787–1865," *Journal of Negro History*, vol. 32, no. 2 (1947), p. 166.

10. In 1821, the New York State constitution was rewritten to require a $250 freehold for black males and a $40 freehold for whites. In addition, black males were required to have paid taxes and live in the state for three years, wherease white males could vote after one year of residence and the payment of taxes or the rendering of highway or military service. Wesley, p. 160.

11. Every other Northern state besides those mentioned earlier placed some type of racial restriction on voting in the antebellum period. This included existing states such as New Jersey, Connecticut, and Pennsylvania, or states entering the union in this period such as Ohio, Illinois, and Indiana.

12. Rhode Island's black population was disenfranchised by statute in 1822 and reenfranchised by the new Constitution drafted in 1842. See Patrick T. Conley, *Democracy in Decline: Rhode Island's Constitutional Development 1776–1841* (Providence: Rhode Island Historical Society, 1977).

13. "Negro Suffrage in the Period of Constitution-Making, 1787–1865," *Journal of Negro History*, vol. 32, no. 2 (1947).

14. Keyssar, *The Right to Vote*, p. xvii.

15. Raymond Aron, *An Essay on Freedom* (New York: An NAL Book, 1970), p. 9.

16. See Ira Katznelson, *City Trenches: Urban Political and the Patterning of Class in the United States* (New York: Pantheon Books, 1981), ch. 1. Katznelson provides a thorough review of the various strains of the American Exceptionalist argument.

17. Alexis de Tocqueville, *Democracy in America*, vol. 1, (New York: 1945), pp. 359–360.

18. Michael Omi and Howard Winant, *Racial Formation in the United States from the 1960s to the 1990s* (New York: Routledge Press, 1994).

19. *Ibid.*, p. 55.

20. *Ibid.*, p. 56.

21. Valelly, *The Two Reconstructions: The Struggle for Black Enfranchisement*. As he lays out in Chapter 1, Valelly takes his cues from three fields of inquiry: historical-institutionalist literature, social movement literature, and rational choice literature.

22. U. S. Bureau of the Census, *Negro Population*, 1790–1915, p. 55.

23. U.S. Census Bureau, *Negro Population*, 1790–1815, p. 51.

24. *Ibid.*, p. 51.

25. Wesley, "Negro Suffrage in 1787–1865," p. 155.

26. *Census of State of New York for 1855*, pp. viii and xi.

27. Rodney Hero, *Faces of Inequality: Social Diversity in American Politics* (New York: Oxford University Press, 1998).

28. Joanne Pope Melish, *Disowning Slavery: Gradual Emancipation and "Race" in New England, 1780–1860* (Ithaca, N.Y.: Cornell University Press, 1998), p. 1.

29. Edmund Morgan, *American Slavery/American Freedom: The Ordeal of Colonial Virginia* (New York: W. W. Norton, 1975). Lerone Bennett, *The Shaping of Black America* (Chicago: Johnson Publishing, 1975). David Roediger, *Wages of Whiteness: Race and the Making of the American Working Class* (New York: Verso Press, 1991). Alexander Saxton, *The Rise and Fall of the White Republic: Class, Politics and Mass Culture in Nineteenth Century*

America (London: Verso Press, 1990). Noel Ignatiev, *How the Irish Became White* (New York: Routledge Press, 1995); Theordore Allen, *The Invention of the White Race* (New York: Verso Press, 1994).

30. Frances Fox Piven and Richard Cloward, *Poor People's Movements: How They Succeed, Why They Fail* (New York: Pantheon Books, 1971), p. 17.

31. Philip A. Klinkner and Rogers M. Smith, *The Unsteady March: The Rise and Decline of Racial Equality in America* (Chicago: University of Chicago Press, 1999), p. 8.

32. See for instance, E.E. Schattschneider, *Party Government* (Westport, Conn.: Greenwood Press, 1942).

33. Valelly, *The Two Reconstructions: The Struggle for Black Enfranchisement*, ch. 1.

34. Paul Frymer, *Uneasy Alliances* (Princeton: Princeton University Press, 1999), p. 7.

35. *Ibid.*, p. 8.

36. See for instance, J. L. Austin, *How to Do Things with Words* (Oxford: Oxford University Press, 1962).

37. See especially Michel Foucault, *Power/Knowledge: Selected Interviews and Other Writings, 1972–1977*, ed. Colin Gordon (New York: Pantheon, 1980).

38. For instance, Richard Delgado contends the following: "Stories, parables, chronicles, and narratives are powerful means of destroying mindset—the bundle of presuppositions, received wisdoms, and shared understandings against a background of which legal and political discourse takes place. These matters are rarely focused on. They are like eyeglasses we have worn a long time. They are nearly invisible; we use them to scan and interpret the world and only rarely examine them for themselves. Ideology—the received wisdom—makes current social arrangements seem fair and natural." Richard Delgado, "Storytelling for Oppositionists and Others: A Plea for Narrative," *Michigan Law Review*, 87 (1989), p. 2413.

39. For more on the role of ideology in the expansion of American political parties, see John Gerring, *Party Ideologies in America, 1828–1996* (Cambridge: Cambridge University Press, 1998). As the United States transitioned from the first-party era to the second-party era, and as political parties expanded from entities there to organize the institutions of government to include masses of voters and complex organizations at the local, state, and national level, the tools that political actors used to organize electoral majorities also expanded. With the onset of the mass-party era, discourse, narrative, and ideology became a more vital means by which political actors sought to organize and then capture a majority of the electorate. It is no coincidence that certain fundamental aspects of the modern political party such as the dissemination of party platforms appear at the moment that the mass political party comes into existence. For party platforms are nothing more than narratives meant to structure the electoral universe discursively, to say something about how that universe works, and why the political party in question should be put in power to guarantee that that universe will continue to work that way. This is another way of suggesting the importance of narrative in partisan coalition formation—but, more important, its heightened significance in all the developments we equate with growth and development of

political parties in the nineteenth century: the expanded electorate, the creation and sustenance of mass-based parties; and the continuation of high levels of voter turnout witnessed for most of the nineteenth century.

40. For a fuller discussion of this, see my "Race Formation, Voting Rights and Democratization in the Antebellum North," *New Political Science*, vol. 27, no. 2 (June 2005), 177–196.

41. Eugene D. Genovese, *Roll Jordan Roll: The World the Slaves Made* (New York: Vintage Books, 1976); Winthrop Jordan, *White over Black: American Attitudes toward the Negro, 1550–1812* (Chapel Hill: North Carolina Press, 1968); James Oakes, *The Ruling Race: A History of American Slaveholders* (New York: W. W. Norton, 1998).

42. Rogers Smith, *Civic Ideals: Conflicting Visions of Citizenship in U.S. History* (New Haven: Yale University Press, 1997).

43. See his "Toward Caste," in *Slavery and Freedom in the Age of the American Revolution*, ed. Ira Berlin and Ronald Hoffman (Charlottesville, Va.: United States Capitol Historical Society, 1983), p. 230.

44. George Frederickson, *The Black Image in the White Mind: The Debate on Afro-American Character and Destiny, 1817–1914* (New York: Harper and Row, 1971), p. 2.

45. For a discussion of this point, see my "Rethinking the End of Black Voting Rights in Antebellum Pennsylvania: Racial Ascriptivism, Partisanship and Political Development in the Keystone State," *Journal of Pennsylvania History*, vol. 72, no. 4 (autumn 2005): 466–504.

46. Part I of Omi and Winant's *Racial Formation in the United States from the 1960s to the 1990s* discusses three approaches or paradigms to race that stand in contrast to their own concept of "racial formation"—ethnicity, class, and nation. On the debate between the "psycho-culturalists" and the "socio-economists," see Allen's *The Invention of the White Race*, Introduction.

Chapter 2

1. "Letter to John Jay," March 14, 1779, *The Papers of Alexander Hamilton* (New York: Columbia University Press, 1961), vol. 2, pp. 17–18.

2. *Ibid.* Emphasis added.

3. *Ibid.*, p. 18.

4. John Jay, *The Winning of the Peace, Unpublished Papers 1780–1784*, ed. Richard Morris (New York: Harper and Row, 1980), p. 705. Emphasis added.

5. DeAlva Stanwood Alexander, *A Political History of the State of New York*, vol. 1 (Port Washington, N.Y.: 1909), pp. 78–94.

6. Dixon Ryan, *The Decline of Aristocracy in the Politics of New York*, (New York: Columbia University, 1919), p. 269n.

7. *Ibid.*, p. 270.

8. See, for instance, Anthony Gronowicz, *Race and Class Politics in New York City before the Civil War* (Boston: Northeastern University Press, 1998), chs. 2 and 3. On Tammany Hall, see, for instance, Gustavus Myers, *The History of Tammany Hall* (New York: Burt Franklin Press, 1917); Jabez D. Hammond, *History of Political Parties in the State of New York*, vol. 1 (Buffalo, N.Y.: Phinney and Company, 1850), ch. 17; Alfred E. Young's *The Democratic*

Republicans of New York: The Origins, 1763–1797 (Chapel Hill: University of North Carolina Press, 1967) mentions in passing the early years of the Tammany Society and both its move away from the Federalists and its support for the French Revolution, p. 208.

9. Gronowicz, p. 269.
10. David Roediger, *The Wages of Whiteness* (New York: Verso Press, 1991).
11. Peter Christopher, "The Freedmen of New Amsterdam," *Journal of the Afro-American Historical and Genealogical Society* 5 (Fall and Winter 1984): 109.
12. Leon A. Higgenbotham Jr., *In the Matter of Color, Race and the American Legal Process: The Colonial Period* (New York: Oxford University Press, 1980), pp. 100–150.
13. Evarts Greene and Virginia Harrington, *American Population before 1790,* (New York: Columbia University Council for Research in the Social Sciences, 1997), pp. 92–105.
14. See, for instance, Harry Reed, *Platform for Change: The Foundations of the Northern Free Black Community, 1775–1865* (East Lansing: Michigan State University Press, 1994), p. 81.
15. Thomas J. Davis, "New York's Long Black Line: A Note on the Growing Slave Population, 1626–1790," *Afro-Americans in New York Life and History* 2 (1978): 41.
16. Reed, *Platform for Change,* p. 81. Such an unusually high number of black conscriptions in the British army may be strong evidence for the harshness of slavery and the overall conditions of black life in New York in the Revolutionary period.
17. New York Sate, *Census of 1855,* p. xi.
18. See Shane White, *Somewhat More Independent: The End of Slavery in New York City, 1770–1810* (Athens: University of Georgia Press, 1991), pp. 28–30. According to White, only seventy-six manumissions occurred in New York City between 1783 and 1800, not a particularly high number considering the high-profile New York Manumission Society.
19. See Rhoda Golden Freeman, *The Free Negro in New York City in the Era before the Civil War* (New York: Garland Publishing, 1994), p. 6.
20. Alvin Kass, *Politics in New York State, 1800–1830,* Syracuse: Syracuse University Press, 1965), p. 18.
21. U.S. Census Bureau, *Negro Population, 1790–1815,* p. 51.
22. Gronowicz, *op. cit.,* p. 30.
23. *Ibid.,* p. 32.
24. *New York Journal and Patriotic Register,* March 16, 1799.
25. Gronowicz, p. 32.
26. Shan White, *Somewhat More Independent,* pp. 156–163.
27. *Ibid.,* p. 156.
28. *Ibid.,* p. 176.
29. *Ibid.,* p. 158.
30. *Ibid.,* p. 161.
31. Herman D. Bloch, *The Circle of Discrimination: An Economic and Social Study of the Black Man in New York* (New York: New York University Press, 1969), p. 26. The numbers are as follows: 8,346 Irish, 3601 white, and 2,574 colored Americans.

32. Reed, pp. 4–5.
33. Quoted in Gronowicz, p. 44.
34. Bloch, p. 27.
35. Leon Litwack, "The Emancipation of the Negro Abolitionist," in *The Antislavery Vanguard,* ed. M. Duberman (Princeton, N.J.: Princeton University Press, 1980), p. 141.
36. Ralph Watkins, "A Survey of the African American Presence in the History of the Downstate New York Area," in *The African American Presence in New York State History: Four Regional Historical Surveys,* ed. Monroe Fordham (Albany: SUNY Press, 1989), p. 7.
37. Carl Lotus Becker, *The History of Political Parties in the Province of New York, 1760–1776* (Madison: University of Wisconsin Press, 1968).
38. *Ibid.,* p. 22.
39. Fox, "The Negro Vote in Old New York," *op. cit.*
40. *Ibid.,* p. 252.
41. Henry P. Johnston, ed., *The Correspondence and Public Papers of John Jay* (New York: Burt Franklin, 1890), I, p. 407.
42. Frank Prescott and Joseph Zimmerman, *The Council of Revision and the Veto of Legislation* (Albany: SUNY Press, 1972), p. 1.
43. C. Z. Lincoln, *The Constitutional History of the State of New York* (Rochester, N.Y.: 1906), p. 172.
44. *Journals of the New York Provincial Congress* (Albany, N.Y., 1842), I, pp. 887–889.
45. See note 1.
46. Phil Klinkner and Rogers Smith, *The Unsteady March: The Rise and Decline of Racial Equality in America* (Chicago: University of Chicago Press, 1999).
47. *New York Journal,* April 15, 1784.
48. *Journal of the Assembly of the State of New York,* February 25, 1785.
49. See Edgar McManus, *A History of Negro Slavery in New York* (Syracuse: Syracuse Press, 1966), p. 162.
50. *Journal of the Senate,* March 9 and 12, 1785.
51. *Ibid.,* March 12, 1785.
52. "Objections by the Council of Revision to a Bill for the Gradual Abolition of Slavery, March 23, 1785" in *Messages from the Governors* (Albany, N.Y.: J. B. Lyon Company, 1909), ed. Charles Z. Lincoln, vol. II, pp. 237–239.
53. *Ibid.,* p. 238.
54. *Ibid.*
55. *Journal of the Senate,* March 21, 1785.
56. *Journal of the Assembly,* March 26, 1785.
57. *New York Gazetteer,* February 4, 1785.
58. *New York Journal, or Weekly Register,* June 22, 1786.
59. Fox, "The Negro Vote in Old New York," p. 254.
60. Jabez D. Hammond's *The History of Political Parties in the State of New York* (Buffalo: Phinney and Co., 1850) is still the definitive work on political party history in New York in the early nineteenth century. See pp. 162–163.
61. Herman Bloch, *The Circle of Discrimination,* op. cit., p. 155.

62. None of the secondary literature on political parties in New York make reference to the impact of black voting in the election of 1800, and nowhere in any of the newspapers of the day—Republican or Federalist—is there evidence of black vote that year.

63. State senate seats were apportioned according to four districts across the state. At this time, there were three senators from each district in the senate.

64. See T. E. V. Smith, *Political Parties and the Places of Meetings in New York City* (New York: New York Historical Society, 1893), p. 10.

65. Joseph Sydney, *An Oration Commemorative of the Abolition of the Slave Trade in the United States* (New York: New York Historical Society, 1809).

66. See note 32.

67. This broadside is quoted in T. E. V. Smith, *Political Parties and Their Places of Meetings*, p. 10.

68. *New York Commercial Advertiser*, April 26, 1809.

69. See *New York Advertiser*, April 26, 1810.

70. Hammond, *History of Political Parties in New York*, vol. 1, pp. 286–287.

71. *Journal of the Senate of the State of New York*, 1811, p. 143.

72. *Messages to the Governors, op. cit.*, pp. 686–688.

73. *Ibid.*, p. 686.

74. *New York Evening Post*, April 27, 1813.

75. *Ibid.*

76. The election of 1813 received considerable attention in the Constitutional Convention of 1821, as we will see shortly. The results of that election and the electoral impact of blacks is in dispute.

77. *New York Spectator*, April 19, 1815.

78. *Ibid.*

79. *Census of the State of New York, 1855*, p. xi.

80. *Ibid.*

81. *Proceedings and Debates of the Constitutional Convention of 1821*, pp. 197–199.

82. Hammond, *History of Political Parties in New York*, vol. 2, p. 2.

83. DeAlva Stanford Alexander, *A Political History of the State of New York*, vol. 1, (Port Washington, N.Y.: 1909), p. 299.

84. Merrill Peterson, *Democracy, Liberty, and Property* (New York: Macmillan Publishing Company, 1966), pp. 137–138.

85. *Reports of the Proceedings and Debates of the New York Constitutional Convention of 1821* (New York: DaCapo Press, 1970), p. 180.

86. *Ibid.*, pp. 180–181.

87. *Ibid.*, p. 181.

88. On the face of it, this appears odd because the Bucktail Republicans were purported to be the party of Jefferson. Van Buren's ambitions for building the Democratic Party in the late 1820s rested on the desire to restore the greatness of the Republican Party founded by Jefferson and Madison. Aldrich demonstrates that Van Buren's ambition in creating a national party meant he had to disavow some of the political rhetoric of Jefferson himself. See John Aldrich, *Why Parties? The Origin and Transformation of Political Parties in America* (Chicago: University of Chicago Press, 1995).

89. *Reports of the Proceedings and Debates of the New York Constitutional Convention of 1821,* pp. 183–184.
90. *Ibid.,* p. 185.
91. *Ibid.,* pp. 185–186.
92. *Ibid.,* p. 186.
93. *Ibid.*
94. *Ibid.,* p. 189.
95. *Ibid.,* pp. 188–189.
96. *Ibid.,* p. 189.
97. Hammond, *History of Political Parties in New York,* vol. 2, p. 21.
98. Quoted in *Jim Crow New York: A Documentary History of Race and Citizenship, 1777–1877* (New York: NYU Press, 2003), p. 166.
99. *Ibid.,* pp. 166–167.
100. *Ibid.,* p. 173.
101. *Ibid.,* p. 183.
102. *Ibid.,* p. 185.
103. *Ibid.,* pp. 184–185.
104. See George Walker, *The Afro-American in New York City, 1827-1860* (New York: Garland Press, 1993), p. 116.

Chapter 3

1. *Dred Scott v. Sandford* 60 U.S. (19 Howard) 393 (1857).
2. *Ibid.*
3. *Ibid.*
4. *Ibid.*
5. The Luzerne County case is cited as *Hobbs v. Fogg,* 6 Watts 553 (1837). The Bucks County case is referred to only as *Opinion of the Honorable John Fox Against the Exercise of Negro Suffrage in Pennsylvania* (Harrisburg, Pa.: Barrett and Parke, 1838). The latter was published as the Pennsylvania Constitutional Convention met to draft a new constitution for the state. As we shall see, Judge John Fox's opinion was instrumental in the convention's successful attempt to place a racial voting restriction in the constitution. There is no evidence that would indicate that Justice Taney based any of his findings on either of the Pennsylvania cases, although he came to the same exact conclusions as Judge John Fox.
6. W. E. B. DuBois, *The Philadelphia Negro: A Social Study* (New York: Schocken Books, 1967), p. 25.
7. Roy Akari, "The Pennsylvania Constitution of 1838," *Pennsylvania Magazine of History and Biography* 48 (1924): 301–333.
8. Lyle L. Rosenberger, "Black Suffrage in Bucks County: The Election of 1837," *Bucks County Historical Society Journal* (Spring 1974): 28–39.
9. Julie Winch, *Philadelphia's Black Elite: Activism, Accommodation, and the Struggle for Autonomy, 1787–1848* (Philadelphia: Temple University Press, 1988); Eric Ledell Smith, "End of Black Voting Rights in Pennsylvania," *Pennsylvania History* 65 (1998): 280.
10. See, for instance, Gary Nash, *Quakers and Politics: Pennsylvania, 1681–1726* (Princeton, N.J.: Princeton University Press, 1968), ch. 1.

11. *Ibid.*, p. 10.
12. Edward Raymond Turner, *The Negro in Pennsylvania, 1639–1861* (New York: Arno Press, 1969), p. 65.
13. *Ibid.*, p. 74.
14. Robert Brunhouse, *The Counter-Revolution in Pennsylvania, 1776–1790* (New York: Octagon Press, 1971), p. 2.
15. DuBois, *The Philadelphia Negro*, pp. 30–31.
16. Thomas Branagan, *Serious Remonstrances* (Philadelphia, 1805), p. 78.
17. Turner, *The Negro in Pennsylvania*, p. 11; DuBois, *The Philadelphia Negro*, p. 13.
18. *Ibid.*, p. 70.
19. Gary Nash, *Forging Freedom: The Formation of Philadelphia's Black Community, 1720–1840* (Cambridge, Mass.: Harvard University Press, 1988), p. 32.
20. DuBois, *The Philadelphia Negro*, pp. 14–15.
21. Vermont had abolished slavery in the constitution drafted in 1777.
22. Nash, *Forging Freedom*, p. 33.
23. U.S. Census Bureau, *Negro Population in the United States, 1790–1915*.
24. Source: Gary Nash, *Forging Freedom*, p. 143.
25. *Ibid.*, pp. 136–137.
26. *Ibid.*, p. 137.
27. *Ibid.*
28. Sanford Higginbotham, *Keystone in the Democratic Arch: Pennsylvania Politics, 1800–1816* (Harrisburg, Pa.: Pennsylvania Historical and Museum Commission, 1952), p. 3.
29. Nash, *Forging Freedom*, p. 157.
30. *Ibid.*, p. 161.
31. *Ibid.*, p. 177.
32. *Ibid.*, p. 205.
33. Cf., *Philadelphia Gazette*, November 24, 1821, February 11, 14, and 18, 1822.
34. *Ibid.*, October 18, 1822.
35. Quoted in Nash, p. 238.
36. James Brewer Stewart, *Holy Warriors: Abolitionists and American Slavery* (New York: Hill and Wang, 1996), pp. 43–44.
37. DuBois, *The Philadelphia Negro*, p. 44.
38. Turner, *The Negro in Pennsylvania*, p. 162.
39. Nash, *Forging Freedom*, p. 2.
40. Alexis de Tocqueville, *Democracy in America*, vol. 1 (New York: Harper and Row, 1966), pp. 315–316.
41. Turner, *The Negro in Pennsylvania*, p. 150.
42. Edward Carter, "A Wild Irishmen Under Every Federalist's Bed: Naturalization in Philadelphia, 1789–1806," *Pennsylvania Magazine of History and Biography*, 94 (July 1970): 331–346.
43. Quoted in Noel Ignatiev, *How the Irish Became White* (New York: Routledge Press, 1995), p. 65.
44. *Ibid.*, especially ch. 5.

45. Richard P. McCormick, *The Second American Party System: Party Formation in the Jacksonian Era* (Chapel Hill: University of North Carolina Press, 1966), p. 134.
46. Carter, "A Wild Irishmen Under Every Federalist Bed," p. 332.
47. Quoted in Philip Shriver Klein, *A Game Without Rules: Pennsylvania Politics, 1817–1832* (Philadelphia: Historical Society of Pennsylvania, 1940), p. 51.
48. Andrew Shankman, *Crucible of American Democracy: The Struggle to Fuse Egalitarianism and Capitalism in Jeffersonian Pennsylvania* (Lawrence: University of Kansas Press, 2004).
49. *Ibid.*, p. 12.
50. R. L. Brunhouse, *The Counterrevolution in Pennsylvania, 1776–1790* (New York: Octagon Books, 1971).
51. McCormick, p. 136.
52. Klein, *A Game Without Rules*, p. 43.
53. Higginbotham, *Keystone in the Democratic Arch*, p. 13.
54. *Lancaster Weekly Journal*, May 17, 1816.
55. Jackson's electors received 101,652 votes to Adams's 50,848.
56. *Crawford Messenger*, March 24, 1831.
57. McCormick, p. 141.
58. Klein explains that Pennsylvanians had despised the Little Magician for a whole host of reasons: first, he had kept then Pennsylvania Governor Simon Snyder from the vice presidential candidacy in 1816; second, he was instrumental in overthrowing DeWitt Clinton in New York, someone popular among Pennsylvania political leaders for his alliance with Jackson in the 1820s; third, he supported the caucus system in 1824; fourth, he had jumped on the Jackson bandwagon only after Pennsylvania had raised him from political obscurity; fifth, he chased the only member of Jackson's cabinet from Pennsylvania out of the administration; sixth, he joined in the attacks against the Second Bank which was housed in Pennsylvania; and, last but not least, he was from New York, Pennsylvania's main rival for national power.
59. Dallas, *Laws of Pennsylvania* II, p. 589.
60. *Journal of the Senate, 1811–1812*, p. 109.
61. *Acts of the Assembly, 1820*, pp. 104–106.
62. *Acts of the Assembly, 1825–26*, pp. 150–155.
63. 16 Peters 542 (1842). Chief Justice Taney agreed in this case that the federal government had full authority in these matters concerning slavery—in contradiction to his decision in *Dred Scott*.
64. Turner, *The Negro in Pennsylvania*, p. 227.
65. Quoted in S. W. Pennypacker, *The Settlement of Germantown* (Philadelphia: 1899), pp. 145ff.
66. In *Views of American Slavery: Anthony Benezet and John Wesley* (New York: Arno Press, 1969), pp. 24–25.
67. In *Benjamin Rush: An Address on the Slavery of Negroes in America* (New York: Arno Press, 1969), pp. 1–2, emphasis added.
68. As Nash and Soderlund point out in the introduction, "to sketch Printer Ben's awkward and shifting relationship to the peculiar institution is to foreshadow several major themes of this book," p. ix.

69. Letter to John Waring, December 17, 1763, in *Benjamin Franklin: Writings* (New York: Library of America, 1987), p. 800.
70. "An Address to the Public from the Pennsylvania Society for Promoting the Abolition of Slavery," in *Benjamin Franklin: Writings* (New York: Library of America, 1987), pp. 1154–1155.
71. Turner, p. 182n48.
72. "Letter to Jean Badollet," February 1, 1793, in *Selected Writings of Albert Gallatin*, ed. E. James Ferguson (New York: Bobbs-Merrill, 1967), pp. 64–65.
73. On this point, see Nash and Solderlund, *Freedom by Degrees: Emancipation in Pennsylvania and Its Aftermath.*
74. Turner, ch. 1.
75. Nash, *Forging Freedom*, p. 31.
76. Noel Ignatiev, *How the Irish Became White*, pp. 51–57; Nash, *Forging Freedom*, pp. 178–180.
77. Quoted in Ignatiev, p. 53.
78. Thomas Branagan, *Serious Remonstrances* (Philadelphia, 1805), p. 58.
79. *Ibid.*, p. 78.
80. *Ibid.*, p. 44.
81. *Ibid.*, p. 68.
82. *Ibid.*, pp. 68 and 73.
83. *Ibid.*, p. 64.
84. *Democratic Press*, January 13, 1813.
85. *Proceedings and Debates of the Convention of Pennsylvania, 1837–1838*, vol. ix, p. 380.
86. Litwack, p. 84. In 1831, Tocqueville observed similar treatment of blacks in Philadelphia. "What becomes of the reign of law in this case?" Tocqueville asked. "The law with us is nothing," was the reply of a white citizen.
87. *Hobbs et al. v. Fogg*, 6 Watts (1837), p. 553.
88. *Ibid.*, p. 554.
89. *Ibid.*
90. *Proceedings and Debates of the Pennsylvania Constitutional Convention of 1837–38*, vol. iii, p. 85.
91. See Henry Mueller, *The Whig Party ...* , 37; also Edward J. Price, *Let the Law Be Just: The Quest for Racial Equality in Pennsylvania, 1780, 1915* (Ph.D. dissertation, Pennsylvania State University, 1973), p. 105.
92. *Bedford Gazette* November 17, 1837.
93. *Pennsylvanian*, October 30 and 31, 1837.
94. *The Opinion of the Honorable John Fox Against the Exercise of Negro Suffrage in Pennsylvania* (Harrisburg: Packer, Barrett and Parke, 1838), p. 8.
95. *Ibid.*, pp. 8–9.
96. *Ibid.*, p. 13.
97. *Proceedings and Debates*, vol. ix, pp. 321.
98. *Ibid.*, vol. ix, pp. 332–333.
99. *Ibid.*, vol. ix, p. 335.
100. *Ibid.*, vol. ix, p. 365.
101. *Ibid.*, vol. x, p. 15.
102. *Ibid.*, vol. x, pp. 45–46.
103. *Ibid.*, vol. x., p. 49. Emphasis added.

104. *Proceedings and Debates*, vol. x, p. 106.
105. Price, *Let the Law Be Just*, p. 116.
106. Cited as 5 Smith 214.
107. DuBois, *The Philadelphia Negro*, pp. 30–31.

Chapter 4

1. Quoted in Dan King, *The Life and Times of Thomas Wilson Dorr with Outlines of the Political History of Rhode Island* (Boston: Dan King, 1859), pp. 205–206.
2. *Ibid.*
3. Quoted in Irving Berdine Richman, *Rhode Island: A Study in Separation* (New York: AMS Press, 1973), p. 302.
4. *Mr. Webster's Argument in the Supreme Court of the United States in the Case of* Martin Luther v. Luther M. Borden and Others, *January 27, 1848* (Washington: Gideon, 1848), pp. 25–26.
5. There are a few works that directly address the black community of Rhode Island in this period. See J. Stanley Lemmons and Michael A. McKenna, "Reenfranchisement of Rhode Island Negroes, 1820–1842," in *Rhode Island History* 30 (February 1971): 3–13; Julian Rammelkamp, "The Providence Negro Community, 1820–1842," in *Rhode Island History* 7 (January 1948): 20–33; Robert Cottrol, *Afro-Yankees: Providence's Black Community in the Antebellum Era* (Westport, Conn.: Greenwood Press, 1982); Irving Bartlett, *From Slavery to Citizen: The Story of the Negro in Rhode Island* (Providence: Rhode Island Urban League, 1947).
6. See Patrick Conley, *Democracy in Decline: Rhode Island's Constitutional Development, 1776–1841* (Providence: Rhode Island Historical Society, 1977), pp. 296–298.
7. *Ibid.*, p. 292.
8. William Goodell, *The Rights and Wrongs of Rhode Island* (Whitesboro: Oneida Institute, 1842), p. 6.
9. The colony passed a law in 1652 stating that "no blacke [*sic*] mankind or white being forced by covenant bond, or otherwise, to serve any man or his assighnes [*sic*] linger than ten years, or until they come to bee twentie-four years ..." The law of indentured servitude was never superceded by later statute. Nonetheless, life-time hereditary slavery existed in Rhode Island until the gradual abolition law of 1784 was passed. See George W. Williams, *The History of the Negro Race in America, 1619–1880* (New York: Arno Press, 1968), pp. 262–281.
10. See Robert Cottrol, *The Afro-Yankees: Providence's Black Community in the Antebellum Era* (Westport, Conn.: Greenwood Press, 1982), pp. 16–17.
11. Sources: William D. Johnson, *Slavery in Rhode Island, 1755–1776*, Rhode Island Historical Society Publications (Providence: Rhode Island Historical Society, 1984), p. 127; Census Bureau, Negro Population, 1790–1915, p. 45.
12. Sources: William D. Johnson, *Slavery in Rhode Island*, p. 127; Census Bureau, *Negro Population, 1790–1915*, p. 45.

13. Joanne Pope Melish makes this point persuasively in *Disowning Slavery: Gradual Emancipation and Race in New England, 1780–1860* (Ithaca, N.Y.: Cornell University Press, 1998).
14. Quoted in Elaine Forman Crane, *A Dependent People: Newport, Rhode Island in the Revolutionary Era* (New York: Fordham University Press, 1985), p. 81.
15. *Ibid.*, pp. 81–82.
16. The remarks were made on December 12, 1820, as Eustis argued against the Missouri Constitution that prohibited free blacks from entering the state. Quoted in William C. Nell, *Colored Patriots of the Revolution* (1855, reprinted New York: Arno Press, 1968), p. 127.
17. Irving H. Bartlett, *From Slave to Citizen: The Story of the Negro in Rhode Island* (Providence: The Urban League of Greater Providence, 1954), p. 21.
18. *Ibid.*
19. Robert Cottrol, *The Afro-Yankees*, p. 50.
20. This is the picture we get from the firsthand account of William J. Brown, whose father was the slave of Moses Brown, and who grew up in Providence during this period. *The Life of William J. Brown* (Providence, H.H. Brown, 1883).
21. The Hardscrabble Riot is recounted in many places, including Brown, *op. cit.*; Bartlett, *From Slavery to Citizen*, ch. 3; Cottrol, pp. 53–55; Melish, pp. 204–205.
22. *Hard Scrabble Calendar: Report of the Trials of Oliver Cummins, Nathaniel G. Metcalf, Gilbert Humes, and Arthur Farrier* (Providence, 1824), p. 4. Quoted in Melish, p. 204.
23. Quoted in Bartlett, p. 29.
24. *Ibid.*
25. Quoted in Melish, p. 205.
26. Bartlett, pp. 32–33.
27. *Ibid.*, p. 37.
28. *Ibid.*
29. Rammelkamp, p. 23.
30. Quoted in Brown, p. 86.
31. Peter J. Coleman, *The Transformation of Rhode Island, 1790–1860* (Providence: Brown University Press, 1963).
32. *Ibid.*, p. 26.
33. *Ibid.*, pp. 39–40.
34. *Ibid.*
35. *Ibid.*, pp. 86–87.
36. See map on page 72 of Coleman.
37. Between the eight expanding towns of the north, there were a total of 173,415 cotton spindles, 6,047 employees, and about $3.8 million in capital accumulation. In all of Rhode Island, there were a total of 237,978 cotton spindles, 9,071 employees in the industry, and $5.5. million in capital accumulation. See Coleman, p. 93.
38. John Gilkeson, *Middleclass Providence, 1820–1940* (Princeton, N.J.: Princeton University Press, 1986), pp. 20, 64–65.

39. Under the original Rhode Island Charter, Newport had six representatives, Portsmouth, Warwick, and Providence had four, and each new town had two. See Marvin Gettleman, *The Dorr Rebellion: A Study in American Radicalism, 1833–1849* (New York: Random House, 1973), p. 4. Gettleman argues that three areas of contention ignited the calls for constitutional reform: the suffrage question, the apportionment scheme of the General Assembly, and the legislative dominance and the lack of separation of powers in the government.

40. Connecticut held a constitutional convention in 1814, replacing its colonial charter.

41. Quoted in Patrick T. Conley, *Democracy in Decline*, p. 62.

42. Elisha Potter, *Considerations on the Questions of Adoption of the Constitution and Extension of the Suffrage in Rhode Island* (Boston: Thomas H. Webb and Co., 1842), p. 10.

43. U. S. Congress, House, *Interference of the Executive in the Affairs of Rhode Island*, Report No. 546, 28 Congr., 1st Session, 1884. Also known and hereafter referred to as *Burke's Report*, this documentary history contains many primary documents produced before, during, and after the Dorr Rebellion; p. 10.

44. Potter., pp. 10–11; *Burke's Report*, p. 11.

45. *Burke's Report*, p. 10.

46. See Conley, pp. 49–50. Citing David Lovejoy's *Rhode Island Politics and the America Revolution, 1760–1776* (Providence, R.I.: Brown University Press, 1958) Conley argues that "Rhode Island's democracy was one of indifference and deference, but a democracy it was."

47. This point was made during the Dorr rebellion by many commentators and was summarized in *Burke's Report* after the conflict had been resolved: "Like all her sister colonies, Rhode Island was, during a long period of time, an agricultural community. Her population was sparse, and it was easy to obtain the requisite amount of land to qualify the citizen for freeman. Few, therefore, were excluded from the enjoyment of the right of suffrage, until the State became a manufacturing and mercantile community, and the circumstances of its people had become substantially changed. This change in the condition, occupations, and circumstances of the people of Rhode Island, demonstrated clearly the injustice of the regulations of the government of the State in relation to suffrage, which operated so as to exclude a large majority of its citizens from the exercise of that individual right." pp. 10–11.

48. Williamson, *American Suffrage: Democracy to Property*, p. 243.

49. See Richard P. McCormick, *The Second American Party System: Party Formation in the Jacksonian Era* (New York: W.W. Norton, 1966), pp. 76–78; Conley, *Democracy in Decline*, chs. 1 and 2; Edward F. Sweet, *The Origins of the Democratic Party in Rhode Island* (unpublished dissertation, Fordham University, 1971), ch. 2.

50. Sweet, p. 23.

51. McCormick, p. 79.

52. From the First to the Sixth Congresses, all but two of the House and Senate representatives are listed as either "pro-administration" or Federalists. See Kenneth Martis, *The Historical Atlas of the Parties in the United States Congress, 1789–1989* (New York: Macmillan Publishing, 1989).
53. See Conley, *Democracy in Decline*, ch. 7.
54. George Burrill, *A Few Observations on the Government of the State of Rhode Island* (Providence, 1807).
55. Federalists won both House seats and one Senate seat in the election of 1808. They won the governor's office in 1811. See Martis, pp. 80–81, and Conley, p. 179.
56. Elisha Potter, Jr. *Considerations on the Questions of the Adoption of a Constitution and Extension of the Suffrage in Rhode Island* (Providence, 1842), quoted in Conley, p. 181.
57. Quoted in Conley, *Democracy in Decline*, p. 187.
58. See Charles Carroll, *Rhode Island: Three Centuries of Democracy* 3 vols. (New York: Lewis, 1932), p. 474.
59. Sweet, p. 30.
60. *Manufacturers' and Farmers' Journal*, April 8, 1822.
61. Digest of Public Laws, 1822, pp. 89–90.
62. Conley, p. 211.
63. *Ibid.*, p. 219.
64. Sweet, p. 224.
65. Conley, pp. 236–237.
66. Seth Luther, *An Address on the Right of Free Suffrage* (Providence, R.I.: S.R Weedon, 1833).
67. Gettleman, p. 19.
68. Luther, p. 12.
69. Gettleman, pp. 22–23.
70. *Manufacturer's and Farmers' Journal*, September 11, 1834.
71. Conley, pp. 267–268; Gettleman, pp. 27–28.
72. Conley, p. 271.
73. As Gettleman points out, Dorr complained that the disenfranchised Rhode Islanders "seemed quite willing to have [tyranny's] foot set upon their necks. Such being the case, they deserve their fate ..." p. 29.
74. Jacob Frieze, *A Concise History of the Efforts to Obtain an Extension of the Suffrage in Rhode Island from the Year 1811 to 1842* (Providence, R.I.: Benjamin Moore, 1842).
75. Conley, p. 274.
76. Quoted in William C. Nell, *Colored Patriots of the Revolution*, p. 126.
77. *Ibid.*, p. 126.
78. *Ibid.*, p. 130.
79. Quoted in Mack Thompson, *Moses Brown: Reluctant Reformer* (Chapel Hill: University of North Carolina Press, 1962), p. 193.
80. Moses Brown, *A Short History of the African Union Meeting and School House* (Providence, R.I.: Brown and Danforth, 1821).
81. *Ibid.*, p. 11.
82. *Ibid.*
83. *Records of the State of Rhode Island*, 10:7.
84. See Robert Cottrol, *The Afro-Yankees*, ch. 2.

85. Joanne Pope Melish, *Disowning Slavery: Gradual Emancipation in and "Race" in New England, 1760–1860*.

86. *Ibid.*, p. 2–3.

87. *Ibid.*, p. 3. This is not completely unlike the contemporary debate over affirmative action. Proponents of the latter argue that thirty-plus years of preferential treatment cannot reverse the historical reality of slavery and institutionalized discrimination, whereas opponents look at the lagging standardized test scores of blacks and argue that the differences are a result of natural ability.

88. *Providence American,* January 18, 1822.

89. *Newport Mercury,* January 19, 1822; *Rhode Island Republican,* February 6, 1822.

90. There is hardly any discussion of the disenfranchisement of blacks to be found in any of the voluminous accounts of the Dorr War and the events that led up to it. Later historians of the Dorr Rebellion (Mowry, Gettleman, Conley) mention the disenfranchisement of blacks in passing but do not offer detailed accounts or explanations of the change. Cottrol suggests that the change in voting laws was a result of the heightening racial conflict between working class whites and blacks in the state. Lemons and McKenna intimate that racial disenfranchisement was due in large measure to the lack of political, social, and economic organization of the black community. See Cottrol, *The Afro-Yankees,* p. 43; J. Stanley Lemons and Michael A. McKenna, "Re-enfranchisement of Rhode Island Negroes," *Rhode Island History,* vol. 30, no. 1 (1971): 3–13. Bartlett has a chapter on the suffrage and Negroes in his brief *From Slavery to Citizen,* but mentions the 1822 change only in passing.

91. See William H. Robinson, *Blacks in 19th Century Rhode Island: An Overview* (Providence, R.I.: Rhode Island Black Heritage Society, 1978), p. 66.

92. *Manufacturers' and Farmers' Journal,* November 27, 1820.

93. *Ibid.*, April 16, 1821.

94. These included marches, songs, the use of banners and slogans ("Tippecanoe and Tyler too" vs. "Little Van"), and bonfires.

95. December 4, 1840.

96. *Providence Journal,* September 15, 1841.

97. *Ibid.*, September 17, 1841.

98. *Providence Journal,* September 27, 1841.

99. Quoted in *Burke's Report,* p. 111.

100. *Ibid.*

101. *Ibid.*

102. *Providence Journal,* October 11, 1841.

103. *Ibid.*

104. *Ibid.*, October 9, 1841.

105. *Ibid.*

106. *Ibid.*

107. *Ibid.*

108. *Ibid.*

109. *New Age and Constitutional Advocate,* October 8, 1841.

110. *The Liberator,* October 29, 1841.
111. *Ibid.,* November 19, 1841.
112. *Petition from the Black Citizens of Rhode Island, 1841* (Rhode Island State Archives).
113. Quoted in Lemons and McKenna, p. 10.
114. Conley, *Democracy in Decline,* p. 336.
115. See, for instance, Lemons and McKenna, "Reenfranchisement of Rhode Island's Negroes," pp. 11–13.
116. Rhode Island House of Representatives, *Journal of the Convention Assembled to Frame a Constitution for the state of Rhode Island, at Newport,* September 12, 1842.
117. Quoted in Lemons and McKenna, p. 11.
118. Conley, p. 345.
119. William Goodell, *Rights and Wrongs of Rhode Island,* pp. 4–5.
120. Quoted in William C. Nell, *Colored Patriots of the Revolution,* p. 131.
121. *Ibid.,* p. 12.
122. Richman, *Rhode Island: A Study in Separatism,* p. 306.
123. Cottrol, *Afro-Yankees,* p. 78.
124. *Providence Journal,* November 6, 1848.

Chapter 5

1. *Roberts v. City of Boston,* 5 Cushing (1849): 206.
2. See Stanley Schultz, *The Culture Factory: Boston Public Schools, 1789–1860* (New York: Oxford University Press, 1973), p. 159.
3. Quoted in Sumner's argument, *Equality Before the Law: Unconstitutionality of Separate Colored Schools in Massachusetts. Argument Before the Supreme Court of Massachusetts, in the case of Sarah C. Roberts v. The City of Boston, December 4, 1849.* Reprinted in *Jim Crow in Boston: The Origin of the Separate But Equal Doctrine,* edited by Leonard Levy and Douglas Jones (New York: DeCapo Press, 1974), p. 180.
4. *Ibid.,* p. 181.
5. *Ibid.,* p. 211.
6. That Sumner's arguments predate the entire contemporary debate on race and the notion of "colorblindness" in Constitution is posited by Andrew Kull in *The Colorblind Constitution* (Cambridge, Mass.: Harvard University Press, 1992). See chapter 3. Curiously, Sumner's belief that colorblindness in the application of the law would lead to more "diversity" has been turned inside out in contemporary debates. It is argued, for instance, that race-based admissions policies lead to more diversity in the academic setting, not less. Conversely, the "colorblind" position staked out by Sumner over 150 years ago is precisely the same position contemporary conservatives take when dealing with race-based remedies. By the standards of the day, Sumner's colorblind argument was certainly considered racially "liberal" if not outright radical.
7. *Sarah C. Roberts v. The City of Boston,* 5 Cush. 198 (1849). Reprinted in *Jim Crow in Boston, op. cit.,* p. 230. Emphasis added. Over the course of the last sixty years, the Supreme Court has arrived at a higher standard for racial

classifications. Beginning with *Caroline Products* (1939) and *Korematsu* (1944), the Court considered any racial classification to be suspect, and thus held to a higher scrutiny than "reasonableness." Strict scrutiny has become the contemporary standard by which the Court considers any racial classification. See for example *Shaw v. Reno* (1993).

8. *Ibid.*, p. 230.
9. It is worth mentioning here that Frederick Douglass was not necessarily a proponent of integration. By the time that the *Roberts* case was argued, Douglass's much publicized split with Garrison was for all intents and purposes irreparable. School integration was one issue the two abolitionists differed on. But the rift essentially turned on their respective readings of the Constitution and their respective views on the usefulness of black political participation through voting.
10. *Roberts v. City of Boston.*, p. 217. See also, Donald Martin Jacobs, "William Lloyd Garrison's *Liberator* and Boston's Blacks, 1830–1865," *New England Quarterly* XLIV, no. 2 (June 1971): 259–277.
11. *Massachusetts House of Representatives, House Report No. 167,* March 17, 1855. The Act was an amendment of an earlier bill passed on March 24, 1845. Levy and Jones, p. 261.
12. George Levesque, *Black Boston: African American Life and Culture in Urban America* (New York: Taylor and Francis, 1994), p. 240.
13. *Ibid.* In reviewing the status of blacks in Massachusetts in 1855, black activist William Nell wrote that "it is safe to say that, in many respects, [Massachusetts'] record is one to be proud of. Her colored citizens ... stand, before the law, on an equality with whites." *Colored Patriots of the Revolution*, p. 111.
14. See Kull, *The Colorblind Constitution, op. cit.*
15. See, for instance, J. Morgan Kousser, "The Supremacy of Equal Rights: The Struggle Against Racial Discrimination in Antebellum Massachusetts and the Foundations of the Fourteenth Amendment," *Northwestern University Law Review* 82:4 (summer 1988): 941–1010.
16. Sumner, *Equality before the Law, op. cit.*, p. 216. Emphasis added.
17. Bruce Laurie, *Beyond Garrison: Antislavery and Social Reform* (Cambridge: Cambridge University Press, 2005), pp. 87–88.
18. *Ibid.*, p. 296.
19. *Ibid.*, p. 292.
20. *Ibid.*, ch. 2.
21. James Oliver Horton and Lois Horton, *Black Bostonians: Family Life and Community Struggle in the Antebellum North* (New York: Homes and Meier, 1979).
22. Ancient Charters and Laws of Massachusetts, pp. 52–53.
23. Cf., George Moore, *Notes on the History of Slavery in Massachusetts* (New York: Negro University Press, 1968), pp. 10–30; George W. Williams, *The History of the Negro Race in America, 1619–1880* (New York: Arno and The New York Times Press, 1968), p. 177.
24. "Free Negroes and Mulattoes," *Mass. House of Representatives, January 16, 1822*, p. 8.
25. Moore, p. 50.
26. Quoted in "Free Negroes and Mulattoes," p. 9.

27. *Ibid.*, p. 10.
28. Williams, *The History of the Negro Race in America, 1619–1880*, p. 184.
29. Moore, p. 61.
30. In response to Judge Sewall's remarks, Judge John Suffin retorted in 1701: "By all which it doth evidently appear both by Scripture and Reason, the practice of the People of God in all Ages, both before and after the giving the Law, and in the times of the Gospel, that there were Bond men, Women and Children commonly kept by holy and good men, and improved in Service; and therefore by the Command of God, *Lev.* 25, 44, and their venerable Example, we may keep bond men, and use them in our Service still; yet with all candor, moderation and Christian prudence, according to their state and condition consonant with the Word of God." Quoted in Williams, p. 217.
31. *Ibid.*
32. *Ibid.*, p. 220.
33. *Ibid.*
34. Levesque, p. 317.
35. *Ibid.*
36. Cf., Emory Washburn, "The Extinction of Slavery in Massachusetts," *Massachusetts Historical Society Collections,* 4th series, IV (1858), p. 339.
37. Paul and John Cuffe, *A Request: To the Selectmen of the Town of Dartmouth,* April 22, 1781.
38. William C. Nell, *The Colored Patriots of the American Revolution* (New York: Arno Press and The New York Times Press, 1968), p. 90.
39. See, for instance, Robert Spector, "The Quock Walker Cases (1781–1783)—Slavery, Its Abolition, and Negro Citizenship in Early Massachusetts," *Journal of Negro History,* vol. 53, no. 1 (January 1968): 12–32; William S. O'Brien, SJ, "Did the Jennison Case Outlaw Slavery in Massachusetts?" *American Journal of Legal History* (April 1961), p. 219–41; John D. Cushing, "The Cushing Court and the Abolition of Slavery in Massachusetts: More Notes on the Quock Walker Case," *American Journal of Legal History,* vol. 5 (1961), pp. 118–144.
40. *Negro Population of the United States, 1790–1915.*
41. Levesque, p. 318.
42. Derived from Joseph Kennedy, *Population of the United States in 1860, Eighth Census,* (Washington, 1864), pp. 601–601; Jesse Chickering, *Statistical View of the Population of Massachusetts, 1765–1840* (Boston, 1846), pp. 132–133; Oliver Warner, *Abstract of the Census of Massachusetts, 1865: With Remarks on the Same, and Supplementary Tables* (Boston, 1867), p. 300.
43. Lemuel Shattuck, *Report to the Committee of the City Council Appointed to Obtain the Census of Boston for the Year 1845* (Boston: Eastburn, 1846), p. 37.
44. Oliver Warner puts the black population of Boston in 1840 at 2,427. See his *Abstract of the Census of Massachusetts, 1865,* pp. 228–231.
45. On the transformation of Massachusetts' economy during this period, see Kinley Brauer, *Cotton versus Conscience: Massachusetts Whig Politics and Western Expansion, 1843–1848* (Lexington: University of Kentucky Press, 1967), ch. 2.
46. Levesque, Table I-10.
47. *Ibid.*, pp. 26–27.

48. *Free Negroes and Mulattoes, op. cit.,* p. 1.
49. *Ibid.,* p. 2.
50. *Ibid.,* p. 3.
51. Oscar Handlin, *Boston's Immigrants: A Study in Acculturation* (Cambridge, Mass.: Harvard University Press, 1979), p. 51.
52. *Ibid.,* compiled from Table V, p. 242.
53. *Ibid.,* p. 52 and Table VI, p. 243.
54. See Stephen Patterson, *Political Parties in Revolutionary Massachusetts* (Madison: University of Wisconsin Press, 1973).
55. Patterson points to four legislative programs that led indirectly to Shay's Rebellion nearly a decade later: abolition of paper currency; a taxation program to decrease the money supply; the repeal of price regulations; and raising of fees for all civil officers. See pp. 178–179.
56. Paul Goodman, *The Democratic-Republicans of Massachusetts: Politics in a Young Republic* (Cambridge: Harvard University Press, 1964), pp. 18–23.
57. *Ibid.,* pp. 112, 137.
58. Ronald Formisano, *The Transformation of Political Culture: Massachusetts Parties, 1790s-1840s* (New York: Oxford University Press, 1983), p. 108.
59. *Ibid.,* p. 34.
60. *Ibid.,* Tables I and III, pp. 348–349.
61. The decline in voter turnout after 1820 occurred because of the statehood status Maine that year.
62. Formisano, p. 118.
63. *Ibid.,* p. 10.
64. *Ibid.,* p. 10.
65. See Kinley Brauer, *Cotton Versus Conscience,* ch. 1.
66. *Ibid.,* p. 15.
67. Laurie, *Beyond Garrison,* p. 51.
68. Brauer, p. 18. See also Michael Holt, *The Rise and Fall of the American Whig Party: Jacksonian Politics and the Onset of the American Civil War* (New York: Oxford University Press, 1999). As both Holt and David Laurie point out, the Conscience Whigs sought to pull the party back to them, but by 1848 they realized it was too late.
69. Brauer, p. 19.
70. March 12, 1845. Quoted in Brauer, pp. 23–24.
71. See for instance, Lawrence Lader, *The Bold Brahmins: New England's War Against Slavery, 1831-1865* (New York: E.P. Dutton and Co., 1961). See also Laurie, p. 153.
72. Brauer, p. 25. Part of the reason that Brauer gives for overtaking the party rests on their desire to regain what they considered to be their rightful place in society and politics.
73. Charles Sumner, "Antislavery Duties of the Whig Party," in *The Works of Charles Sumner* vol. I (Boston: 1870–1883), p. 306.
74. Brauer, p. 233.
75. See Formisano, pp. 329–331.
76. A.B. Darling, "Jacksonian Democracy in Massachusetts, 1824–1848," *American Historical Review,* vol. 29, no. 2 (1924), p. 272.
77. Brauer, p. 20.

78. Dale Baum, *The Civil War Party System: The Case of Massachusetts, 1848–1876* (Chapel Hill: University of North Carolina Press, 1984), pp. 24–25.
79. Darling, pp. 280–281.
80. Formisano points out that Darling and Schlesinger agree on this point, while Oscar and Mary Handlin have a different take on the Massachusetts Democrats. See *The Transformation of Political Culture, op. cit.*, p. 317.
81. Darling, p. 285.
82. Levesque, *Black Boston,* pp. 231–238.
83. *Ibid.*, p. 238.
84. Darling, "Jacksonian Democracy in Massachusetts," p. 282.
85. Handlin points out that the Irish in Boston, as elsewhere, remained decidedly against abolition from the 1830s to the 1850s. He refers to a song sung by Irish laborers in the city at the time in which they believed that "when the Negroes shall be free / To cut the throats of all they see / Then this dear land will come to be / The den of foul rascality." *Boston's Immigrants, op. cit.*, p. 133.
86. Baum, *The Civil War Party System,* p. 25.
87. Formisano, *Transformation of Political Culture,* p. 330.
88. So much has been written about abolitionism and its impact on American politics. For a concise history of the impact of abolition and antislavery on Massachusetts, see Richard S. Newman, *The Transformation of American Abolitionism: Fighting Slavery in the Early Republic* (Chapel Hill: University of North Carolina Press, 2002).
89. See Benjamin Quarles, *Black Abolitionists* (New York: Oxford University Press, 1969), p. 18, and *Documents of Upheaval: Selections from William Lloyd Garrison's The Liberator, 1831–1865,* ed. Truman Nelson (New York: Hill and Wang, 1966), p. xii.
90. *The Liberator,* January 1, 1831.
91. Donald M. Jacobs, "William Lloyd Garrison's *Liberator* and Boston's Blacks, 1830–1865," *New England Quarterly,* vol. 44, no. 2 (June 1971): 260.
92. Aileen Kraditor, *Means and Ends in American Abolitionism: Garrison and His Critics on Strategies and Tactics, 1834–1850* (New York: Pantheon Books, 1969), p. 119.
93. Quoted in Wesley, "The Participation of Negroes in Anti Slavery Political Parties," p. 33.
94. The number of works on the subject are too numerous to mention. I have found Kraditor's work (*op. cit*) to be especially illuminating from the perspective of strategy. Quarles *Black Abolitionists* touches on the subject from the perspective of black leaders of the times. Gerald Sorin's *Abolitionism: A New Perspective* (New York: Praeger Publishers, 1972) is also absorbing. Newman's *The Transformation of American Abolitionism* (op. cit.) is also an excellent analysis.
95. Wesley, p. 34.
96. *Ibid.*, p. 39.
97. Brauer, p. 22.
98. Laurie, ch. 3.
99. Eric Foner, "Politics and Prejudice: The Free Soil Party and the Negro, 1849–1852," *Journal of Negro History,* 50 (1965): 239.

100. *Ibid.*, p. 239. Foner also makes this point in his *Free Soil, Free Labor, Free Men: The Ideology of the Republican Party before the Civil War* (New York: Oxford Press, 1995).

101. *North Star,* January 12, 1849. Quoted in Foner, "Politics and Prejudice," p. 255.

102. Quoted in *ibid.*, p. 250.

103. Baum, *The Civil War Party System*, p. 27.

104. Foner, *Free Soil, Free Labor, Free Men*, pp. 250–253.

105. Baum, *The Civil War Party System*, p. 24.

106. Winthrop Jordan, *White over Black: American Attitudes toward the Negro, 1550–1812* (Chapel Hill: University of North Carolina Press, 1968), p. 287.

107. Mary Stoughton Locke, *Anti-Slavery in America, 1619–1808* (Gloucester, Mass.: Peter Smith Publishing, 1965), p. 50.

108. James Otis, *The Rights of The British Colonies Asserted and Proved* (Boston, 1764), pp. 29–30.

109. See Gary Nash, *Race and Revolution* (Madison, Wisc.: Madison House Publishing, 1990), p. 8.

110. *Ibid.*, p. 281.

111. Quoted in *ibid.*, p. 9.

112. Samuel Webster, *Address to My Country on Slavery*, in Coffin, *Sketch of the History of Newbury*, p. 338.

113. Bernard Bailyn, *Ideological Origins of the American Revolution* (Cambridge: Harvard Press, 1967), p. 239.

114. Quoted in Nash, p. 173.

115. J. E. A. Smith, *History of Pittsfield*, pp. 366 and 368.

116. Quoted in *Massachusetts Law Quarterly* (March 1958): 68. In 1874, the Chief Justice of the Massachusetts Supreme Court, Horace Gray, read this passage before the Massachusetts Historical Society and stated that "the reasonable conclusion seems to be that the doctrine that slavery was abolished in this Commonwealth by the Declaration of Rights in 1781 … [was] distinctly affirmed by the chief justice [Cushing] and the jury instructed accordingly [and] thereby conclusively established as the law of the Commonwealth."

117. "Letter to Robert J. Evans, June 8, 1819," in *The Selected Writings of John and John Quincy Adams,* edited by Adrienne Koch and William Peden (New York: Alfred Knopf, 1946), pp. 209–210.

118. *Annals of Congress,* 5 Congress, 2 session, 1310–1311.

119. *On the Missouri Question: Delivered in the Congress of the United States, December 12th, 1820.*

120. *Annals of Congress,* 16 Cong. 2 Sess., pp. 88–89.

121. *Ibid.*

122. *Minority Report of the Joint Special Committee,* Massachusetts Senate Docs. No. 92 (April 12th, 1836), pp. 6–10.

123. Quoted in Levesque, *Black Boston*, p. 239.

124. *Register of Debates in Congress,* vol. 2, pt. 1, 1579–1580.

125. Jonathan Earle, "Marcus Morton and the Dilemma of Jacksonian Antislavery in Massachusetts, 1817–1849," *The Massachusetts Historical Review* NA 2002. www.historycooperative.org/journals/mhr/4/earle.html.

126. Quoted in *ibid.*

127. *Ibid.*

128. *Ibid.*
129. Samuel Eliot Morrison, *Harrison Gray Otis, 1765–1848: Urbane Federalist* (Boston: Houghton Mifflin, 1969), p. 429.
130. See Brauer, *Cotton versus Conscience,* pp. 99–100.
131. Webster to Benjamin Silliman, January 29, 1838, quoted in Brauer, p. 42.
132. Quoted in Brauer, p. 95.
133. Reprinted in *The Daniel Webster Reader,* ed. Bertha Rothe (New York: Oceana Publications, 1956), pp. 243–244.
134. Quoted in Lader, p. 155.
135. Quoted in Lawrence Lader, *The Bold Brahmins,* p. 153.
136. *Ibid.,* pp. 409–410.
137. In 1852, Palfrey defended blacks against the Southern charge of inferiority and drafted a resolution in the state convention that year which insisted that the rights "of our colored citizens going to other states must be protected." Quoted in Foner, "Politics and Prejudice," p. 245. Foner makes the argument that some of the Free Soilers of Massachusetts were uncertain about Negro equality and hence labels them "prejudiced." I argue here that Palfrey's stance is typical of the paternalistic views on race of the time: though uncertain on the question of inferiority, white political leaders nonetheless pushed for the equal rights of citizenship.
138. See Brauer, *Cotton versus Conscience,* pp. 244–245.
139. "The Right Sort of Politics," Liberty Tract No. 2, 1843, *Massachusetts Historical Society,* Box E441, pp. 2–3.
140. "The National Liberty Convention," September 1843, *Massachusetts Historical Society,* Box E441, pp. 3–5.
141. *The Liberator,* January 1, 1831.
142. *Thoughts on African Colonization* (Boston, 1832, reprinted in New York: Arno Press and The New York Times Press, 1968), p. 71.
143. *The Liberator,* April 23, 1831.
144. *The Transformation of American Abolitionism,* ch. 5.
145. *Thoughts on African Colonization,* pp. 145–146.
146. *Ibid.,* pp. 129–131.
147. *Ibid.,* p. 129.
148. John Vashon, printed in William Lloyd Garrison's *Thoughts,* "A Voice from Pittsburgh," September 1, 1831, pp. 34–35.
149. Quoted in *Thoughts on African Colonization,* pp. 12–13.
150. John L. Thomas, *The Liberator: William Lloyd Garrison* (Boston: Houghton Mifflin, 1963), p. 4.
151. Quoted in Lader, p. 269.
152. *Ibid.,* pp. 220–221.
153. In *Beyond Garrison,* Laurie calls him "self-serving" (p. 112) and "opportunistic" (p. 46).
154. Quoted in Gerald Sorin, *Abolitionism: A New Perspective,* p. 82.
155. Jacobs, p. 278.

Chapter 6

1. The story is recounted in Robert Dallek's magisterial *Flawed Giant: Lyndon Johnson and His Times* (New York: Oxford University Press, 1998), p. 120.
2. Much of this data can be found on Dave Leip's wonderful website Atlas of U.S. Presidential Elections, http://uselectionatlas.org/.
3. See Numan V. Bartley and Hugh D. Graham, *Southern Politics and the Second Reconstruction* (Baltimore: Johns Hopkins University, 1975), p. 190.
4. http://www.thegreenpapers.org.
5. V. O. Key, *Southern Politics in State and Nation* (New York: Alfred Knopf, 1949).
6. Richard Valelly, *The Two Reconstructions: The Struggle for Black Enfranchisement.*
7. http://www.nndp.com.
8. See, for instance, "Forum: Timing and Sequence in Political Processes," *Studies in American Political Development* 14 (Spring 2000): 72–119.
9. Sean Wilentz, *The Rise of American Democracy: From Jefferson to Lincoln* (New York: W.W. Norton, 2006).
10. See, for instance, John Aldrich, *Why Parties? The Origins and Transformation of Political Parties in America* (Chicago: University of Chicago Press, 1995).
11. Robert V. Remini, *Van Buren and the Making of the Democratic Party* (New York: W.W. Norton, 1970).
12. Richard Valelly, *The Two Reconstructions,* chs. 2–5.
13. *Plessy v. Ferguson,* 163 U.S. 537 (1896).
14. *Ibid.*
15. See, for instance, Frances Fox Piven and Richard Cloward, *Poor People's Movements: Why They Succeed, How They Fail* (New York: Vintage 1979).
16. Paul Frymer, *Uneasy Alliances* (Princeton, N.J.: Princeton University Press, 1999).
17. Daryl Michael Scott, *Contempt and Pity: Social Policy and the Image of the Damaged Black Psyche, 1880–1996* (Chapel Hill: University of North Carolina Press, 1997).
18. *Brown v. Board of Education,* 347 U.S. 483 (1954).

Selected Bibliography

Primary Sources

Government Documents

Acts of the Assembly of Pennsylvania
Ancient Charters and Laws of Massachusetts
Annals of Congress, 5 Congress, 2 Session.
Brown v. Board of Education, 347 U.S. 483 1954.
Census of State of New York for 1855
Digest of Public Laws of Rhode Island, 1822
Dred Scott v. Sandford 60 U.S. 19 Howard 393 1857.
Hobbs v. Fogg, 6 Watts 553 1837.
Journal of the Assembly of the State of New York
Journals of the New York Provincial Congress. Albany, N.Y., 1842.
Journal of the Senate of New York
Journal of the Senate of Pennsylvania
Laws of Pennsylvania
Massachusetts House of Representatives House Reports
Minority Report of the Joint Special Committee. Massachusetts Senate Docs.
    April 12, 1836.
Plessy v. Ferguson, 163 U.S. 537 1896.
Proceedings and Debates of the Convention of Pennsylvania, 1837–1838.
Records of the State of Rhode Island.
Register of Debates in Congress, vol. 2, pt. 1, 1579–1580.
Reports of the Proceedings and Debates of the New York Constitutional Conven-
    tion of 1821. New York: DaCapo Press, 1970.
Rhode Island House of Representatives. Journal of the Convention Assembled to
    Frame a Constitution for the state of Rhode Island, at Newport, September
    12, 1842.
Roberts v. City of Boston, 5 Cushing (1849).

U. S. Bureau of the Census, *Negro Population*, 1790–1915, p. 55.
U. S. Congress, House of Representatives. *Interference of the Executive in the Affairs of Rhode Island*, Report N0.546, 28 Congress, 1st Session, 1884.

Newspapers

Bedford Gazette
Crawford Messenger
Democratic Press of Philadelphia
Lancaster Weekly Journal
Manufacturers' and Farmers' Journal
Newport Mercury
New Age and Constitutional Advocate
New York Commercial Advertiser
New York Evening Post
New York Gazetteer
New York Journal
New York Journal and Patriotic Register
New York Spectator
North Star
Pennsylvanian
Philadelphia Gazette
Providence American
Providence Journal
Rhode Island Republican
The Liberator
Weekly Register

Speeches, Pamphlets, and Printed Collections

Adams, John, and John Quincy Adams. *The Selected Writings of John and John Quincy Adams*. Edited by Adrienne Koch and William Peden. New York: Alfred Knopf, 1946.
Benezet, Anthony, and John Wesley. *Views of American Slavery*. New York: Arno Press, 1969.
Branagan, Thomas. *Serious Remonstrances*. Philadelphia: Philadelphia Historical Society, 1805.
Brown, Moses. *A Short History of the African Union Meeting and School House*. Providence, R.I.: Brown and Danforth, 1821.
Brown, William J. *The Life of William J. Brown*. Providence, R.I.: H.H. Brown, 1883.
Burrill, George. *A Few Observations on the Government of the State of Rhode Island*. Providence, R.I., 1807.
Chickering, Jesse. *Statistical View of the Population of Massachusetts, 1765–1840*. Boston, 1846.
Cuffe, Paul, and John Cuffe. *A Request. To the Selectmen of the Town of Dartmouth*, April 22, 1781.
Fox, John. *The Opinion of the Honorable John Fox Against the Exercise of Negro Suffrage in Pennsylvania*. Harrisburg, Pa.: Packer, Barrett and Parke, 1838.
Franklin, Benjamin. *Benjamin Franklin: Writings*. New York: Library of America, 1987.

Frieze, Jacob. *A Concise History of the Efforts to Obtain an Extension of the Suffrage in Rhode Island from the Year 1811 to 1842.* Providence, R.I.: Benjamin Moore, 1842.

Gallatin, Albert. "Letter to Jean Badollet," February 1, 1793. *Selected Writings of Albert Gallatin.* Ed. E. James Ferguson. New York: Bobbs-Merrill.

Garrison, William Lloyd. *Documents of Upheaval: Selections from William Lloyd Garrison's The Liberator, 1831–1865.* Ed. Truman Nelson. New York: Hill and Wang, 1966.

Garrison, William Lloyd. *Thoughts on African Colonization.* Boston, 1832. Reprinted in New York: Arno Press and The New York Times Press, 1968.

Goodell, William. *The Rights and Wrongs of Rhode Island.* Whitesboro, N.Y.: Oneida Institute, 1842.

Hamilton, Alexander. *The Papers of Alexander Hamilton.* New York: Columbia University Press, 1961.

Hammond, Jabez D. *The History of Political Parties in the State of New York.* Buffalo, N.Y.: Phinney and Co., 1850.

Jay, John. *The Winning of the Peace, Unpublished Papers 1780–1784.* Ed. Richard Morris New York: Harper and Row, 1980.

Jay, John. *The Correspondence and Public Papers of John Jay.* Ed. Henry P. Johnston. New York: Burt Franklin, 1890.

Liberty Party. "The Right Sort of Politics," Liberty Tract No. 2, 1843, *Massachusetts Historical Society,* Box E441.

Liberty Party. "The National Liberty Convention," September 1843, *Massachusetts Historical Society,* Box E441.

Luther, Seth. *An Address on the Right of Free Suffrage* Providence, R.I.: S.R Weedon, 1833.

Messages from the Governors. Ed. Charles Z. Lincoln. Albany, N.Y.: J.B. Lyon Company, 1909.

Nell, William C. *Colored Patriots of the Revolution.* 1855. Reprinted in New York: Arno Press, 1968.

Otis, James. *The Rights of the British Colonies Asserted and Proved.* Boston, 1764.

Petition from the Black Citizens of Rhode Island, 1841. Rhode Island State Archives.

Potter, Elisha. *Considerations on the Questions of Adoption of the Constitution and Extension of the Suffrage in Rhode Island.* Boston: Thomas H. Webb and Co., 1842.

Rush, Benjamin. *Benjamin Rush: An Address on the Slavery of Negroes in America.* New York: Arno Press, 1969.

Smith, J. E. A. *The History of Pittsfield (Berkshire County), Massachusetts.* Boston: Lee and Shepard, 1869.

Sumner, Charles. *Equality Before the Law: Unconstitutionality of Separate Colored Schools in Massachusetts. Argument before the Supreme Court of Massachusetts, in the Case of* Sarah C. Roberts v. The City of Boston, *December 4, 1849.* Reprinted in *Jim Crow in Boston: The Origin of the Separate but Equal Doctrine.* Ed. Leonard Levy and Douglas Jones. New York: DeCapo Press, 1974.

Sumner, Charles. "Antislavery Duties of the Whig Party." *The Works of Charles Sumner.* Boston: 1870–1883.

Sydney, Joseph. *An Oration Commemorative of the Abolition of the Slave Trade in the United States.* New York: New York Historical Society, 1809.

Warner, Oliver. *Abstract of the Census of Massachusetts, 1865.* Boston, 1867.

Washburn, Emory. "The Extinction of Slavery in Massachusetts." *Massachusetts Historical Society Collections,* 4th series, IV. 1858.

Webster, Daniel. *Address to My Country on Slavery.* In Coffin, Joshua. *Sketch of the History of Newbury.* Boston: S.G. Drake, 1845.

Webster, Daniel. *Mr. Webster's Argument in the Supreme Court of the United States in the case of* Martin Luther v. Luther M. Borden and Others. Washington: Gideon, 1848.

Webster, Daniel. *The Daniel Webster Reader.* Ed. Bertha Rothe. New York: Oceana Publications, 1956.

Secondary Sources

Akari, Roy. "The Pennsylvania Constitution of 1838." *Pennsylvania Magazine of History and Biography* 48 (1924): 301–333.

Aldrich, John. *Why Parties? The Origins and Transformation of Political Parties in America.* Chicago: University of Chicago Press, 1995.

Alexander, DeAlva Stanwood. *A Political History of the State of New York.* Port Washington, N.Y.: 1909.

Allen, Theodore. *The Invention of the White Race.* New York: Verso Press, 1994.

Aron, Raymond. *An Essay on Freedom.* New York: An NAL Book, 1970.

Atlas of U.S. Presidential Elections, http://uselectionatlas.org/.

Austin, J.L. *How to Do Things with Words.* Oxford: Oxford University Press, 1962.

Bailyn, Bernard. *Ideological Origins of the American Revolution.* Cambridge, Mass.: Harvard Press, 1967.

Bartley, Numan V., and Hugh D. Graham, *Southern Politics and the Second Reconstruction.* Baltimore: Johns Hopkins University, 1975.

Baum, Dale. *The Civil War Party System: The Case of Massachusetts, 1848–1876.* Chapel Hill: University of North Carolina Press, 1984.

Becker, Carl Lotus. *The History of Political Parties in the Province of New York, 1760–1776.* Madison: University of Wisconsin Press, 1968.

Bennett, Lerone. *The Shaping of Black America.* New York: Penguin Reprint, 1993.

Bloch, Herman D. *The Circle of Discrimination: An Economic and Social Study of the Black Man in New York.* New York: New York University Press, 1969.

Bartlett, Irving. *From Slavery to Citizen: The Story of the Negro in Rhode Island.* Providence: Rhode Island Urban League, 1947.

Brauer, Kinley. *Cotton versus Conscience: Massachusetts Whig Politics and Western Expansion, 1843–1848.* Lexington: University of Kentucky Press, 1967.

Brunhouse, Robert. *The Counter-Revolution in Pennsylvania, 1776–1790.* New York: Octagon Press, 1971.

Bush, George W. "President Bush Signs Voting Rights Act Reauthorization and Amendments Act of 2006," July 27, 2006. http://www.whitehouse.gov/news/releases/2006/07/20060727.html.

Carroll, Charles. *Rhode Island: Three Centuries of Democracy.* New York: Lewis, 1932.

Carter, Edward. "A Wild Irishmen Under Every Federalist's Bed: Naturalization in Philadelphia, 1789–1806." *Pennsylvania Magazine of History and Biography* 94 (July 1970): 331–346.

Christopher, Peter. "The Freedmen of New Amsterdam." *Journal of the Afro-American Historical and Genealogical Society.* Volume 5, Fall and Winter 1984.

Coleman, Peter J. *The Transformation of Rhode Island, 1790–1860.* Providence, R.I.: Brown University Press, 1963.

Conley, Patrick. *Democracy in Decline: Rhode Island's Constitutional Development, 1776–1841.* Providence, R.I.: Rhode Island Historical Society, 1977.

Cottrol, Robert. *Afro-Yankees: Providence's Black Community in the Antebellum Era.* Westport, Conn.: Greenwood Press, 1982.

Crane, Elaine Forman. *A Dependent People: Newport, Rhode Island in the Revolutionary Era.* New York: Fordham University Press, 1985.

Cushing, John D. "The Cushing Court and the Abolition of Slavery in Massachusetts: More Notes on the Quock Walker Case." *American Journal of Legal History,* vol. 5 (1961): pp. 118–144.

Dallek, Robert. *Flawed Giant: Lyndon Johnson and His Times.* New York: Oxford University Press, 1998.

Darling, A. B. "Jacksonian Democracy in Massachusetts, 1824–1848." *American Historical Review,* vol. 29, no. 2 (1924).

Davis, Thomas J. "New York's Long Black Line: A Note on the Growing Slave Population, 1626–1790." *Afro-Americans in New York Life and History,* vol. 2 (1978).

Delgado, Richard. "Storytelling for Oppositionists and Others: A Plea for Narrative." *87 Michigan Law Review* (1989): 2413.

DuBois, W. E. B. *The Philadelphia Negro: A Social Study.* New York: Schocken Books, 1967.

Earle, Jonathan. "Marcus Morton and the Dilemma of Jacksonian Antislavery in Massachusetts, 1817–1849." *The Massachusetts Historical Review,* NA, 2002. www.historycooperative.org/journals/mhr/4/earle.html.

Foner, Eric. "Politics and Prejudice: The Free Soil Party and the Negro, 1849–1852." *The Journal of Negro History,* vol. 50, no. 4 (Oct. 1965): 239–256.

Foner, Eric. *Free Labor, Free Men: The Ideology of the Republican Party before the Civil War.* New York: Oxford Press, 1995.

"Forum: Timing and Sequence in Political Processes," *Studies in American Political Development* 14 (Spring 2000): 72–119.

Formisano, Ronald. *The Transformation of Political Culture: Massachusetts Parties, 1790s-1840s.* New York: Oxford University Press, 1983.

Foucault, Michel. *Power/Knowledge: Selected Interviews and Other Writings, 1972–1977.* Ed. Colin Gordon. New York: Pantheon, 1980.

Frederickson, George. *The Black Image in the White Mind: The Debate on Afro-American Character and Destiny, 1817–1914.* New York: Harper and Row, 1971.

Freeman, Rhoda Golden. *The Free Negro in New York City in the Era before the Civil War.* New York: Garland Publishing, 1994.

Frymer, Paul. *Uneasy Alliances: Race and Party Competition in America.* Princeton, N.J.: Princeton University Press, 1999.

Gellman, David N., and David Quigley, eds. *Jim Crow New York: A Documentary History of Race and Citizenship, 1777–1877.* New York: NYU Press, 2003.

Genovese, Eugene D. *Roll Jordan Roll: The World the Slaves Made.* New York: Vintage Books, 1976.

Gerring, John. *Party Ideologies in America, 1828–1996.* Oxford: Cambridge University Press, 1998.

Gettleman, Marvin. *The Dorr Rebellion: A Study in American Radicalism, 1833–1849.* New York: Random House, 1973.

Gilkeson, John. *Middleclass Providence, 1820–1940.* Princeton, N.J.: Princeton University Press, 1986.

Goodman, Paul. *The Democratic-Republicans of Massachusetts: Politics in a Young Republic.* Cambridge, Mass.: Harvard University Press, 1964.

Greene, Evarts and Virginia Harrington. *American Population before 1790.* New York: Columbia University Council for Research in the Social Sciences.

Green Papers, The. http://www.thegreenpapers.org.

Gronowicz, Anthony. *Race and Class Politics in New York City before the Civil War.* Boston: Northeastern University Press, 1998.

Hammond, Jabez D. *History of Political Parties in the State of New York.* Buffalo, N.Y.: Phinney and Company, 1850.

Handlin, Oscar. *Boston's Immigrants: A Study in Acculturation.* Cambridge, Mass.: Harvard University Press, 1979.

Hayduk, Ron. *Democracy for All: Restoring Immigrant Voting Rights in the United States.* New York: Routledge Press, 2006.

Higginbotham, Jr., Leon A. *In the Matter of Color, Race and the American Legal Process: The Colonial Period.* New York: Oxford University Press, 1980.

Higginbotham, Sanford. *Keystone in the Democratic Arch: Pennsylvania Politics, 1800–1816.* Harrisburg: Pennsylvania Historical and Museum Commission, 1952.

Hero, Rodney. *Faces of Inequality: Social Diversity in American Politics.* New York: Oxford University Press, 1998.

Holt, Michael. *The Rise and Fall of the American Whig Party: Jacksonian Politics and the Onset of the American Civil War.* New York: Oxford University Press, 1999.

Horton, James Oliver, and Lois Horton. *Black Bostonians: Family Life and Community Struggle in the Antebellum North.* New York: Homes and Meier, 1979.

Ignatiev, Noel. *How the Irish Became White.* New York: Routledge Press, 1995.

Jacobs, Donald Martin. "William Lloyd Garrison's Liberator and Boston's Blacks, 1830–1865." *New England Quarterly* XLIV, no. 2 (June 1971): 259–277.

Johnson, William D. *Slavery in Rhode Island, 1755–1776.* Providence: Rhode Island Historical Society Publications, 1984.

Jordan, Winthrop. *White over Black: American Attitudes toward the Negro, 1550–1812.* Chapel Hill: North Carolina Press, 1968.

Kass, Alvin. *Politics in New York State, 1800–1830.* Syracuse, N.Y.: Syracuse University Press, 1965.

Katznelson, Ira. *City Trenches: Urban Political and the Patterning of Class in the United States.* New York: Pantheon Books, 1981.

Kennedy, Joseph. *Population of the United States in 1860, Eighth Census.* Washington, 1864.

Key, V. O. *Southern Politics in State and Nation.* New York: Alfred Knopf, 1949.

Keyssar, Alexander. *The Right to Vote: The Contested History of Democracy in the United States.* New York: Basic Books, 2000.

King, Dan. *The Life and Times of Thomas Wilson Dorr with Outlines of the Political History of Rhode Island.* Boston: Dan King, 1859.

Klein, Philip Shriver. *A Game without Rules: Pennsylvania Politics, 1817–1832.* Philadelphia: Historical Society of Pennsylvania, 1940.

Klinkner, Philip A., and Rogers M. Smith. *The Unsteady March: The Rise and Decline of Racial Equality in America*. Chicago: University of Chicago Press, 1999.

Kousser, J. Morgan. "The Supremacy of Equal Rights: The Struggle against Racial Discrimination in Antebellum Massachusetts and the Foundations of the Fourteenth Amendment." *Northwestern University Law Review* 82:4 (Summer 1988): 941–1010.

Kraditor, Aileen. *Means and Ends in American Abolitionism: Garrison and His Critics on Strategies and Tactics, 1834–1850*. New York: Pantheon Books, 1969.

Kull, Andrew. *The Colorblind Constitution*. Cambridge, Mass.: Harvard University Press, 1992.

Lader, Lawrence. *The Bold Brahmins: New England's War against Slavery, 1831–1865*. New York: E.P. Dutton and Co., 1961.

Laurie, Bruce. *Beyond Garrison: Antislavery and Social Reform*. Cambridge: Cambridge University Press, 2005.

Lemmons, Stanley and Michael A. McKenna. "Reenfranchisement of Rhode Island Negroes, 1820–1842." *Rhode Island History* 30 (February 1971): 3–13.

Lincoln, C. Z. *The Constitutional History of the State of New York*. Rochester, N.Y.: 1906.

Litwack, Leon. "The Emancipation of the Negro Abolitionist," *The Antislavery Vanguard*. Edited by Martin Duberman. Princeton, N.J.: Princeton University Press, 1980.

Locke, Mary Stoughton. *Anti-Slavery in America, 1619–1808*. Gloucester, Mass.: Peter Smith Publishing, 1965.

Lovejoy, David. *Rhode Island Politics and the America Revolution, 1760–1776*. Providence, R.I.: Brown University Press, 1958.

Lovejoy, David. *North of Slavery: The Negro in the Free States*. Chicago: University of Chicago Press, 1965.

MacLeod, Duncan. "Toward Caste." *Slavery and Freedom in the Age of the American Revolution*. Ed. Ira Berlin and Ronald Hoffman. Charlottesville, Va.: United States Capitol Historical Society, 1983.

Malone, Christopher. "Race Formation, Voting Rights and Democratization in the Antebellum North." *New Political Science*, vol. 27, no. 2 (June 2005): 177–198.

Malone, Christopher."Rethinking the End of Black Voting Rights in Antebellum Pennsylvania: Racial Ascriptivism, Partisanship and Political Development in the Keystone State." *Pennsylvania History*, vol. 72, no. 4 (autumn 2005): 466–504.

Martis, Kenneth. *The Historical Atlas of the Parties in the United States Congress, 1789–1989*. New York: Macmillan Publishing, 1989.

McCormick, Richard P. *The Second American Party System: Party Formation in the Jacksonian Era*. Chapel Hill: University of North Carolina Press, 1966.

McManus, Edgar. *A History of Negro Slavery in New York*. Syracuse, N.Y.: Syracuse University Press, 1966.

Melish, Joanne Pope. *Disowning Slavery: Gradual Emancipation and "Race" in New England, 1780–1860*. Ithaca, N.Y.: Cornell University Press, 1998.

Moore, George. *Notes on the History of Slavery in Massachusetts*. New York: Negro University Press, 1968.

Morgan, Edmund. *American Slavery/American Freedom: The Ordeal of Colonial Virginia*. New York: W.W. Norton, 2005.

Morrison, Samuel Eliot. *Harrison Gray Otis, 1765–1848: Urbane Federalist*. Boston: Houghton Mifflin, 1969.

Mueller, Henry Richard. *The Whig Party of Pennsylvania*. New York: Columbia University Press, 1921.

Myers, Gustavus. *The History of Tammany Hall*. New York: Burt Franklin Press, 1917.

Nash, Gary. *Quakers and Politics: Pennsylvania, 1681–1726*. Princeton, N.J.: Princeton University Press, 1968.

Nash, Gary. *Forging Freedom: The Formation of Philadelphia's Black Community, 1720–1840*. Cambridge, Mass.: Harvard University Press, 1988.

Nash, Gary. *Race and Revolution*. Madison, Wisc.: Madison House Publishing, 1990.

Nash, Gary and Jean Solderlund. *Freedom by Degrees: Emancipation in Pennsylvania and Its Aftermath*. New York: Oxford University Press, 1991.

Newman, Richard S. *The Transformation of American Abolitionism: Fighting Slavery in the Early Republic*. Chapel Hill: University of North Carolina Press, 2002.

NNDP. http://www.nndp.com.

Oakes, James. *The Ruling Race: A History of American Slaveholders*. New York: Norton and Company, 1998.

O'Brien, S.J., William S. "Did the Jennison Case Outlaw Slavery in Massachusetts?" *American Journal of Legal History* (April 1961): 219–241.

Omi, Michael, and Howard Winant. *Racial Formation in the United States from the 1960s to the 1990s*. New York: Routledge Press, 1994.

Patterson, Stephen. *Political Parties in Revolutionary Massachusetts*. Madison: University of Wisconsin Press, 1973.

Pennypacker, S. W. *The Settlement of Germantown*. Philadelphia, 1899.

Peterson, Merrill. *Democracy, Liberty, and Property*. New York: Macmillan Publishing Company, 1966.

Piven, Frances Fox, and Richard Cloward. *Poor People's Movements: Why They Succeed, How They Fail*. New York: Vintage 1979.

Prescott, Frank, and Joseph Zimmerman. *The Council of Revision and the Veto of Legislation*. Albany: SUNY Press, 1972.

Price, Edward J. *Let the Law Be Just: The Quest for Racial Equality in Pennsylvania, 1780, 1915*. Ph.D. dissertation, Pennsylvania State University, 1973.

Rammelkamp, Julian. "The Providence Negro Community, 1820–1842." *Rhode Island History* 7 (January 1948): pp. 20–33.

Reed, Harry. *Platform for Change: The Foundations of the Northern Free Black Community, 1775–1865*. East Lansing: Michigan State University Press, 1994.

Remini, Robert V. *Van Buren and the Making of the Democratic Party*. New York: W. W. Norton, 1970.

Richman, Irving Berdine. *Rhode Island: A Study in Separation*. New York: AMS Press, 1973.

Robinson, William H. *Blacks in 19th Century Rhode Island: An Overview*. Providence, R.I.: Rhode Island Black Heritage Society, 1978.

Roediger, David. *Wages of Whiteness: Race and the Making of the American Working Class*. New York: Verso Press, 1991.

Rosenberger, Lyle L. "Black Suffrage in Bucks County: The Election of 1837." *Bucks County Historical Society Journal* (Spring 1974): 28–39.

Ryan, Dixon. *The Decline of Aristocracy in the Politics of New York*. New York: Columbia University, 1919.

Saxton, Alexander. *The Rise and Fall of the White Republic: Class, Politics and Mass Culture in Nineteenth Century America*. London: Verso Press, 1990.

Schattschneider, E.E. *Party Government*. Westport, Conn.: Greenwood Press, 1942.

Schultz, Stanley. *The Culture Factory: Boston Public Schools, 1789–1860*. New York: Oxford Press, 1973.

Scott, Daryl Michael. *Contempt and Pity: Social Policy and the Image of the Damaged Black Psyche, 1880–1996*. Chapel Hill: University of North Carolina Press, 1997.

Shankman, Andrew. *Crucible of American Democracy: The Struggle to Fuse Egalitarianism and Capitalism in Jeffersonian Pennsylvania*. Lawrence: University of Kansas Press, 2004.

Smith, Eric Ledell. "End of Black Voting Rights in Pennsylvania." *Pennsylvania History* 65 (1998).

Smith, Rogers. *Civic Ideals: Conflicting Visions of US Citizenship*. New Haven: Yale University Press, 1997.

Smith, T. E. V. *Political Parties and the Places of Meetings in New York City*. New York: New York Historical Society, 1893.

Sorin, Gerald. *Abolitionism: A New Perspective*. New York: Praeger, 1972.

Spector, Robert. "The Quock Walker Cases (1781–1783)—Slavery, Its Abolition, and Negro Citizenship in Early Massachusetts." *Journal of Negro History*, vol. 53, no. 1 (January 1968): 12–32.

Stewart, James Brewer. *Holy Warriors: Abolitionists and American Slavery*. New York: Hill and Wang, 1996.

Sweet, Edward F. *The Origins of the Democratic Party in Rhode Island*. Ph.D. dissertation, Fordham University, 1971.

Thomas, John L. *The Liberator: William Lloyd Garrison*. Boston: Houghton Mifflin, 1963.

Thompson, Mack. *Moses Brown: Reluctant Reformer*. Chapel Hill: University of North Carolina Press, 1962.

Tocqueville, Alexis. *Democracy in America*. New York: Alfred A. Knopf, 1948.

Turner, Edward Raymond. *The Negro in Pennsylvania, 1639–1861*. New York: Arno Press, 1969.

Valelly, Richard. *The Two Reconstructions: The Struggle for Black Enfranchisement*. Chicago: University of Chicago Press, 2004.

Warner, Oliver. *Abstract of the Census of Massachusetts, 1865: With Remarks on the Same, and Supplementary Tables*. Boston, 1867.

Watkins, Ralph. "A Survey of the African American Presence in the History of the Downstate New York Area." *The African American Presence in New York State History: Four Regional Historical Surveys*. Ed. Monroe Fordham. Albany: SUNY Press, 1989.

Wesley, Charles. "Negro Suffrage in the Period of Constitution-Making, 1787–1865," *Journal of Negro History*, vol. 32, no. 2 (1947).

Wesley, Charles. "The Participation of Negroes in Anti Slavery Political Parties." *The Journal of Negro History*, vol. 29, no. 1 (Jan. 1944): 32–74.

White, Shane. *Somewhat More Independent: The End of Slavery in New York City, 1770–1810*. Athens: University of Georgia Press, 1991.

Wilentz, Sean. *The Rise of American Democracy: From Jefferson to Lincoln.* New York: Norton Press, 2006.

Williams, George W. *The History of the Negro Race in America, 1619–1880.* New York: Arno Press, 1968.

Williamson, Chilton. *American Suffrage: Democracy to Property.* Princeton, N.J.: Princeton University Press, 1968.

Winch, Julie. *Philadelphia's Black Elite: Activism, Accommodation, and the Struggle for Autonomy, 1787–1848.* Philadelphia: Temple University, 1988.

Young, Alfred E. *The Democratic Republicans of New York: The Origins, 1763–1797.* Chapel Hill: University of North Carolina Press, 1967.

Index

A

Abolition Act of 1780, 85–86
Abolition bill; *see also* Gradual abolition
    bill
    Brown in 1784 and, 125
    John Jay signing, 39
    in Massachusetts, 174
    in Pennsylvania, 37, 72
Abolitionism; *see also* Abolitionist
    movement
    Daniel Webster and, 181
    in Massachusetts, 21, 148, 159–173
    in Philadelphia, 71
    in Rhode Island, 140
    throughout antebellum North, 145
    William Garrison and, 150, 186–191,
      192
Abolitionist movement
    Boston and, 155, 158–159, 168,
      172–173
    Irish immigrants and, 166
    paternalism and, 148
    in Philadelphia, 59–60, 70–72, 79, 81
    in Rhode Island, 105, 139–140
    schism of, 170
    Wiiliam Garrison and, 192
Abolition law. *see* Gradual abolition
    laws
Abyssinian Baptist Church, 33
Adams, Charles Francis, 164, 184
Adams, John, 144, 153, 159, 175

Adams, John Quincy
    battle on Gag Rule against
      antislavery petitions, 164–165
    election of, 77, 147, 160, 163
    stance on slavery, 183–184
Adams, Samuel, 159
An Address on the Right of Free Suffrage
    (Luther), 121
An Address to the Inhabitants of the
    British Settlements on the
    Slavery of Negroes in America
    (Rush), 83
A Few Observations on the Government
    of the State of Rhode Island
    (Burrill), 118
African Americans, *see* Blacks
African Baptist Church, 143
African Benevolent Society, 109
African Methodist Episcopal Zion
    Church, 33
Africans, the Dutch and, 28
African Union Meeting House, 112
Age, right to vote and, 4
"Age of the Common Man", 120–121
Akari, Roy, 60
Alien and Seditions Acts, 25, 74
Allen, Charles, 164, 165
Allen, Richard, 69, 70
Allen, Theodore, 11
American and Foreign Anti-Slavery
    Society, 170
American Anti-Slavery Society, 71, 170

American Citizenship (Newspaper), 31
American Colonization Society, 70, 71, 188
American democracy; *see also* Democratic Party; Democrats
    Alexis de Tocqueville and, 6–7
    race prejudice and, 1
American politics
    in Antebellum North, 6–8
    Civil Rights Movement and, 197
    Civil War and, 199–200
American Revolution, 29, 34–35, 187
American Slavery/American Freedom: The Ordeal of Colonial Virginia (Morgan), 11
American society, 6
Andrews, William, 19
Annual Meeting of the Friends, 83
Antebellum North
    American politics in, 6–8
    black enfranchisement in, 3–4, 5
    free black communities across, 32–33
    racial belief systems across, 15–16
    right to vote in, 5–6
Anti-Masons, 77
Anti-Mason-Whig coalition, 78
Antislavery movement
    in Massachusetts, 170–171, 181
    Philadelphia as ground zero of, 59–60
A Refutation of the Charge of Abolitionism ... Against the Hon. Marcus Morton (Henshaw), 181
Arnold, Benjamin, 132–134
Aron, Raymond, 6
Asher, Jeremiah, 113
"Atlanta Compromise" speech, 201
"Attention!! People of Colour", 43
Atwell, Samuel, 101
Austin, J. L., 15

B

Bancroft, George, 180
Becker, Carl, 34–35
Becket, Thomas Jefferson, 97
Bedford Gazette, 93

Beecher, Lyman, 169
Bell, Derrick, 15
Benezet, Anthony, 61, 69, 83
Bennett, Lerone, 11
Benoit (slave), 24
Benson, Egbert, 36
"Between freedom and bondage" (Wesley), 5
Beyond Garrison: Antislavery and Social Reform (Laurie), 148
"Bill to Prevent Frauds at Elections, and For Other Purposes," 42–43
Binns, John, 90, 98
Birney, James, 170
Black churches, 33–34
Black males; *see also* Blacks
    in Massachusetts, 146, 153
    in New York, 8–9, 26, 47, 128
    rights to vote, 3– 6
    Van Buren and disfranchisement of, 26
Black population/density; *see also* Blacks
    in Massachusetts during 1790–1860, 155–156
    in New York during 1703–1790, 29
    in New York during 1790–1860, 30
    in Philadelphia during 1780–1830, 67–68
    by region and states during 1790–1850, 9
    in Rhode Island during 1708–1774, 107
    in Rhode Island during 1790–1820, 108
Blacks; *see also* Black males; Black population/density; Disenfranchisement of blacks; Employment of blacks; Free blacks; Reenfranchisement of blacks; Voting
    enfranchisement of, 3, 5, 8
    federalists and, 40–41
    manumission of, 8–9
    Massachusetts and education of, 143–145
    mental ability of, 23–34
    in Northern states, 7, 8–10
Blight, David, 19
Bloch, Herman, 32, 33, 39

Boder, F. L., 93
Body of Liberties, 151
Boston, population and density in, 156
Boston Manufacturing Company, 163
Boston Port Bill, 115
Boutwell, George, 168
Branagan,Thomas, 63, 87–90, 92, 98
Bray Associates, 84
Bridgham, Samuel, 119
Brooks, John, 162
Brown, Henry Billings (Justice), 145,
      201–202
Brown, Moses, 114
Brown v. Board of Education, 145
Bryant, William Cullen, 138
Bucktail Republicans, 19, 25, 26, 44,
      53–55
Burr, Aaron, 37
Burrill, George, 118, 121
Bush, George W., 1, 2, 3, 206

C

Calhoun, John, 167, 180
Carter, Edward, 73, 75
Carter, Jimmy, 196
Charles II, 60, 64
Charter of Rhode Island, 115
Cherry Street School, 69
The Circle of Discrimination (Bloch), 39
*Civic Ideals: Conflicting Visions of U.S.
      Citizenship* (Smith), 4
Civil Rights Act, 195, 196, 203
Civil Rights Movement, 197
Civil War
      abolitionism before, 73
      American politics and, 199–200
      in Massachusetts, 146, 154, 155
      moral absolutism and, 191
      racial ascriptivism during, 17
      Republicans during, 168, 171, 197
Clark, Kenneth, 204
Clarke, Robert, 49–50
Class, in Rhode Island amid Dorr War,
      101–107
Clay, Cassius, 164
Clay, Henry, 121, 181, 182, 183
Clay American System, 163

Clinton, Bill, 196
Clinton, DeWitt, 39
Coleman, Peter, 113, 114, 120
Collens, Richard, 154
Collins, Charles, 122
Colonial period
      economic and social conditions from,
            28–34
      racial ascriptivism in Pennsylvania
            during, 86–87
      in Rhode Island during, 115–123
Colorblindness, concept of, 203, 205, 206
"Color-conscious," Democratic Party
      and, 205
Colored American (Newspaper), 34
*Colored Patriots of the American
      Revolution* (Cuff), 154
Commercial Advertiser (News paper), 33
Competing rational narratives, in New
      York, 34–45
Conscience Whigs, 148, 164–165, 168
Constitutional change in Old New York,
      23–28
Constitutional Convention
      of 1777, 36, 37
      of 1779, 150
      of 1780, 174
      of 1787, 175
      of 1789, 86
      of 1821, 25, 30, 34–53, 72
      of 1834, 122
      of 1837–1838, 17, 20, 63, 91–98
      of 1841, 136, 137
      of 1853, 180
Constitutional development, in Rhode
      Island, 115–123
Constitutional Party, 122–123
Constitutional reform, in Rhode Island,
      105, 117, 118–121, 121
Continental Congress, 23
Cotton Whigs, 148, 164–165
Council of Appointments, in New York
      Constitution, 36, 37
Council of Revision,, in New York
      Constitution, 36, 42–45
Crawford Messenger, 77
Crow, Jim, 2

Crucible of American Democracy: The Struggle to Fuse Egalitarianism and Capitalism in Jeffersonian Pennsylvania (Shankman), 75
Crummell, Alexander, 113, 132–133
Cuffe, Paul, 70, 154, 174
Cummins, Oliver, 110
Cushing, William (Chief Justice), 175

D

Darlington, William, 96
Darusmont, Fanny Wright, 59
Declaration of Independence, 49, 95, 184, 186, 188
The Decline of Aristocracy in the Politics of New York, 35
Delgado, Richard, 15
Democracy for All: Restoring Immigrant Voting Rights in the United States (Hayduk), 4
Democracy in America (de Tocqueville), 1
Democratic Party; *see also* Democrats
  in 1965, 196
  Ignatiev's role in, 74
  of Massachusetts, 150, 158–159, 165–168, 172, 180–181
  in New York, 55
  in Pennsylvania, 13, 60, 77, 78–79
  in Rhode Island, 130
Democratic Press (Newspaper), 90
Democratic Republicans
  in early nineteenth century, 26
  in New York, 36, 40
  in Pennsylvania, 75, 77–79, 118
Democrats; *see also* Democratic Party; Democratic Republicans
  Irish community and, 74
  in Massachusetts, 165–166
  New York Equal Rights and, 130
  in Pennsylvania, 13, 20, 26, 75, 77–79
  in Rhode Island, 121, 122, 130, 141
  suffrage restriction and, 97
Demographic changes
  in Massachusetts, 149, 151–159
  in New York, 53
  in Pennsylvania, 64, 68, 72–73

  in Rhode Island, 104, 115, 139, 141
Disenfranchisement of blacks
  in America, 3–4, 15, 18
  Constitutional Convention of 1837–1838 and, 91–98
  males, Van Buren and of, 26
  in Massachusetts, 15
  in New York, 3–4, 15, 18, 26
  in Pennsylvania, 15, 57–99
  in Rhode Island, 120
"Doll Test", 204
Dorr, Thomas Wilson
  in 1842, 134, 137–138
  on his 1840 election, 129–130
  rebellion of, 138, 141–142, 148
  on suffrage clause, 134–135
  trial and conflict of, 101–107, 122, 123
Dorr War in Rhode Island
  disenfranchisement amid, 123–129
  race and class amid, 101–107
  reenfranchisement during, 6, 13–14, 101–107, 129–138
  suffrage rights during, 36–37
Douglass, Frederick, 101–107, 135, 139, 171
Dred Scott, 57, 58, 99
DuBois, W. E. B.
  about Philadelphia, 59, 66
  on black community of Philadelphia, 68, 71
  on political development of Pennsylvania, 62
  on transformation of Pennsylvania, 98–99
"Duke's Law", 28
Durfee, Job, 101, 102
Dutch rule, Africans and, 28
Dutch West India Company, 28

E

Earle, Thomas, 95, 170
Eastwood, Asa, 52
Economic conditions
  of black community in Rhode Island, 112–115
  from Colonial Period to 1821, 28–34
  gradual abolition and, 31

in Pennsylvania, 99
slavery in Pennsylvania and, 61
Economic structure, of racial conflict,
   8–12
Electoral votes, 196
Emancipation, in Northern states, 10
Emerson, Ralph Waldo, 183
Employment of blacks
   Civil Rights Act and, 203–204
   discrimination in, 203
   in Pennsylvania, 65, 67, 79, 112
   in Rhode Island, 129
   vs. whites, 32, 129
Enfranchisement of blacks, 3, 5, 8
English rule, Africans and, 28
Equal rights, 154, 171, 185, 201
Essay on Freedom (Raymond), 6
Eustis, John, 108
Eustis, William, 176–177, 178
Evening Post, 138
Everett, Edward, 179

F

The Federalist, 24
Federalist Party/Federalists; see also
   Republican Party/Republicans
   in 1826, 160
   blacks and, 40
   Irish migration and, 74
   in New York, 25, 34
   in the northern states, 75
   politics with race and, 24
   in Rhode Island, 118, 119
First Great Awakening, 152
First-Party period, consensus in,
   175–177
First Reconstruction, 197, 200–201
Florida, voting for blacks in, 2
Fogg, William, 90, 97
Forbes, John Murray, 183
Forten, James, 70
Foster, Frances Smith, 19
Foucault, Michel, 15
Fox, Dixon Ryan, 26, 35
Fox, John, 93, 94, 98
Franklin, Benjamin, 79, 84–85, 95
Fredrickson, George, 16

Free African Union Society, 109
Free blacks
   Abolition Act of 1780 and, 86
   after emergence from slavery, 10
   in Massachusetts, 21, 155
   in New York, 29–30, 44
   in New York City, 55
   in the Northern states, 8
   in Pennsylvania, 66, 68
   Pennsylvania and kidnapping of, 80
   in Rhode Island, 109
   South Carolina law and, 167
   total number in the United States, 8
Freedom by Degrees: Emancipation in
   Pennsylvania and its Aftermath
   (Nash and Soderlund), 84
Free Soilers, 145, 150, 165
Free Soil Party, 148
   Democrats alliance with, 166, 168
   formation of, 170–171
   Liberty Party members and, 170
   in Massachusetts, 184
   merger with Liberty Party, 185
   Whigs in 1840s and, 55
Frymer, Paul, 12–13, 14, 203
Fugitive Slave Act of 1793, 80
Fugitive Slave Bill, 182–183

G

Gag Rule, 147, 165, 184
Gallatin, Albert, 86, 96
Garrison, William Lloyd
   abolitionism and, 145, 150, 186–193
   as abolitionist, 72, 102, 106
   abolitionists in Massachusetts and,
      148
   about Sarah Roberts case, 145
   publishing in The Liberator, 135,
      168–170
General Court of Massachusetts Bay, 173
"General Meeting of the Electors of
   Colour", 40
The Genius of Universal Emancipation
   (Lundy), 168
Genovese, Eugene, 16
Gerry, Elbridge, 175
Gettleman, Marvin, 121, 122

Gibbs, William, 119
Gibson, John, 97–98
Goldwater, Barry, 195–196, 198
Goodell, William, 106, 140
Gore, Al, 196
The Government of American Cities
    (Munro), 4
Gracchus, Tiberius, 102
Gradual abolition bill; *see also* Abolition
    bill
    in 1799, 24, 39
Gradual abolition laws, 169
    in New York, 24–25, 30–31, 46
    in Pennsylvania, 64–72, 85, 90, 93,
       109
    during Revolutionary War, 10
    in Rhode Island, 127
Graham, Maryemma, 19
"Great Negro Plot of 1741", 28
Green, Thomas, 132
Gronowicz, Anthony, 31, 33

H

Haitian Emigration Society, 70
Hale, John, 171
Hall, Prince, 143
Hamilton, Alexander, 33, 79
    action regarding manumitting slaves,
       37
    on conscription of Negro soldiers in
       Revolutionary Army, 23–24
    as founder of NY Manumission
       Society, 39
    John Adams and, 159
Hammond, Jabez, 42
Hancock, John, 95, 159, 162
Hard Scrabble Calendar, 110–111
Hard Scrabble Riot, 110–112
Harlan, John Marshall (Justice),
    202–203, 204
Harris, Leslie, 19
Harrison, William Henry, 78, 129
Hartford Convention in 1814, 160–161
Hayduk, Ron, 4, 5
Hazard, James, 113
Henry, Patrick, 95
Henshaw, David, 167, 168, 181

Hero, Rodney, 10
Higginbotham, Leon, 28
Higginbotham, Sanford, 76
*The History of Political parties in the
    Province of New York,* 35
Hobbs, Hiram, 90, 91, 97
Hobbs v. Fogg, 97
Hodges, Graham Russell, 19
*Holy Warriors: The Abolitionists and
    American Slavery,* 71
Hopkins, Samuel, 108
Horton, James, 19, 151
Horton, Lois, 19, 151
How the Irish Became White (Ignatiev),
    11
Humphrey, Hubert, 196

I

Ideological change, in Old New York,
    23–28
Ignatiev, Noel, 11, 74, 87
Immigration to New York, 29–31
Independence Day celebration, in
    Pennsylvania, 69
The Invention of the White Race (Allen),
    11
Irish immigration
    in early nineteenth century, 172
    in Massachusetts, 158
    in Philadelphia, 73–74, 76
    in Rhode Island, 114

J

Jackson, Andrew, 77, 96–97
Jackson, Edmund, 145r
Jackson, Francis, 145
Jay, John, 23– 25, 33
Jay, Peter, 47–48
Jefferson, Thomas, 25, 26, 95, 118, 162
Jefferson's Embargo of 1804, 32, 118
Jenks, Phineas, 92
Jim Crow, 206
    in Massachusetts, 193
    reversing effects of, 205
    the Second Reconstruction and, 197

as strategy, 201
Whiteness as Property during, 202
Johnson, Lyndon, 195, 196, 197, 198, 203
Jones, Absalom, 69, 70
Jordan, Winthrop, 16, 173
Julian, George, 171

K

Kachline, Jacob, 93
Kerry, John, 196
Key, V. O., 197
Keyssar, Alexander, 4, 5
The Keystone in the Democratic Arch
  (Higginbotham), 76
Kidnapping, first act against, 80
King, Rufus, 24
King, Samuel, 138
King Cotton, 164
Klein, Philip Shriver, 76
Know-Nothing Party, 145, 148
Kraditor, Aileen, 169

L

Lancaster Weekly Journal, 77
Laurens, Henry, 23
Laurie, Bruce, 148–149, 150–151, 170
Law and Order Party, 37, 104, 106, 137,
  138
Lawrence, Abbott, 164, 181, 184
Lay, Benjamin, 61, 83
Legal Constitution, in Rhode Island, 137
Levitical Code, 151
The Liberator (Garrison), 135, 168, 169,
  186, 187, 189
Liberty Party, 181, 191
  about, 170–171
  in Massachusetts, 145, 148, 185–186
  Whigs in 1840s and, 55
Lincoln, Abraham, 55, 198
Litwach, Leon, 33
Livingston, Robert, 38–39
Locofocos, 130
Lowell, Frances Cabot, 163
Lundy, Benjamin, 168
Luther, Seth, 121–122

Luther v. Borden, 102, 103
Lyman, Theodore, 151, 157

M

Maclay, William, 94–95
Macleod, Duncan, 16
Madison, James, 70, 95, 176
Manufacturers' and Farmers' Journal,
  119, 128– 129
Marsh, Metcalf, 122
Marshall, John, 95
Marshall, Thurgood (Justice), 205–206
Martin, Benjamin, 92, 94
Massachusetts
  from abolitionism to rise of radical
    Republicans, 168–173
  conditions for blacks in, 7, 13
  consensus in the first-party period,
    175–177
  Democratic Party of, 180–181
  demographic development in,
    151–159
  discourse of racial paternalism in,
    173–191
  party competition in the First-party
    period, 159–163
  race, partisanship and abolition in,
    159–173
  racial paternalism in, 143–151
  racial structure of partisan
    competition in, 14
  rise and demise of Whig Party,
    163–165
  rising conflict and nationalization
    of race in second-party era,
    178–179
  slavery in, 10
  Whig Party in, 181–185
Massachusetts Abolition Society, 170
Massachusetts Declaration of Rights,
  144
"Massachusetts Exceptionalism," 148
McCormick, Richard, 74–75, 78
McKinley, William, 201

Melish, Joanne Pope, 11
Memorial of Thirty Thousand Disenfranchised Citizens of Philadelphia to the Honorable Senate and House of Representatives (Petition), 99
Mercer, Charles Fenton, 70, 71
Mifflin, Thomas, 76, 80
Missouri Compromise of 1820, 57, 156
Monroe, James, 160, 163
Moore, Ely, 138
Morgan, Edmund, 11
Morton, Marcus, 167, 168, 180–181
Mowry, Nathaniel, 133
Moyers, Bill, 195, 205
"Mr. Madison's War", 43
Munro, William, 4

N

Nash, Gary, 60, 65, 72, 87
Nationalization
    of party politics, 195–206
    of race, in second-party era in Massachusetts, 178–179
Nativism, 74, 140, 142
Naturalization Act in 1797, 74
Negro soldiers, conscription of, 23
Nell, William C., 145, 154
New Age and Constitutional Advocate, 135
Newman, Richard, 188
New Netherland, 28
New York
    blacks in, 7, 8–9, 13, 28–34
    number of blacks in, 29–31, 44
    old, constitutional and ideological change in, 23–28
    politics, partisanship, and competing racial narratives in, 34–45
    process of emancipation in, 10
    race and suffrage in the Constitutional Convention of 1821, 45–53
    race formation and voting rights in, 53–55
    racial structure of partisan competition in, 13

New York Commercial Advertiser, 41
The New York Constitution, 36
New York Constitutional Convention, 36
New York Equal Rights Democrats, 130
New York Evening Post, 43
New York Free African School, 33, 34
New York Gazetteer, 39
New York Journal, 31, 37
New York Manumission Society, 24, 33, 39
New York Society for the Encouragement of Faithful Domestics, 32
New York Spectator, 41
Niger, Alfred, 113, 132, 136
Nixon, Richard, 196
Northern States. *see* Antebellum North
The North Star, 171

O

Oakes, James, 16
Obama, Barak, 198
Occupations of blacks, 32
Omi, Michael, 7–8, 14
Otis, Harrison Gray, 74
Otis, James, 173–174, 177, 178

P

Painter, Nell Irvin, 19
Palfrey, John, 184
Parker, Ransom, 113
Parker, Theodore, 145
Partisan competition/conflict; *see also* Partisanship
    disenfranchisement of blacks and, 63
    racial structure of, 12–14
    in Rhode Island from colonial times to 1840, 115–123
Partisanship
    in the Democratic Arch, 1770–1838, 72–82
    in Massachusetts, 159–173
    in New York, 25, 34–35
    in Pennsylvania, 99

political life and, 15
in Rhode Island, 106–107, 117, 120, 141
Pastorius, Francis Daniel, 82–83
Paternalism. see Racial paternalism
Patriotic Register, 31
"Peace Ticket", 43
Penn, William, 60, 64, 82, 93
Pennsylvania
in 1780–1838, 64–72
from Colonial times to 1837, 82–91
conditions for blacks in, 7, 13
creation of White Republic in, 57–64
disfranchisement of blacks in, 57–99
first act against kidnapping in, 80
partisanship in the democratic arch 1702–1838, 72–82
process of emancipation in, 10
racial structure of partisan competition in, 13
right to vote for African Americans in, 5–6
transformation in racial politics of, 98–99
Pennsylvania Abolition Society (PAS), 68, 69, 79–82, 84–85, 90
Pennsylvania Constitutional Convention of 1837–1838, 17
"The Pennsylvania Society for Promoting the Abolition of Slavery, for the Relief of Free Negroes, Unlawfully Held in Bondage, and for the Improvement of the African Race.". see Pennsylvania Abolition Society (PAS)
People' Convention, 134, 135
People's Constitution, 136, 137
"People's Constitutional Convention", 131
Peterson, Carla, 19
Philadelphia. see Pennsylvania
Philadelphia Gazette, 69
The Philadelphia Negro, 62, 66, 98
Phillips, Stephen, 184
Phillips, Wendell, 145
Pickering, Thomas, 153
Pierce, Franklin, 171
Platt, Thomas C. (Judge), 52

Plessy, Homer, 202
Plessy v. Ferguson (1896), 144, 145, 201
Political actors, 14–15, 16
Political discourse, 14–15
Politics in New York, 34–45
"Politics of the Revolutionary Center", 162
Post nati statutes, 10
Potter, Elisha, 139
Preliminary Essay on the Oppression of the Exiled Sons of Africa (Branagan), 88
Price, Edward, 97
Prigg v. Pennsylvania, 81
Providence Home Guard, 138
Providence Journal, 131, 132, 133

Q

Quakers
in Pennsylvania, 60–62, 64–65, 82–83
in Rhode Island, 108
Quock Walker cases of 1783, 153, 154

R

Race; see also Race riots; Racial ascriptivism; Racial conflicts/hostilities; Racial paternalism
Antebellum North and formation of, 6–8
concept of, 19
in the Constitutional Convention of 1821, 45–53
in ideological formation of political parties, 27
in Massachusetts, 159–173, 178–179
in Pennsylvania, 65–66, 71, 82–91
prejudice, American democracy and, 1, 2, 7
in Rhode Island, 101–107, 141–142
Race riots
in Pennsylvania, 59, 60, 71, 90
in Rhode Island, 110, 112, 126
Racial ascriptivism; see also Racial paternalism
in Massachusetts, 147–148, 158

in Pennsylvania, 86–90
prevalence of, 201
racial paternalism and, 20
in Rhode Island, 140
suffrage movement and, 140
by the time of Civil War, 17
Racial coalition formation, structure of, 14–18
Racial conflicts/hostilities
economic structure of, 8–12
in Pennsylvania, 63
Pennsylvania Irish population and, 74
in Philadelphia, 70, 72–73
in Rhode Island, 112
Racial Formation in the United States from the 1960s to the 1990s (Omi and Winant), 7–8
Racial paternalism, 16, 17; see also Racial ascriptivism
Benjamin Franklin and, 84
in Massachusetts, 143–151, 173–191
in Pennsylvania, 81–82, 83, 86
Platt on, 52–53
racial ascriptivism and, 20
in Rhode Island, 124–126, 140–141
versions of, 16–17
Racial structure, of partisan competition, 12–14
Racing formation in New York, 53–55
Radical Republicans, in Massachusetts, 168–173
Rael, Patrick, 19
Raynor, Kenneth, 179
Reconstruction period, 1, 3, 4
Redemption, 3
Reed, Harry, 32
Reenfranchisement of blacks
during 1841–1843, 129–138
during Dorr War, 6, 101–107
during 1770s–1840, 123–129
Remond, Charles Lenox, 145
Republican Party/Republicans; see also Federalist Party/Federalists; Law and Order Party; Whig Party/Whigs
in 1973, 196
blacks and, 40–41
Irish and, 74

in Massachusetts, 148
in New York in late 1850s, 55
in Pennsylvania, 74–75
War of 1812 and, 43
Revolutionary and Confederation years, 24, 29
Revolutionary Army, 23
Revolutionary era, 16, 25
Revolutionary War, 27, 30, 66, 84–85, 108–109
Rhode Island
during 1841–1843, 129–138
amid Dorr War, 101–107
blacks during 1770s–1840 in, 107–115
from colonial times to 1840, 115–123
process of emancipation in, 10
racial structure of partisan competition in, 13–14, 15
during 1770s–1840, 123–129
treatment of blacks in, 5–6
Rhode Island Anti-Slavery Society, 135
Rhode Island Suffrage Association, 133
Rights of the British Colonies (Otis), 173–174
Right to vote
see Voting rights
The Right to Vote: The Contested History of Democracy in the United States (Keyssar), 4
The Rise and Fall of the White Republic (Saxton), 11
The Rise of American Democracy: Jefferson to Lincoln (Wilentz), 199
Roberts, Sarah, 143, 144, 145
Roberts v. City of Boston, 144, 145, 146, 147
Roediger, David, 11, 27
Roosevelt, Eleanor, 203
Roosevelt, Franklin, 203
Roosevelt, Teddy, 201
Root, Erastus, 48–49
Rorschach test, 4
Rosenberger, Lyle, 60
Ross, James, 75
Ross, Stephen, 46–47
Rush, Benjamin, 83–84

S

Sandiford, Ralph, 61, 83
Saxton, Alexander, 11
Schattschneider, E. E., 5
Scott, Daryl Michael, 204
Scott, Winfield, 171
The Second American Party System
    (McCormick), 74
Second Reconstruction, 195, 197, 204,
    205, 206
Serious Remonstrances Addressed to the
    Citizens of Northern States,
    and Their Representatives
    (Branagan), 88, 90
Sewell, Samuel, 152
Shankman, Andrew, 75, 76
Shaw, Lemuel (Justice), 144–145
Simmons, James, 129
Slater, Samuel, 114
Slave population
    in New York, 30
    in Philadelphia, 66
    in Rhode Island, 109
    in South Carolina, 23
Slavery
    in Massachusetts, 150, 151–159, 168,
        173–174, 180–185
    in New York, 28–30
    New York Gazetteer attacking, 39
    in Pennsylvania, 37, 64–72, 151–152
    in wake of Revolutionary War, 10–11
Smith, Eric Ledell, 60
Smith, Roger, 4, 5
Social conditions
    of African Americans in New York,
        28–34
    of black community in Rhode Island,
        114
    from Colonial Period to 1821, 28–24
    in Pennsylvania in 1780–1838, 64–72
"Social diversity", 10
Society Friends' Shelter for Colored
    Orphans, 72
Society of Friends, 61, 64, 84
Socioeconomic changes, blacks in Rhode
    Island and, 107–115
South Carolina, 167, 178–179
Southeby, William, 65

Southern Politics in State and Nation
    (Key), 197
Southern Slave Power, 167
South states of United States, political
    parties and, 195–196
Spencer, William, 134
Stamp Act, 35, 174
State Constitution of Massachusetts, 144
Sterigere, John, 92, 95–96
Stevens, Thaddeus, 93, 97
Stewart, Brewer, 71
Stewart, James Brewer, 19
Strong, Caleb, 175
Suffrage; *see also* Suffrage movement
    Alfred Nigel on, 136–137
    for blacks, 25–26
    in the Constitutional Convention of
        1821, 45–53
    Democrats and restriction of, 97
    Dorr movement in Rhode Island and,
        102
    to taxpaying males in Pennsylvania,
        76
    Thomas Green, 132
    "Town Born" on, 131
Suffrage Association, 131, 132, 135
Suffrage movement, 102, 105, 106,
    129–131, 139–140
Sumner, Charles, 143–144, 145–146, 164,
    165, 185
Sydney, Joseph, 40
"System of 1896", 201

T

Taney, Roger (Justice), 17, 57–59, 93, 94,
    103
Taylor, Zachary, 13, 164, 165, 168, 182
Thatcher, George, 175
The Shaping of Black America (Bennett),
    11
Thoughts on African Colonization
    (Garrison), 187, 189
Tilden, Samuel, 138
Tillinghast, Joseph L., 111
Tocqueville, Alexis de, 6–7, 72
Tompkins, Daniel, 41, 43

"Town Born", 131
Transformation of Rhode Island,
1790–1860 (Coleman), 113
Treaty of Paris, 29
Tucker, Mark, 102
Turner, Edward, 72–73, 81
Turner, Nat, 59, 68
Tyler, John, 137

U

U. S. Constitution
  Fifteenth Amendment to, 3–4, 26,
    60, 202
  Fourteenth Amendment, 144, 145
  Pennsylvania and drafting of, 85
  Twenty-Fourth Amendment of, 3
Uneasy Alliances (Frymer), 12–13

V

Valelly, Richard
  analysis of two reconstructions,
    12–13
  on black enfranchisement, 5, 8, 197,
    201
Van Buren, Martin, 129, 142
  in 1835, 78
  in 1848, 168, 171
  on benefits of parties, 15
  building Democratic Party, 200
  Constitutional Convention of 1821
    and, 45–4 6, 50–52, 54–55
  on disfranchising blacks, 25–26
  Whigs support in Massachusetts for,
    165
Vashon, John, 189
Voting; *see also* Voting rights
  blacks and problems in, 2
  of blacks in New York election, 44
  in Massachusetts, 154
  in New York, 23–55
  in Pennsylvania, 59, 92
  in Rhode Island, 106, 113, 116, 118,
    128
Voting rights
  in the Antebellum North, 5–6, 198,
    200

  in 1830s, 6–7
  history of, 4–5
  Marcus Morton and, 180
  in Massachusetts, 5, 148–149, 172,
    179
  in New York, 5–6, 53–55
  in Pennsylvania, 58, 60, 89
  in Rhode Island, 5–6
Voting Rights Act of 1965, 1, 2, 3, 205
Voting Rights Act Reauthorization and
    Amendments Act of 2006, 1,
    2, 3
Voting Rights Reauthorization Act of
    2006, 196

W

Wages of Whiteness: Race and the
    Making of the American
    Working Class (Roediger), 11
Walker, David, 186
Wallace, George, 196
Walnut Street prison, 68
Waring, John, 84
War of 1812
  black community and, 32
  competition for governors office in
    Massachusetts during, 160
  constitutional reform on eve of, 118
  Massachusetts and partisanship in
    and during, 160
  Pennsylvania and, 76–77, 90
  Philadelphia as refuge for blacks at
    end of, 66
  Republicans and, 43
  Rhode Island during, 114, 118
  state constitutions following, 128
Warren, Earl (Chief Justice), 145, 204
"War Ticket", 43
Washington, Booker T., 201
Washington Benevolent Society, 41
Watts, J. C., 197
Wayland, Francis, 102
Wealth of black community, in Rhode
    Island, 112–113
Webster, Daniel, 102–103, 163, 181–183,
    184

Webster, Samuel, 174
Wesley, Charles, 5
Wheeler, Henry T., 110
Whig-Anti-Mason coalition, 97
Whig Party/Whigs; *see also* Conscience
     Whigs; Cotton Whigs
  in Massachusetts, 163–165, 181–185
  in New York, 26, 36, 55
  in Pennsylvania, 13, 63, 77
  in Rhode Island, 13–14, 104, 123,
    129, 142
White, Shane, 31–32
Whitefield, George, 84
White males, states restricting the
    franchise to, 4
White Over Black (Jordan), 173
White population
  in Boston, 156–157
  in Philadelphia, 66–67
  in Rhode Island, 107–108

White Republic of Pennsylvania,
    creation of, 57–64
Why Americans Don't Vote (Piven and
    Cloward), 4
Wilentz, Sean, 199
Williams, Patricia, 15
Williams, Peter, 33
Williams, Roger, 134
Williamson, Chilton, 116
Wilson, Woodrow, 201
Winant, Howard, 7–8, 14
Winch, Julie, 60
Women, right to vote of, 4
Woodward, George, 95
Woolman, John, 83, 108

Y

Yellin, Jean Fagan, 19
Young, Samuel, 25, 46, 50, 52